YIE

T

NONE

Cede Nullis

The History Of
The King's Own
Yorkshire Light Infantry

VOLUME VII

1945 - 1968

Malcolm K. Johnson

This book is published by Propagator Press, an imprint of:

AM S Educational
Woodside Trading Estate
Low Lane
Horsforth
Leeds LS18 5NY

ISBN   1 86029 803 6

Designed by Propagator Press
Printed in Great Britain

Her Majesty Queen Elizabeth The Queen Mother
Colonel-in-Chief The Kings Own Yorkshire Light Infantry
1927-1968   *Regt Painting*

The Colonels Of The Regiment 1927-1968

Fig: 2 Gen Sir Charles Deedes
1927 – 1947   Regt Archive

Fig: 3 Major Gen William Robb
1947 – 1950   Regt Archive

Fig: 4 Lt Gen Sir Harold Redman
1950 – 1960   Regt Archive

Fig: 5 Lt Gen Sir Roger Bower
1960 – 1966   Regt Archive

Fig: 6 Major Gen John Deedes
1966 – 1968   Regt Archive

Honorary Colonels
4th Territorial Battalion
1948 - 1968

Fig: 7 Lt Col Tom Chadwick   1948 – 1955   Regt Archive

Fig: 8 Lt Col Michael Kaye   1955 – 1966   Regt Archive

Fig: 9 Lt Col Edgar Baker   1966 – 1968 Regt Archive

This history is dedicated to

all those who served with

The King's Own Yorkshire Light Infantry

in the period

1945 – 1968

and especially those who died

or were killed

while serving with the Regiment

during this time

Yield To None

The History Of
The King's Own Yorkshire Light Infantry

Volume VII

1945 – 1968

Contents Page

Acknowledgements

My sincere thanks go to all those whose names appear in the Bibliography and the Reference section. The framework of the book has been taken from the Regimental Journal *The Bugle*, and I am indebted to the many editors and contributors who were involved with its production. This final volume of the Regiment's history covers a period of 23 years and has been pieced together with the active cooperation of many of the participants. The work deviates from the norm in that much of the primary source material has not yet found its way into any archive but has been in the hands of former members of the Regiment who are still very much alive – and Yorkshiremen too, with all that that implies.

The initial request for stories, anecdotes, photographs, or any relevant material, produced a mass of information, with the result that it has not been possible to include quotations from all those who contributed. The source of each quotation used has been footnoted, and where described as a 'Memoir' the full text can be found in the Regimental archive. All the material, whether included or not, will be held in the Regimental archive for this period.

There are a number of people, however, who should be thanked for their particular contributions. The current Regimental Secretary, Major Michael Deedes, must be credited with having the original idea for producing this final volume of the Regiment's history. His willing cooperation at every stage of the operation has been much appreciated. On the many occasions that I visited the Light Infantry Office (Yorkshire), the staff at Minden House, Captain Reg Robinson, and Mrs Viv Lewis, always provided that degree of efficient assistance every researcher hopes to find on his quest for information. Major Deedes' predecessor, Colonel John Cowley, who served with the Regiment for much of the time in question, was subjected to frequent visits and telephone calls during the course of which his memory of individuals and events was taxed to the full. At the Malay Veterans Association annual reunions, Tom Morgan, John (Jock) Scurr, John Barnes, and the other veterans readily answered questions about events over fifty years before: John Barnes contributed the whole of Appendix 6, the story of *The Minden Post*. A copy of the penultimate draft of the book was sent to a number of retired officers who were willing not only to read it, but also to comment and check its historical accuracy. This proved to be a most valuable exercise and I am indebted to Major General Anthony Makepeace-Warne, Brigadier Roger Preston, Colonel John Cowley, Colonel Colin Huxley, Colonel Brian Lees, Lieutenant Colonel Peter Fleming, Lieutenant Colonel Ashley 'Tinny' Tinson, Major John Hutton and Captain Roy Ackling for their comments.

I must also thank Michael Ball, Head of the Department of Printed Books at the National Army Museum, for providing answers to a number of questions that baffled my usual sources of information. Stephen Lane and Christopher Oakford, of the Ministry of Defence's Department of Army Casualties post Second World War at Upavon, Wiltshire, and Catherine Witt, of the Enquiries Section of the Commonwealth War Graves Commission were most helpful in checking the list of soldiers who died while serving with the Regiment. Geoff Preece, Head of Museums and Art Galleries for Doncaster Metropolitan Borough Council, and his staff at the Museum have always been most helpful on the many occasions that I visited the Regimental Museum. Major M. Young, Deputy Commanding Officer of the North Saskatchewan Regiment, kindly allowed me to reproduce much of his work on the history of that Regiment, which forms part of Appendix 5. Mr Brian Ford, a historian and former colleague, read one of the later drafts and provided a valuable and independent assessment of the historical content. The historian, Dr George Betts, who joined the Regiment in Malaya in May 1949 as a National Service Commissioned officer, not only provided a great deal of source material, but also much sound advice and encouragement.

I have received many photographs from individual contributors, but mention must be made of the huge number from the KOYLI/2LI website made available by former Corporal Peter Shields, Malcolm Moore and Les Parkin. Those photographs not used in the book will be placed in the Regimental archive. Photographs labelled IWM are produced by kind permission of the Imperial War Museum. Mike Parsons and Victoria Keys of Propagator Press assisted in the final preparation of the book, and this was much appreciated.

As ever, I would like to thank my wife for her continued support and advice, especially her patient reading, and re-reading of the manuscript from the earliest to the final drafts.

Finally, given all the help that has been forthcoming, any errors in the book are entirely my responsibility.

Malcolm K. Johnson
Doncaster 2005

Author's Notes

Emergency:

The term Emergency has been used throughout this history to describe the periods of terrorist activity that occurred in each of the former colonies. The use of this word stems directly from the attempt by successive British governments to avoid using the word 'war'. Having just experienced six years of World War, public opinion in Britain was unwilling to sanction involvement in any further wars, no matter how minor. (The exception being the Korean War.) The Emergencies in Malaya, Kenya, and Cyprus could, however, be more accurately described as civil wars, with rival groups drawn from the civil population fighting each other for the right to rule the country once the British had left. In most cases, the tactics adopted by the terrorists resulted in the killing of far more of the civilian population than members of the security forces.

Serjeant:

The spelling of the rank of Serjeant, with a 'j' rather than a 'g', has been maintained at the request of many members of the Regiment. In replying to a letter in the autumn 1963 edition of *The Bugle* that ended, 'let no-one take our "j's" and make them "g's".' the editor pointed out –
' "Standing Orders of the KOYLI – 1933" has the following note: "The spelling used in King's Regulations is adopted for the words SERJEANT, PIQUET and WAGON (not sergeant, picquet and waggon)." Queen's Regulations, Para. 391, Sec.VII, as amended 10/5/63, shows Sergeant with a "G". The change was made in 1951. – (Ed).'
Although not all of the previous six volumes of the Regimental History used the letter 'j' rather than a 'g', it was felt appropriate that the tradition be maintained in this final volume.

Maps:

It has not been possible to include the name of every town and village mentioned in the text. This is especially true of the maps illustrating the Malaya and Borneo periods when KOYLI patrols visited, and were involved in actions near, very small villages and settlements.

Place names:	When the former colonies gained their independence, many chose to renames towns, regions, and even the country – Southern Rhodesia became Zimbabwe, and the name of its former capital, Salisbury, was changed to Harare. A number of name changes were made in Malaya – the former Province Wellesley changed to Pinang, and the village of Grik became Gerik, while Bidor changed but one letter to become Bidur. In the town of Aden, the area known to 1st KOYLI as Tawahi is now At-Tawahi; Maalla has had a number of spellings including Ma'ala, Ma'alla, and Ma'Allah, while Khormaksar is shown on some maps as Khaur Maksar. The Aden Protectorate became South Yemen in 1968, with Aden as its capital, and in 1990 North and South Yemen merged into the single country of Yemen. Since 1968, many of the villages 'up country' have made either complete, or very significant changes to their names. Throughout the text, the names that were used by the KOYLI at the time have been maintained.
Ranks and Awards	The rank, decorations and awards of those named in the text are those that were applicable at the time. The final rank, together with a complete list of all decorations and awards, has not always been given, even in the Index of Names. Exceptions have been made in the Reference section where the final rank of a named source has been used.
Names:	During the early part of the Battalion's tour of Malaya, there were two officers with identical surnames names, and almost identical initials. The third editor of *The Minden Post* was Captain J.M. Hutton who was known as Black John, not to be confused with – Lieutenant J.M.C. Hutton known simply as John.
Appendix 3:	For the years 1945 to 1948, the name of the battalion (and in some cases the name of the company) in which the soldier was serving at the time of his death has been recorded. The amalgamation of the 1st and 2nd Battalions in November 1948 made this unnecessary.
Footnotes:	Where quotation marks are shown, and no footnote number given, the quotation has been taken from *The Bugle*. Notes labelled 'Memoir' have been made available by the named sources, and a copy of the whole contribution forms part of the archive of this final period of the Regiment's History.

List Of Maps

1. **GERMANY 1945 – 1968**
   Three tours of Germany were undertaken in this period, 1st KOYLI Battalion HQ were located in the underlined towns.

2. **MALAYA 1947 – 1951**
   KOYLI operational responsibility extended throughout the states of Perlis, Kedah and Province Wellesley (now named Pinang), plus the island of Penang. Many operations were also carried out in Perak.

3. **KENYA 1954 – 1955**
   The 1st KOYLI's main area of operation was to the west of Mount Kenya in the Aberdare Range.

4. **ADEN 1955 – 1956**
   The town of Aden and the immediate surroundings.

5. **THE ADEN PROTECTORATE 1955 – 1956**
   1st KOYLI's initial HQ was at RAF Khormaksar, but companies trained at Dhala, and forays were made to parts of the western sheikdoms.

6. **CYPRUS 1955 – 1957**
   Numerous roads criss-cross the whole island. Remote tracks in the Troodos and Kyrenia areas were frequently used by EOKA.

7. **BRUNEI AND THE ISLAND OF BORNEO 1961 – 1964**
   With few roads, rivers provide the principal means of transportation. For 1st KOYLI, helicopters became an important means of moving troops over this difficult jungle terrain.

8. **HABILAYN January – March 1966**
   The area surrounding Habilayn and the airstrip.

List Of Illustrations

Frontispiece
1. Her Majesty Queen Elizabeth The Queen Mother
   Colonel-in-Chief The King's Own Yorkshire Light Infantry 1927-1968   Regt. Painting

The Colonels of the Regiment
2. Gen Sir Charles Deedes   1927 - 1947   Regt Archive
3. Major Gen William Robb   1947 - 1950   Regt Archive
4. Lt Gen Sir Harold Redman   1950 - 1960   Regt Archive
5. Lt Gen Sir Roger Bower   1960 - 1966   Regt Archive
6. Major Gen John Deedes   1966 - 1968   Regt Archive

Honorary Colonels of the 4th KOYLI (TA)
7. Lt Col Tom Chadwick   1948 - 1955   Regt Archive
8. Lt Col Michael Kaye   1955 - 1966   Regt Archive
9. Lt Col Edgar Barker   1966 - 1968   Regt Archive

Germany 1945 – 1947
10. Marching through the City of Leeds after the Freedom ceremony, 1945 .   Yorks Post
11. The Minden Memorial, Germany   Regt Archive
12. KOYLI Bugle Platoon marching through Minden, 1947.   Regt Archive

Malaya 1947 – 1951
13. A patrol from 'C' Coy in the Kuala Kangsar area, 1949.   J. Scurr
14. Part of 'C' Company being transported to Alor Star, 1949.   J. Scurr
15. Travelling to Kroh before 'Operation Betong', Feb 1951.   Dr G.M. Betts
16. Preparing to leave Kroh on 'Operation Betong', Feb 1951.   Dr G.M. Betts
17. Gen Sir Charles Keighley C-in-C FARELF, inspecting 11 Platoon,
    Kulim, June 1951.   Dr G.M. Betts

Germany 1951 – 1954
18. HM Queen Elizabeth with Officers 1st KOYLI, Strensall, Oct 1951.   Regt Archive
19. An East German watchtower overlooking the British sector of Berlin, 1953.
    P. Shield
20. Lt Gen Sir Richard Gale, C-in-C BAOR, Lt Col Nic Pope, and Major Healing
    observe 2Lt J.S. Cowley's Anti-Tank Gun Platoon at work in Berlin, 1953.
    Col J.S. Cowley
21. Sjt L. Raveney's MMG Platoon being inspected by GOC Northern
    Command, Lt Gen Sir Geoffrey Evans, and Lt Col Pope, Strensall, 1954.
    Regt Archive

Kenya 1954 – 1955
22. The Anti-Tank Platoon's camp cookhouse during Op. 'Searchlight II'
    in the Aberdares, Aug 1955.   Sir David Goodall
23. 2Lt David Goodall's patrol – Op.'Torchlight I' in the Aberdares
    L:R. Rear: Pte Sayer, 2Lt Goodall, L/Cpl Thomson, Joshua (Kikuyu Tracker)
    Front: Pte O'Toole, Pte Wales, Pte Moffat, Aug 1955.   Sir David Goodall
24. Capt Dick Unett, Lt John Cowley, Capt Tom Cairns (MO) at about 15,500 ft
    on Mt Kenya, 1955.   Col. J.S. Cowley
25. Cpl Atkinson (standing) and his team prepare for a Mortar shoot at Hall's
    Farm, Kenya, 1955.   Sir David Goodall

xiii

Aden   1954 – 1956

26. Dhala Camp, 80 miles north of Aden.   P. Sheild
27. Dhala market – L:R Capt Mike Tibbets (MO), Capt Tim Green,
    2Lt Dan Dyas.   Sir David Goodall
28. Op. 'Flagday'. On the way to show the Flag, and collect the money
    L:R. Pte Lawson, Pte Johnson, 2Lt David Goodall, 1956.   Sir David Goodall
29. Op. 'Flagday' 2Lt Brian Dale and Sjt Ashcroft making camp
    on the first day, 1956.   Sir David Goodall
30. Three houses in Ahwar were blown up as part of the fine, 1956.   Sir David Goodall

Cyprus 1955 – 1957

31. FM Sir John Harding, Governor of Cyprus, with Lt Col John Deedes
    during a visit to 1ˢᵗ KOYLI at Limni, 1956.   Col. J.S. Cowley
32. A well-armed signaller in the Troodos mountains, 1956.   Regt Archive
33. CSM F.H. Dolby leading a mobile night curfew patrol in Nicosia, 1956.   Regt Archive
34. 'D' Coy removing a barbed wire barricade in Nicosia, August1956.   Col. J.S. Cowley

Germany 1957 – 1961

35. Honour Guard for the Under Secretary of State for Defence,
    Christopher Soames. Hilden, 1961.   Capt. R. Ackling
36. The last National Servicemen leave the Regiment, Hilden, 10 July, 1961. Regt Archive
37. HM the QM with Officers 1ˢᵗ KOYLI, Pontefract, 28 Oct 1961.   Regt Archive
38. Parading 4ᵗʰ KOYLI's new Colours, 3 Aug 1962.   Regt Archive

Borneo 1961 – 1964

39. L/Cpl P. Oberg, with Pte Woodall and a Recce Platoon patrol following,
    crossing a native bridge in the Borneo jungle.   P. Shield
40. A patrol preparing for operations in the jungle.
    2ⁿᵈ from L, Pte Trigg Nicholls, 4ᵗʰ from L: Cpl Milton Baden Powell Starky.
                                                                                           P. Shield
41. Boats on the river are the main method of civilian transport in Borneo. Regt Archive
42. A KOYLI patrol making its way through the Borneo jungle.   IWM
43. Helicopters and fixed wing aircraft on the airstrip at Bareo, 1964.   IWM
44. This elevated machine gun position formed part of the defence system
    guarding the important airstrip at Bareo.   P.Shield

Aden 1964 – 1966

44. Searchlight and trailer landed by helicopter on one of the highest buildings
    in Maalla, 1965.   Regt Archive
45. The 'Cap Badge' picket overlooked the Wadi Taym, 1966   P. Shield
46. 'B' Company on a training march. L:R. Pte Street, Cpl Mellors, Pte Curtiss,
    Sjt Moss, Ptes Alder, Healey, Mountain, Wroe and Brant, 1966.   Regt Archive
48. 'A' Company going up country from Radfan Camp, 1965.   P. Shield
49. L/Cpl Loveday and part of 'D' Company, waiting to be taken by
    helicopter from Habilayn airstrip, 1966.   P. Shield
50. 4ᵗʰ KOYLI on exercise at Thetford Camp, 1965.
    L:R. -?-, Major J.M.P. Naylor, Sjt Oates, Lt T.J. Crowther.   Regt Archive

Germany 1966 – 1968

51. Pte Lloyd, and Pte Matthews (driver) on a stretch of the Berlin border.   Regt Archive
52. Berlin Tattoo, 1968.   P. Shield
53. Allied Forces Day Parade, 1968.   Regt Archive
54. Vesting Day 10 July, 1968.   P. Shield
55. Colours and Regimental Silver of 1ˢᵗ KOYLI.   Regt Archive

Foreword

This concluding volume of the history of the Regiment covers the period from 1945, and the post-Second World War adjustments to the Army, to the formation of the Light Infantry on 10th July 1968.

These twenty-three years proved to be a period of intense activity and heavy engagement. Against the background of the cold war, the Regiment was called upon to conduct operations in many theatres, some familiar, and some new to the Regiment. Throughout the earlier years, we were heavily dependant upon the National Service entry to the Regiment, and it is proper that their generous contribution be remembered.

I am deeply grateful to Malcolm Johnson for his diligent research and sympathetic telling of the Regiment's story, and to those members of the Regiment who contributed in diverse ways to the production of this history.

It is only natural that we should mourn the passing of our Regiment, but we should do so conscious of a history of comradeship, adversity borne with courage and cheerfulness and the consolation of a job well done – CEDE NULLIS.

Salisbury
A Makepeace-Warne
Major General
January 2005

Introduction

Post War Problems

The war in Europe ended at midnight 8 May 1945, but it was 2 September before the final act of the Second World War took place with the Japanese signing of the terms of surrender on board the United States battleship Missouri. At the end of the First World War Britain's armed forces emerged far stronger than they had been in 1914. Britain and its empire had made a major contribution towards victory, and the defeat of Germany in 1918 removed, for the time being at least, her most dangerous political, economic, and colonial rival. During the early 1920s, the army dealt with a number of problems in the Middle East, and closer to home in Ireland, but eventually resumed its former peacetime role of policing the empire.

In 1945 Britain's position was much more unsure. Her commitments, as outlined in the government's Defence White Paper of June 1946, were, (1) to ensure Germany and Japan complied with the terms of surrender, (2) to assist with the occupation of Austria, (3) to assist in the national recovery of Greece, (4) to carry out the country's responsibilities in Palestine, (5) to oversee the end of Japanese occupation of Allied territories in South East Asia, and finally, (6) to maintain both internal security within the Empire and safeguard communications with the scattered bases throughout the world.

The initial post-war fear of Britain and France had been the resurgence of Germany, which resulted in the signing of the Brussels Treaty in March 1948. This concern was soon to be replaced by the far more serious problem of the lack of agreement between the two super-powers, the United States of America and the Soviet Union, over the future of Germany and Soviet policy in eastern Europe. Added to the formidable list of Britain's responsibilities was extreme pressure from the United States for Britain to take the lead in producing an international force for the defence of Western Europe against the growing threat from the Soviet Union and her Communist satellites. With chaos prevailing throughout Europe, Britain was the only western European nation with a viable military force on the continent. Nevertheless, had she been faced with a determined attack from the east, Britain would have been unable to provide little more than a token resistance to the Red Army without substantial help from the United States. The country was thus faced with the responsibilities of a world power, but lacked the financial means to fulfill its obligations unaided.

For military planners in Britain, the main problem was a lack of manpower. Those men who had been called up for 'wartime service only' were expecting to be demobilized on the principle of 'first in – first out'. There were some instances of dissatisfaction but, in general, demobilization after the Second World War was achieved without the huge disturbances that followed the unfair process adopted in 1918-19. However, if promises were to be honoured, and justice done, a way was needed to produce the numbers of men to enable the armed forces to fulfill the nation's commitments. The problem was a complicated one, given the nation's enormous effort during six years of total war.

In July 1946, the first priority of the newly appointed Chief of the Imperial General Staff (CIGS), Field Marshal Montgomery, (he succeeded Field Marshal Viscount Alanbrooke) was to find sufficient troops to enable the army to meet the demands being placed upon it. Montgomery proposed that a period of 18 months conscription (National Service) be established for all males over the age of 18 years. In the face of considerable opposition from many quarters, a Bill to this effect was passed by Parliament in the following November. (An amendment to the Bill was passed on 1 April 1947 reducing the period of service from 18 to 12 months, but this proved to be impractical and was never implemented.) The CIGS planned to produce an army of 305,000 men, with the ranks of a revitalised Territorial Army being filled by ex-National Servicemen who would serve for a period of six-years on the reserve list. National Service (conscription being a word to be avoided in peacetime), and the debate on its effectiveness, persists to this day. At the time, however, the Treasury, supported by Herbert Morrison and Sir Stafford Cripps, was against the idea, considering it wasteful of valuable manpower and thereby uneconomical. With Prime Minister Attlee in favour, and strong support from Montgomery, who wished to see ever more men in the army, and whose word in the immediate post-war years carried much weight, the Bill was passed.

A White Paper published in February 1947 suggested that withdrawal from the Dutch East Indies and Japan in the Far East, and Venezia-Giulia and Trieste in Europe, together with the evacuation of all troops from a newly independent India, would allow for a reduction in service personnel of 500,000 men and women during the current year. Withdrawal from India would indeed produce substantial savings, but it was to be almost two decades before the garrisons guarding the lifeline to the subcontinent were evacuated. A start was made on this in August 1947 when plans were announced for the withdrawal of some 200,000 men from these overseas stations, a move that it was hoped would be completed by March 1948.

The difficult problem of maintaining British influence in world affairs led the Foreign Secretary, Ernest Bevin, to develop a strategy of persuading the USA to reject isolationism and, as a matter of self-interest, continue to provide US troops to guarantee the security of Western Europe. Bevin worked tirelessly on plans to create a North Atlantic Treaty Organization

(NATO), and his efforts were finally rewarded when the treaty was signed in April 1949. Together with most of Britain's policy-makers at the time, Bevin and his foreign office advisors assumed that, with Europe secure, Britain would be able to concentrate a greater proportion of her effort, especially her military resources, to its more traditional interests outside Europe. No longer a super-power, it was nevertheless felt by many that Britain could remain a great power, while at the same time reducing its imperial commitments. In this way such specific overseas assets as Malayan rubber and Middle Eastern oil could be safeguarded, while Britain's position in Asia and Africa would ensure its influence could be maintained into the foreseeable future.

During the three decades immediately following the end of the Second World War, Britain's politicians attempted to provide a sound economy and full employment, while at the same time improving the country's social services, which were to become an increasing drain on the national exchequer. Britain's diminishing economic power resulted in a failure to generate sufficient resources to fund her strategic defense aspirations in both Europe and the Empire. The armed forces became involved in a protracted, and piecemeal withdrawal from the responsibilities of Empire. The final chapter of the history of the King's Own Yorkshire Light Infantry (KOYLI) is closely interwoven with this process for the Regiment served in Europe, the Middle and Far East, and was involved in almost all of the engagements, variously described as Emergencies, Troubles, or Anti-Terrorist Actions, that were to take place during this time.

1

Release and Reassignment

Arriving in France from the Middle East in February 1945, 1st KOYLI took part in the final weeks of the campaign in northwest Europe. As part of 15th Infantry Brigade, 5th Division, the Battalion fired its last shots of the Second World War at Potrau and Buchen on the Elbe-Lubeck Canal. By 8 May, the day on which the German Army surrendered to the Western Allies, it had crossed the river Elbe and reached the town of Ratzeburg 17 miles south of the port of Lubeck. On the last day of the war 1/4th KOYLI, 146th Infantry Brigade, 49th Division, was in the Grebe Line, near the Dutch town of Ede, where a partial truce had been in operation for some time to allow Royal Army Service Corps (RASC) convoys to carry much needed food to Amsterdam, Rotterdam and The Hague. The following day 1/4th KOYLI moved into Utrecht and began disarming elements of the German Army. The 8th KOYLI, formed in 1940, and later converted to 94th Light Anti-Aircraft (LAA) Regiment Royal Artillery (RA), had landed in Normandy as part of the Guards Armoured Division. It too ended the war in northern Germany on the estuary of the river Elbe near Lubeck.

The rapid disintegration of the German armies in northern Italy on 2 May 1945 came as a surprise to 2/4th KOYLI, which was completing its preparations for yet another offensive in Italy. The Battalion was quickly moved to the area of Capporetto and Plezzo in northeastern Italy where it encountered the Yugoslavian troops of Marshal Tito. The Yugoslavian communists were intent upon occupying that part of Italy, which they had recently conquered, and were busily changing road signs and street names from Italian to Serbo-Croat. Tact and diplomacy were needed in this very difficult situation and, after discussions, Tito's men finally agreed to withdraw. The 5th KOYLI, which had been converted in 1938 to 53rd LAA Regiment RA, was serving with 8th Army, and ended the war in Forli, 36 miles northwest of the coastal resort of Rimini in Italy. The 57th LAA Regiment RA (the second line unit of the 53rd), which also served with 8th Army in North Africa and Italy, was eventually transferred to Greece where it was disbanded shortly after 8 May 1945. The 9th KOYLI, which had been formed from the Yorkshire Dragoons in February 1942, had also fought in Italy, but had been broken up before the end of 1944, most of the men being transferred to 2/4th KOYLI, 138th Infantry Brigade, 46th Division. When the war in Europe ended there were three KOYLI units in England – the Regimental Depot was at Strensall Barracks, York, which was also the home of No 6 Holding Battalion, while No 6 Infantry Training Centre was based at Berwick-on-Tweed.

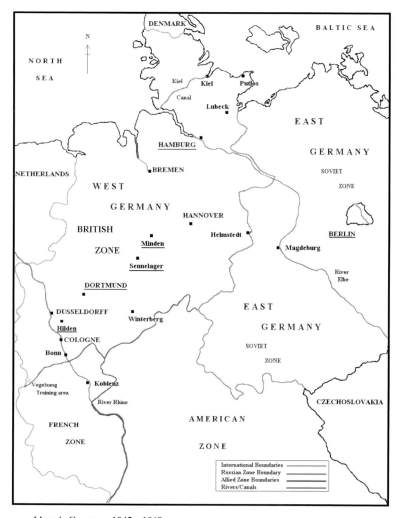

Map: 1 **Germany 1945 – 1968**
Three tours in Germany were undertaken in this period. 1ˢᵗ KOYLI Battalion HQ were located in the underlined towns.

News of the Japanese surrender reached 2nd KOYLI at Sultan's Battery, Mysore, southern India, where it was carrying out jungle training in preparation for the planned invasion of Malaya. Having 'toiled like beasts of burden, up slippery, mud-covered hillsides, with filled packalls swinging from bamboo poles', come VJ Day the Battalion '[emerged] from this arboreal fastness [where] our vision was bounded by teak trees and dense clumps of lantana,' and moved to Bethmangala near the Kolar gold fields.[1]

In November came a change of Commanding Officer (CO), Lieutenant Colonel W.S.F. Hickie OBE, replacing Lieutenant Colonel B.W. Wood. November also brought a move northwards to Malthone in the Madhya Pradesh Province of central India. Once the site of a Rajput fort, Malthone village was little more than a collection of mud huts, but had the distinction of being the location of one of General Orde Wingate's 'Chindit' training camps. Here, in a tented camp with the main buildings made of stone, the Battalion stayed until April 1946. Despite the continual departure of personnel back to England, 2nd KOYLI continued to grow and almost reached 1,200 men. Many of the newcomers were from other services including the Royal Navy, Royal Marines, Royal Air Force, and a large contingent from the Royal Artillery. For many, especially the former Naval and Air Force personnel, life in an infantry battalion must have come as quite a shock. The weather at Malthone, particularly during the winter months, was pleasant and healthy, but the main problem was dust, which crept into everything. One noted absentee at this time was, 'The well known character, Company Serjeant Major J.P. Howson MM, [who] has disappeared into the wilds of Burma to seek untold treasures, left hidden in the 1942 campaign. We hope the ship has been built that is capable of carrying the "loot".'[2] Unfortunately, as Lieutenant Colonel Hickie reported in the next edition of *The Bugle*, very little of the buried treasure was retrieved.

Also in India was another converted battalion of the Regiment. The 7th KOYLI, which had become 149th Regiment of the Royal Armoured Corps (RAC), arrived from England in 1941 and played a prominent part in the relief of Kohima, April 1944, and the fighting in the Imphal Plain. After being re-equipped with Churchill tanks, it too had been preparing to re-enter the struggle against the Japanese in Malaya, but the dropping of the atomic bomb brought about a decisive end to the war in the east.

On 4 October 1944, Leeds City Council had passed a resolution conferring on the Regiment the Freedom of the City, 'in recognition of your long and historical association with this City in which Regiment so many of our sons have been proud to serve'. The formal ceremony to mark this occasion took place on the 7 June 1945 when General Sir Charles Deedes KCB, CMG, DSO, Colonel of the Regiment, accepted from the Lord Mayor of Leeds, Alderman C.V. Walker, a Scroll recording this resolution.[3] Following the ceremony, the Guard of Honour, 100 members of No 6 Holding Battalion, with bayonets fixed, drums beating, colours unfurled, and led by the Regimental Band, marched to the Civic Hall through streets lined with thousands of cheering people.

In Germany, 1st KOYLI moved to Neuhaldensleben, near Magdeburg at the beginning of June 1945, and on 1 July it was involved in 'Operation Hammer'. The agreed boundaries between the Allied Zones of occupation and the Russian Zone placed the area held by 1st KOYLI outside the Allied Zone. The object of the operation was to achieve an ordered transfer of the area to the Headquarters staff and 100 men of the 12th USSR Guards Corps. Following a cordial meeting between the KOYLI and the Russians, at noon, 2 July, a Russian Lieutenant Colonel, accompanied by six other ranks and a woman interpreter, presented himself at Battalion Headquarters.

Fig: 10 Marching through the city of Leeds after the Freedom ceremony 1945
Yorks Post

His claim to take command of all troops in Neuhaldensleben having been politely and successfully contested, he left with his party to set up an office with the Burgomaster. [4]

By 3 July, all the arrangements had been completed and the 1st Battalion moved west to Wolfenbuttel, 50 miles east of Hanover, where it was established in the former German 'Flak' Barracks. The cordial relationship with the Russians, which had accompanied the immediate ending of hostilities, was soon to be replaced by mutual suspicion, and the Battalion's close proximity to the new frontier with the Russian Zone required strict attention to detail, much tact, and a high level of military efficiency.

In early 1946, 1st KOYLI not only relocated, but also changed Division, leaving 5th Infantry to join 7th Armoured, the famous Desert Rats, where it became part of 131st Lorried Infantry Brigade. (The title must have had a rather incongruous ring for a regiment of Light Infantry.) The 1st Battalion established its Headquarters (HQ) at Bergedorf, a suburb of Hamburg, where the main duty was to guard some 7,000 captured German SS troops and former guards of the Nazi concentration camps at Neuengamme, another suburb of Hamburg. It was believed that in these camps, known as the Neuengamme-Ring, more than 82,000 Jews had died after being literally worked to death, their bodies filling a huge grave estimated by Private Basil Mason to be 'about the size of a football pitch.' Many of the 'old hands' in the Battalion had departed and been replaced by young conscripts who saw for themselves ample evidence of the purpose of the camp.

The two incinerators, used to burn the bodies of the unfortunates at Neuengamme, still rear their ugly heads above the squat, green-painted living huts. Outside one of the incinerators are the charred remnants of thousands of pairs of boots and shoes, in themselves mute testimony to the sufferings once endured here by Jewry. One day, I saw, caught up in the barbed wire, a small child's bootee.[5]

The German prisoners of war (POWs) were subjected to a long process of interrogation and, of the fifteen placed on trial before a War Crimes Court in Hamburg, eleven were hanged; one of the latter being the camp's former commandant. Despite the former status and reputation of the inmates, Private Mason believed that relations between the men of 1st KOYLI and their prisoners were relatively humane, 'they were simply defeated enemies', although he did understand the hostility felt by many of his comrades who had lost relatives and friends in the war.[6]

At the beginning of June 1945, 1/4th KOYLI left Utrecht for the area around Meschede, Nordrhein-Westfalen. Officially the 1/4th's immediate tasks were guarding camps containing Displaced Persons (DPs), ex- POWs – mostly Russians and Poles – and enforcing law and order, but 'B' Company's scribe saw the work in a different light. 'We became a combination of welfare workers, CID and wholesale provision dealers.'[7] The rumours of a move, which had been circulating for some time, were about to be proved correct. In a classic example of bureaucratic logic, in November 1/4th KOYLI moved from Meschede westwards to Calais, then journeyed through southern France and on to Switzerland before finally reaching Italy, where it settled into a crowded transit camp on the edge of Lake Como. With Battalion HQ at Bergamo, the rifle companies were dispersed around the area north of Milan.

Following its brush with the Yugoslavian troops in Plezzo in early May 1945, the 2/4th KOYLI travelled via Trevisio across the Alps into Austria. 'Along the route could be seen the final and overwhelming defeat of the German forces – thousands of prisoners, large dumps of material, and hastily abandoned guns, equipment and kit strewn along the sides of the road.'[8] The Battalion moved into the area of Wolfsberg and set up its HQ in the village of Twimberg. For the companies, which were dispersed over a wide area, the main tasks were security patrols, de-Nazification duties, collecting arms, guarding POWs, and escorting former Allied POWs and DPs to concentration areas in preparation for their return home. In August came yet another move, this time to Mureck close to the Yugoslav border, which was followed by the final move to Murzzuschlag on the main road from Graz to Vienna.

In early 1946, an 'A' Company's contributor to *The Bugle* had written, 'If everything goes as planned, we shall be in Austria by the time this is printed... Shall we be sorry to leave Italy? NOT A BIT!'[9] Everything did go according to plan and on 24 March 1946, 1/4th KOYLI arrived in

8

Murzzuschlag, Austria, to relieve 2/4th KOYLI. The 2/4th was disbanded the same day and those who were not returning to England remained to be absorbed by the 1/4th. This process, together with the continuing return of men to civilian life, brought many changes in personnel to 1/4th KOYLI as it settled down to its occupation duties. One of the saddest consequences of the change was the transfer from 49th (West Riding) Division to 46th (North Midlands) Division – exchanging the Polar Bear shoulder flash for the Oak Tree. The change proved short lived, and a mere six months after the move to Austria 1/4th KOYLI too was placed in suspended animation. This time, however, there was to be a significant difference. The Battalion returned to the United Kingdom (UK) from Austria in June, and was disbanded on 16 August 1946, but 60 men of 'C' Company remained in Austria under a new title, 'Z' Vienna Police Company, The KOYLI, with Major R.D. Moore in command and Captain P. Strickland as 2nd i/c. The Company's task was to assist with the policing of the streets of Vienna, which they did 'and look smart in S.D. peaked caps, green hosetops, white anklets and belts and green on white chevrons.'[10]

The 8th KOYLI (94th LAA), based at Stolberg, Germany, was also employed in security patrols, the processing of DPs, and many of the tasks that had fallen to the occupying powers, but on 9 January 1946, it too was disbanded. In late May 1945, 5th KOYLI (53rd LAA) left the Forli area for Udine, where it performed similar tasks to those being carried out by other KOYLI battalions in Germany and Austria. Another move in July dispersed the 53rd LAA batteries to such exotic locations as Rome, Bologna, Rimini and Florence. One more move in September took it to the Milan area, before it finally returned to Udine in May 1946 where it was relieved of all duties.

In early June 1946, 1st KOYLI was happy to leave Bergedorf, and Neuengamme, and the odious duty of guarding the SS and former

Fig: 11 The Minden Memorial, Germany
Regt Archive

guards of the death camps. The new location could not have been a more appropriate one – Minden. Here, the Battalion was concentrated in the former Nazi SS Gneisenau Barracks where, on 1 August, the Colonel of the

Regiment addressed the whole Battalion and took the salute at the Minden Day Parade. In similar language to that used on 1 August nearly 200 years previously, Sir Charles greeted the parade with, 'Colonel Ridout, officers,

Fig: 12 KOYLI Bugle Platoon marching through Minden, 1947
Regt Archive

non-commissioned officers and private men of the 51st Regiment'. In his short address Sir Charles made references to the Regiment's history and ended by saying that, as he stood on the field of Minden, he was confident that The King's Own Yorkshire Light Infantry would ever carry out its duty to its Sovereign and its country as it had in the past.

In January 1946, Her Majesty Queen Elizabeth's traditional gift to the Regiment of a consignment of Christmas puddings duly arrived in India.[11] Having consumed the 'puds', 2nd KOYLI began serious training at various locations, some up to 85 miles away from the camp. The first contribution by 7th KOYLI (149th Royal Armoured Corps) to the first edition of the Regimental Journal *The Bugle*, which reappeared in January 1946, read, 'What the future holds for us, no one knows; one hopes for a speedy decision, as nothing is more frustrating than hanging about with no certain knowledge as to the future.'[12] The uncertainty was ended on 28 February 1946 when the Regiment was disbanded at Ahmednagar. The Regiment had lost its fighting vehicles the previous December and had latterly been used in an infantry role. The personnel were distributed between 146th RAC, 43rd Royal Tank Regiment, the RAC Depot, and 3rd Carabineers.

The concerns of 7th KOYLI were shared by many thousands of men on all fronts in the months immediately following the end of the war. All three services had greatly expanded since 1939, but demobilizing over 4.6 million men could not be accomplished in a matter of days, especially given the

10

commitments that victory had brought with it. To avoid the demobilization chaos that had followed the end of the First World War, officers, and men were placed in numbered Age/Service Groups (A/S Groups), which created a definite order of priority for return to civilian life. This scheme was introduced as soon as it became practicable and by the end of 1945 was beginning to have some appreciable effect, but not for many of those in the Far East.

For 2nd KOYLI, the year 1946 began with some concern for the situation in India. 'By now Internal Security was looming up before us as an urgent subject to be mastered by one and all.'[13] Discontent and rioting, which preceded and followed the British withdrawal from India in August 1947, were already beginning to surface. On the last day of February 1946, trouble in Jubbulpore caused 'C' Company to make a swift return to Malthone, but on arrival, it discovered that the situation was quiet and no action was required. At Easter, 2nd KOYLI moved south to the semi-hill station of Nasik, where it took up residence in the tented No 5 Camp of the Homeward Bound Trooping Depot. Any ideas of moving from here to 'Dear Old Blighty' were quickly dashed when orders for another move were received, and on 1 June the Battalion made the journey to No 2 Camp at Kalyan, some 40 miles from Bombay. The move to Kalyan meant the Battalion left 19th Indian Infantry Brigade, 8th Indian Division, and joined the newly raised 29th British Brigade Group, which included 1st Somersets, 1st Glosters and 28th Field Regiment RA.

Another expedition by Company Serjeant Major Howson to the interior of Burma in search of 2nd KOYLI's silver again proved fruitless, the only positive find being a typewriter, 'now a prize sought after by the rest of the Battalion'. Lieutenant Colonel Hickie's account of the fate of the Battalion's silver provided distressing reading, but fortunately, 'The Colours, after being carried out of Burma in the Regimental Serjeant Major's pack [RSM Guest], were entrusted to His Excellency the Viceroy for safe custody.'[14] Howson did eventually have some success and, when Serjeant Major of the Training Company at the Depot, explained to the Adjutant, Captain P.G. Fleming, how he had recovered the 2nd Battalion Commanding Officer's Bugle, lost with the rest of the Battalion's silver. Whilst searching in Burma, Howson spotted this fine instrument, chased with the crest and battle honours of the Battalion, slung over the shoulder of a Burmese policeman. The policeman was persuaded to part with the bugle, ' "Big John" Howson could be very persuasive'.

It was at Kalyan that some members of the Battalion experienced their first monsoon rain when, 'The thunder rolled and the rain lashed down in fury until it was impossible to see a yard through it.'[15] The stay at Kalyan lasted until September when the Battalion returned to the relative comfort of Deolali, and the mis-named Homeward Bound Training Depot, soon to be renamed Minden Lines. One of the first duties for the Battalion was patrolling Nasik City, which provided quite a change from the normal routine.

The growing aspirations of Indian nationalism ensured that, once the war with Japan had been brought to a satisfactory conclusion, Britain would be under pressure to negotiate the granting of independence. In 1946 the commercial benefits of holding on to India were far outweighed by the cost of trying to placate a reluctant continent and the British Prime Minister, Clement Attlee, announced that power would be transferred not later than June 1948. It soon became obvious that the Muslim and Hindu politicians could not negotiate an amicable solution to the problem of self-government, and reluctantly the British proposed the country be partitioned. Not wishing to be caught on the wrong side of any future border between the two faiths, huge movements of population began, especially in the Punjab. Rioting and disturbances took place and during the four month period July-October 1946, the British government announced that some 5,018 people had been killed and 18,320 injured; figures that were to rise considerably in the early months of 1947. The date for independence, and the creation of the two states of India and Pakistan, was set for 15 August 1947.

As time passed, many servicemen experienced what they considered were unnecessary delays to their return to 'Civvy Street', and there were some, particularly those in the Far East, whose patience was very sorely tried. In Deolali, Lieutenant Colonel Hickie issued a letter to all ranks of 2nd KOYLI urging those who were bent on writing to their Member of Parliament (MP) to save time and write to him instead. In a 'Special Bugle Call' of 18 November 1946, he pointed out that writing to them (MPs), 'is a waste of time, because in the end your letter returns to me and I have to answer it'. Private J. Heald was at pains to point out, 'I must stress our discontent was NOT with Colonel Hickie or our beloved regiment. Every man I knew had the greatest respect for our battalion ...'[16]

During the course of 1946, the Regiment was granted the privilege of the freedom of the City of Wakefield, 1 June; the Boroughs of Dewsbury and Batley, 29 June; and the Borough of Doncaster, 20 October. On each occasion, the Colonel of the Regiment was present to receive the Commemorative Scroll on behalf of the Regiment. In the ceremonies at Wakefield, Dewsbury and Batley, the Guard of Honour was provided by the 1/4th Battalion, but with the disbandment of the 1/4th in August, the Training Battalion from Berwick provided the Guard of Honour at the ceremony in Doncaster. Members of the Regimental Association took part in each ceremony, and as the men who had served their country during the war returned to their homes, so the membership of the various branches of the Association throughout the county, and indeed the country, began to grow. By late November 1946, the Regimental Depot and the 51st Primary Training Centre (PTC) had moved from Strensall to Ranby Camp, Retford, in Nottinghamshire. The KOYLI was now reduced to two regular battalions,

12

plus 'C' Company, 1/4th KOYLI, better known as 'Z' Garrison Police Company, Vienna (KOYLI).

In the weeks immediately following the ending of hostilities Germany had been divided into four zones, roughly corresponding to the areas occupied by the Allied armies when the fighting stopped. The British occupied the northern zone eastwards to the River Elbe; the Americans the southern zone to the border with Switzerland and eastwards to the Czechoslovakian border. A similar arrangement also divided Austria with, in the cases of Germany and Austria, the smaller French zones laying to the west behind the American zones. The Russian Zone extended over the whole of eastern Germany and eastern Austria. In each zone, the Allies were responsible for all aspects of government, and this proved to be a daunting task. Disarming and guarding the many thousands of German troops who had surrendered was made more difficult by the movement of hundreds of thousands of DPs who were criss-crossing the country trying to find ways of returning to their homes, or desperately fleeing westwards to avoid being trapped in the Soviet Zone.

The winter of 1946-47 was one of the worst on record, and while those in the UK shivered, conditions in Europe were desperate, especially in Germany where both food and fuel were in short supply. In January 1947, 'A' Company, 1st Battalion, was detached from Minden to the forests around Fallingbostel where the men felled timber, much of which formed the cargo of the first post war German commercial ship to leave Hamburg for the UK. For the remaining companies, their time was spent in training, but occasionally they provided Security Patrols in the neighbouring German towns. The monthly Security Check, an attempt to catch up with the local 'Black Marketeers', often produced evidence to show that illicit foodstuffs – plus coffee, petrol and other desirables – were constantly being traded. One patrol's enthusiasm to apprehend those responsible for the theft of a Humber Snipe car from within the barrier of Minden resulted in an embarrassing situation. A Humber Snipe having just passed it, the patrol stealthily crept up on a figure seen carefully covering the bonnet of the car with a large rug. Once the patrol was in place its leader's opening, 'Good evening', brought forth a blistering, 'What are you doing here?' from Brigadier Gordon, the former Commander of 131st Lorried Infantry Brigade! Later the patrol's leader admitted, 'We were admonished, and after a short conversation we proceeded on our way. The stolen car was found later by the Garrison CMP'.[17]

Some time in 1947, 'Z' Company moved to Villach in Corinthia and was re-named 'Z' Railway Police Company (Austria) KOYLI. Because widespread thieving from trains was taking place, the Company was given the task of providing escorts on trains carrying supplies from ports in Holland and Germany through to Austria and Italy. On one occasion, a train almost crossed the border into Yugoslavia, the production of a pistol being the only means by which the Zug Fuehrer (guard) could be persuaded to send it back on the correct route.[18] Many years later Lance-Corporal D. Lochrie remembered, 'There was a lot of pilfering and black market, so it was the job of the KOYLI to see that it reached its destination safely. I was very proud to be part of this service. The KOYLI did a great job.'[19] It was 'Z' Company's proud boast that, during their time in Austria, nothing was pilfered from any train they guarded. The Company had the honour of providing the train guard when Field Marshal Montgomery visited Austria, but by August 1948 it had lost its last KOYLI CO, Major P. Strickland, and

It was with a sad heart that I hauled down the Company flag. The green banner with the golden bugle and crown had proudly floated over the Police Headquarters in Vienna and the Railway Police Headquarters in Styria.[20]

The 1st Battalion spent May 1947 at Vögelsang, where it carried out infantry/tank exercises. Vögelsang, the site of a former Nazi Political and Kultur School, to the south west of Cologne, still showed some evidence of the cult of 'Aryan Supremacy' in the form of bas-reliefs. American strafing had caused a great deal of damage both here and in many of the surrounding villages in the days following the Battle of the Bulge in early 1945. The exposed position of the camp and the absence of running water were minor distractions to the soldiers, their chief concern being the total lack of any form of entertainment!

Earlier in the year Captain T. Reynolds MC, who had succeeded Major G.B. Whitworth as OC 'C' Company, received a warning order that he was to be posted to Wakefield, to become Adjutant of 4th KOYLI (TA) which was to be reactivated on 1 May. The CO of the reformed 4th Battalion was to be Lieutenant Colonel M.A.C.P. Kaye, with Major J.R. Haslegrave OBE, 2nd i/c; both officers had family connections with the Battalion stretching back into the previous century. The 4th Battalion was to join 149th Infantry Brigade (TA) of 50th Northumbrian Division. On the same date, 1 May, the former 53rd and 57th LAA Regiments in Doncaster were also to be reactivated, but with new numbers and titles, 553rd (KOYLI) LAA Regiment, RA (TA), and 557th Mixed (KOYLI) Heavy Anti-Aircraft (HAA) Regiment RA (TA). It was the government's intention that time expired National Servicemen would serve as reservists in TA units such as these.

While a number of Minden Day celebrations were taking place in Germany, Austria, and India, the main celebration in 1947 was held in York. The day began with a ceremony at York Minster, which was attended by the Colonel-in-Chief of the Regiment, Her Majesty Queen Elizabeth, General Sir Charles Deedes, and representatives of every unit of the Regiment. During the ceremony, a Book of Honour, containing the names of 1,200 members of the Regiment who had lost their lives in the war of 1939-1945, was handed to the Dean for safe keeping in the Regimental Chapel. This particular Minden Day also marked the transfer of the

Colonelcy of the Regiment from General Sir Charles Deedes, who had been Colonel for over 20 years, to Major General William Robb CBE, DSO, MC. At a ceremony following lunch in the Officers' Mess at Queen Elizabeth Barracks, Strensall, Her Majesty presented Sir Charles with a silver statuette of a Light Infantryman and a Souvenir Book, which had been subscribed to by all ranks and units of the Regiment. At the same ceremony, Her Majesty presented Company Serjeant Major R.W.L. Steerment with the Military Medal for Gallantry in Burma, and Corporal T. Wright with the Long Service and Good Conduct Medal.

At a ceremony in Deolali, 19 April 1947, the Colours of 2nd KOYLI, which had been in the safekeeping of the Viceroy since 1942, were returned to the Battalion. Major General Whistler, CB, DSO, GOC British Troops in India, was unable to be present, and in his absence Brigadier I.H. Good DSO, 29th British Brigade Group, took the salute. As a steady stream of officers and men returned to the UK for demobilization, replacements continued to be found from other regiments and very small drafts from the UK. One development, however, was greeted with great enthusiasm. 'An occasion which should go down in the Annals of the Regimental History was the day when we were issued with spring beds. If this is Monty's army – give us more!'[21] On a visit to the 2nd Battalion in June, Major General Whistler gave a vivid commentary on the life of other British units in India, as well as a shrewd summary of the present unsettled situation. The transfer into 2nd KOYLI of large drafts from 7th Worcesters and 1st Glosters at the end of May was part of the process of withdrawal before India's independence. In sharp contrast to what was happening further north, on 2 June, 4 Platoon was loaned to 'D' Company to take part in a Flag March in the town of Malegaon, some 75 miles from Deolali. 'Instead of brickbats and acid from the inhabitants, flowers and tea were freely given. The sight of Officers and a Serjeant Major being garlanded caused hilarity, but when the 'Strong' men of the Platoon were given sprays of flowers and sprinkled with scent, who can say that the red faces were entirely due to sunburn?' [22] This type of reception was not unusual, and in many instances, it was only the presence of small detachments of British soldiers, often commanded by National Service or Non Commissioned Officers, that provided the refugees from both sides with protection from rioting fanatics. If the newly empowered politicians were thankful to see the British soldiers leave, all too often the route of the departing troops was lined with crowds genuinely saddened at their leaving.

On 15 September, just days before 2nd KOYLI left India, it was presented with the trophies of the 1st Battalion The Great Indian Peninsular (GIP) Railway Regiment. Following India's Independence, 1st GIP Railway Regiment, part of the Auxiliary Force (India), had been disbanded and, knowing that 2nd KOYLI had lost most of its regimental silver, generously offered its own trophies as replacements.

Deolali had been the newly formed 2nd Madras European Light Infantry's first station in 1839, so it was fitting that it should be 2nd KOYLI's last station in India.[23] Perhaps even more poignant was the fact that when the 2nd Battalion left India for the last time on 24 September, it should be from the port of Madras, the place where it was raised and, coincidently, the port at which the 51st had arrived in April 1799. Since its formation in 1839, 2nd Madras European LI/2nd KOYLI had spent a mere 21 years at home; although, it could be argued that India was its home. On the morning of 29 September, the troopship *HMT Devonshire* sailed down the Straits of Malacca, rounded the Island and at 2 pm docked in the port of Singapore. The 2nd Battalion was greeted by two officers who were to play a significant part in the Regiment's future, Major General H. Redman CBE, Chief of Staff Far East Land Forces (FARELF) and Major N.S. Pope DSO, both of whom were stationed in Singapore. Before the Battalion was a 500-mile train journey via Kuala Lumpur and Ipoh to Taiping, where it detrained in the early hours of 1 October. The final destination was Glugor Barracks, on the island of Penang, where 2nd KOYLI was to form part of 99th Infantry Brigade, 17th (Gurkha) Infantry Division, but circumstances dictated that it would spend some time in Taiping before it reached Glugor.

While the 2nd Battalion was saying its final farewells to India, Lieutenant Colonel D.G.B. Ridout OBE, was imparting momentous news to the 1st Battalion in Minden. The substance and source of his communication was revealed in the Times, 'War Office announced last night that all infantry regiments are to be reduced to one regular battalion each.'[24] Individual battalions, however, were not the only ones under threat; indeed, the whole of the regimental system was being questioned. In both World Wars, especially in the Second, the regimental system of recruitment and replacement had had to give way to expediency. The inability of regiments to provide significant numbers for drafts had resulted in the available reinforcements being posted to those battalions in greatest need, irrespective of regiment. The answer, it was argued, was to copy the German and American system and produce a Corps of Infantry, with unit numbers replacing names. This notion was strongly resisted, one of the principal opponents being Field Marshal Sir William Slim GCB, GBE, DSO, MC, who had succeeded Field Marshal Montgomery as CIGS. The necessary reduction in numbers, and a greater emphasis on technical and support services, were beginning to put a great strain on the retention of the regimental system – but it was retained. The price of survival was now to be paid. The editorial of *The Bugle* began,

> The Army having no politics it is with some trepidation that we thank providence being already Nationalised nothing worse has happened to the K.O.Y.L.I. than reorganisation. We are spared liquidation, though in our humble position we would not venture to say by how much.[25]

The 1st KOYLI, 51st Primary Training Centre, and the small representation at the Light Infantry Basic Training Centre, were to be run down and finally disbanded by April 1948. The editor of *The Bugle* expressed the hope that the 51st would be amalgamated with the 105th to form one battalion bearing the name of the 1st Battalion 51st and 105th Foot, but at this stage, nothing was known for certain. Why was the 1st Battalion chosen to go into 'suspended animation'? Simple economics dictated that transferring the 1st Battalion to Malaya to replace the 2nd Battalion would have been too costly, especially to a government starved of resources.

An advance party, commanded by Captain J. Storie, left Minden on 11 December bound for the 1st Battalion's last station, Fort Tregantle near Plymouth. Before the final departure, 350 soldiers were transferred to the Oxfordshire and Buckinghamshire Light Infantry (Oxf and Bucks LI) and, on 16 December 1947, the remnants of the 1st Battalion left Minden. Travelling from the Hook to Devonport, the Battalion was greeted on the dockside by the Regimental Band. Major General Robb visited the Battalion on 11 February 1948, and took the salute at a parade when the Regimental Colours were carried for the last time by the original 51st. The 1st Battalion, now reduced to cadre, remained in existence until the end of April 1948 when the last Battalion Order was issued which read 'The 1st Battalion is now dead, long live the new 1st Battalion 51st/105th '. In concluding his final contribution to *The Bugle*, Lieutenant Colonel Ridout wrote

> May the old 51st wish the 105th all good wishes for the future, and we pass to them the sole responsibility for keeping the King's Own Yorkshire Light Infantry on the map.[26]

1   *The Bugle*, 1946, Vol. 38.1 pp 13/14 'Victory over Japan' – VJ Day
2   *Ibid*, 1946, Vol. 38.2 p 20
3   Alderman Walker had been commissioned into the 11th Battalion of the Regiment in 1914.
4   Ellenberger, Brig. G.F. *History of the King's Own Yorkshire Light Infantry, Volume VI 1939-1948*, Gale and Polden, Aldershot, 1961, p 168
5   *The Bugle*, 1946, Vol. 38.3 p 54 Life in a Former German Concentration Camp. Guarding the "SS" at Neuengamme. A 1st Battalion Commitment.
6   Mason, Pte B. Conversations with the author.
7   *The Bugle*, 1946, Vol. 38.1 p 22
8   *Ibid*, 1946, Vol. 38.2 p 25
9   *Ibid*, 1946, Vol. 38.3 p 32 'A' Company notes.
10 *Ibid*, 1946, Vol. 38.4 p 34

[11] For many years Queen Elizabeth had provided the Regiment with Christmas puddings, a tradition that she continued until the Regiment was disbanded in 1968.

[12] *The Bugle* 1946 Vol. 38.1 p 27 Production of *The Bugle* had been suspended during the Second World War, as it had been throughout the First World War.

[13] *The Bugle*, 1946, Vol. 38.2 p 20 'B' Company notes

[14] *Ibid*, 1946, Vol. 38.3 pp 26-28

[15] *The Bugle*, 1946, Vol. 38.4 pp 29/30

[16] Heald, Pte J. Letter to the author, and original copy of *Special Bugle Call*. Regt. Archive. Lt Col Hickie's letter was printed in a *Special Bugle Call*. The first edition of the *Bugle Call*, a daily news-sheet produced by the Battalion's education staff, was issued on 1 July 1946. The idea of a news-sheet was revived when 2nd KOYLI arrived in Malaya and resulted in the publication of *The Minden Post*.

[17] *The Bugle*, 1947, Vol. 39.1 p19

[18] *The Bugle*, 1949, Vol. 41.1 p 43 Notes contributed by CSM H.J. Keay,

[19] Lochrie. Cpl D. In 2002, Cpl Lochrie was a pensioner of the Royal Hospital Chelsea. Memoir Regt. Archive.

[20] *The Bugle*, 1949, Vol. 41.1 p 43 Notes contributed by CSM H.J. Keay. 'Z' Company was based at Villach, but the HQ for the Railway Police was in the neighbouring province of Styria.

[21] *The Bugle*, 1947, Vol. 39.2 p 28 'A' Company notes.

[22] *Ibid*, 1947, Vol. 39.3 p 47

[23] The 2nd Madras became the 105th Madras in 1861, and 2nd KOYLI in 1881.

[24] *The Times*, 15 October 1947.

[25] *The Bugle*, 1948, Vol. 40.1 p 1

[26] *Ibid*, 1948, Vol. 40.1 p 18

2

Malaya

In the immediate post-war period, the British Army in Malaya was deployed to counter a perceived threat of military invasion by either the Soviet Union or China.[1] Malaya's natural resources included tin and timber, but her most important asset was rubber – of which she produced approximately 50% of the world's supply. The sudden Japanese surrender in August 1945 forestalled the planned invasion of Malaya, an operation for which 2nd KOYLI had been training. During the brief period between the end of Japanese rule and the return of the British, there was an increase in communal strife, racial violence, and an ever-growing crime wave. With the arrival of British troops, responsibility for the country temporarily passed to the British Military Administration, but the imposition of martial law was slow to quell the civil unrest that was occurring throughout the country.

Malaya was divided into a number of political areas with Penang, Malacca, and Singapore being ruled as Crown Colonies and known collectively as the Straits Settlements. Some of the states were part of a Federation, each being ruled by a Sultan with the assistance of a British Resident advisor: the Sultans of those states that were not part of the Federation had a higher degree of independence. Control of the country's overall administration, defence, and foreign policy was in the hands of the British High Commissioner. Malaya's population, excluding Singapore, was fewer than 5 millions with native Malays accounting for 44%, immigrant Chinese 38.5% and Indians 10.5%.

The granting of independence to India and Pakistan in August 1947, and Burma in January 1948, encouraged many in Malaya, especially the Malayan Communist Party (MCP), a mainly Chinese organisation led by Chin Peng, to work for independence. The formation of the Federation of Malaya on 1 February 1948 coincided with the Soviet Cominform's Calcutta Youth Conference, where it was agreed that armed struggle would be the means by which South-East Asia would be released from imperial domination. These two separate events, significant though they were, are not thought to have been the principal reason for Malaya's slide into terrorist activity. In his book *My Side of History*, Chin Peng maintains that the murders were carried out by a militant splinter group as revenge for heavy-handed strike breaking by the authorities.[2] In the coming months unrest, much of it instigated by communist action groups, spread throughout most of South East Asia including Burma, Indo-China, Indonesia and the Philippines. Malaya, the most stable of all the European colonies, was developing a prosperous economy and, with the growth of the important commercial centre and port of Singapore was a prize the communists could not ignore.

Map: 2. **Malaya 1947 – 1951**
KOYLI operational responsibility extended throughout the states of Perlis,
Kedah and Province Wellesley (now named Pinang), plus the island of Penang.
Many operations were also carried out in Perak.

The Malayan People's Anti Japanese Army (MPAJA), a resistance organisation encouraged and armed by the British, had been based on the MCP. With the increasing intensity of the communist inspired strikes and riots, following the establishment of the Federation of Malaya, the British High Commissioner, Sir Edward Gent DSO, MC, was urged to ban the MCP, but he resisted. Chin Peng, who had been awarded the OBE for his leadership of the MPAJA during the war, had hidden away many of the arms the British had supplied to his organisation. Peng now prepared the MCP to go underground and become the Malayan Races Liberation Army (MRLA). Originally estimated to number approximately 4,000, the MRLA set out on a campaign of murder, economic sabotage, coercion, and terror. Despite its title, support for the MRLA came mainly from the Chinese, and while many were hard-working traders who dominated the economy, there were over half a million landless Chinese living near the edge of the jungle. These people were to become the terrorist's chief source of food, information, money and recruits, and were later referred to by the troops as 'squatters'.

The 2nd KOYLI arrived in Taiping on 1 October 1947, its much-reduced strength initially restricting its operational capability. The first patrol, to the coastal village of Lumut, a two-hour drive southwards from Taiping, was mounted by 'C' Company. Following a cross country Flag March of 12 miles, accompanied by Police Guides and Interpreters, the patrol of one officer and 24 men, went out at night through the villages and along the main road, but the countryside was quiet. The Battalion's first casualties, Privates J.S. Morton and D. Mayoh, of 'D' Company, were killed in a road accident on 11 November when the three ton truck in which they were returning from a swimming trip crashed over a small bridge.

The various schemes for returning men to the UK – A/S Groups, LIAP, and Python – seriously reduced the Battalion's numbers; some 250 NCOs and privates had been left behind in India.[3] (The return of A/S groups 65-72 shortly after the Battalion's arrival in Malaya also took a heavy toll.) Between the end of December 1947 and early January 1948 three large drafts from the UK, plus two from the 2nd Durham Light Infantry, brought 15 NCOs and 533 soldiers to the ranks of 2nd KOYLI. But the demobilization of wartime conscripts, and a slow response to the recruitment of regular soldiers, resulted in the UK bound A/S group 76 reaching Singapore before being ordered to return to Penang; a Whitehall decision that was not well received by the group.

The nature of the tasks required of the Army in Malaya, the geography of the country, and the need to provide a quick reaction over a wide area, brought about a significant increase in the independence of each rifle company. The topography of northern Malaya, mainly rubber plantations and tropical jungles covering steep sided valleys and high peaks, with isolated settlements linked by narrow and often badly maintained roads, posed particular difficulties for the re-supply of troops. To deal with this a number of training exercises with the RAF were carried out, two of which were Cotswold I and Cotswold II.

My first task with 6 Platoon was to manhandle a jeep and trailer into a Dakota aircraft. Then, about thirty-two strong, we flew with these vehicles to Kota Bahru. I noticed the railway and the road below looked about half an inch wide and fervently hoped that the bottom wouldn't fall out of the plane.[4]

During these three-day air exercises, whole rifle companies were transported from Taiping to Kota Bharu on the northeast coast near the border with Thailand. Throughout, parachute drops from Dakotas supplied the companies, while overhead Spitfires simulated close air support. This type of combined services operation had its origins in the Chindit's Burma Campaigns of 1943-44. Techniques first used in Burma were further developed in Malaya, and would later be used by the Army in its fight against terrorism in many parts of the world. During the coming years the infantryman would become increasingly reliant on aircraft, especially the helicopter, for transportation, re-supply and fire support, but these forms of close cooperation were unavailable in Malaya at this time.

In the first week of December, 2nd Lieutenant G. Rose joined 'C' Company and was immediately ordered to take 7 Platoon, plus signallers, Motor Transport (MT) drivers and a medical orderly, to Grik, which *The Bugle* described as 'a rather small and seemingly insignificant town' on the border with Siam (Thailand). After a week settling in, the District Officer asked the Company's assistance to rescue some 200 Chinese who were in danger of drowning. Torrential rain had caused the river to rise by 18 feet and it was now 300 yards wide and approximately 28 feet deep. A boat was found some seven miles away and used to evacuate 60 people on the first day alone. Over the next three days and nights, 250 people were rescued and transported the five miles to Grik. Extra supplies for the detachment were dropped from RAF Dakotas, and this small band of KOYLI soon became local heroes, their reputation quickly spreading throughout the district.

In January 1948, Lieutenant Colonel Hickie left the Battalion to take up a staff appointment, command passing to Lieutenant Colonel A.B. Brown OBE who arrived in March. The new CO, who had been severely wounded while serving with 1/4th KOYLI in Normandy in 1944 and had lost an arm, was to be affectionately known to his men as 'Wingy'. On 6 January, 'A' and 'C' Companies moved to Ipoh, 60 miles south of Taiping, where they operated independently of the Battalion, a procedure that was to become familiar to all companies over the coming years.

The long awaited move to permanent quarters in Glugor Barracks on the island of Penang was finally completed by the end of May 1948. In early July the casual observer walking round the barracks may have wondered at the absence of soldiers, and been forgiven for thinking this was indeed a 'cushy posting' in a quiet backwater of Empire. Nothing could have been further from the truth.

On 16 June, the European managers of three rubber estates near Sungei Siput, approximately 15 miles north of Ipoh, were murdered, and the High Commissioner immediately declared a State of Emergency in Perak. The following day the State of Emergency was extended to the whole of Malaya and, three days after the murders, Sir Edward Gent DSO, MC visited the Battalion. Immediately following this visit, 'B' Company was sent to the Caledonian Estate, one of those attacked, where it carried out offensive patrols in the nearby hills. To deal with the possibility of further outbreaks of terrorism, the other 2nd KOYLI rifle companies, and HQ Company, were deployed over a wide area of northern Malaya, and soon the Battalion's operational area was estimated to be the size of Wales. From this time onwards, the successful application of lessons learned on jungle exercises became increasingly important to the young soldiers in their task of seeking out and destroying the terrorists.

The newly appointed GOC Malaya District, Major General C.H. Boucher CB, CBE, DSO, quickly responded to the situation. His plan had three elements: break up insurgent concentrations, attempt to bring them to battle before they were ready, and drive them away from urban areas and into the jungles where they could be followed by soldiers and police, supported by the RAF. The GOC believed that it was important to keep the insurgents on the move and deprive them of supplies and recruits. To garrison Malaya Major General Boucher had eleven battalions of infantry and one British field regiment of the Royal Artillery. The infantry consisted of six Gurkha, two Malay and three British battalions; two of the British battalions were in Singapore leaving 2nd KOYLI the only British troops on the mainland.

When 2nd KOYLI arrived in Malaya, responsibility for security operations rested with the Malay Federation's Commissioner of Police, whose force could request army assistance should it be required. The 2nd KOYLI quickly became aware of the degree of civilian unrest and, in common with the Malayan Police Force and other branches of the Security Forces, the term 'bandit' came into common usage. This expression seriously underestimated the potential of the opposition. With a significant number of British trained guerrilla fighters in their ranks, and a specific political and military objective in mind, the communist terrorists initially provided a stern test for the security forces. In the early stages of the campaign, their superior knowledge of the country allowed them to exploit the element of surprise with some success, which forced the troops into a mainly reactive role. Establishing camps in the jungle, the bandits would emerge to carry out acts of terrorism, intimidate the local population, or simply forage for food, which was almost impossible to find in the jungle.

At battalion level, counter-terrorist operations had their own particular difficulties. Physically identifying terrorists was not usually a problem since men and women of the MRLA wore a simple uniform.[5] Their supporters, however, wore no distinctive dress, and could appear as workers peacefully going about their business. Another difficulty was the absence of a recognised geographical front line, leaving the patrols open to attack from any direction. A swept area might reveal no bandits, but it could not be assumed that thereafter it was entirely safe: it could become contaminated within hours of the troops leaving. A typical patrol would consist of some 20 men led by a junior officer.

> We would prepare the night before. In those days, 5 days was about the limit without re-supply. There were no specialised ration packs; tins of bully beef, biscuits, "mutton scotch-style" and other goodies would be distributed for the patrol to carry, together with reserve ammunition, 2" mortar bombs, cooking pots etc etc. There were no air-drops; everything had to be accounted for – even jungle boot laces.[6]

By 1948, many of the jungle fighters who had been successful against the Japanese had left the army, and the valuable lessons learned had gone with them; this also applied to the Gurkha battalions. A number of soldiers in 2nd KOYLI had jungle experience, one of the most experienced being Major D.S. Sutcliffe, OC 'B' Company, who had been with the wartime Force 136, originally formed to help the Malayan people to use guerrilla tactics against the Japanese. In late August 1948, 17 men from the Demonstration Platoon were sent to the Jungle Warfare Wing of the Far East Training Centre at Johore Bahru; the Commandant of the School being Lieutenant Colonel Walter Walker DSO, who had commanded a battalion of Gurkhas in Burma during the war. For most recruits in the early days, there had been almost no jungle warfare training in the UK. Private H.J.B. Swarbrick, who joined 7 July 1949, gave an account of his training. Following his ten weeks basic training there followed a further six during which Lieutenant Ryall and Serjeant O'Hare (Som LI) and Lieutenant Clinton (DCLI), 'gave us some valuable information on ways of jungle fighting [and] we also learned some new weapons, Sten, 2-in. Mortar and PIAT.' Following their arrival at Glugor Barracks, Private Swarbrick's draft was sent to Kroh for four weeks training under the watchful eyes of Lieutenant J.H.W. Haddon, Serjeant Robson and Corporal Goodall, who introduced them to the EY Rifle (which was capable of firing grenades), and firing the Bren Gun from the hip.[7] Many years later Captain R. Ackling also remembered 'CSM A. Taylor and Cpl T. Walters were two very gifted Weapons Training instructors' who

Fig: 13 A patrol from 'C' Coy in the Kuala Kangsar area, 1949   *J Scurr*

imparted valuable information to the newly arrived at Glugor.[8] Among those to benefit was 2nd Lieutenant J.E. Crisp who recalled,

> There was no specific training in the UK as far as I can remember… When we arrived in Penang, three officers and about thirty to forty other ranks, we went on a familiarisation course run by the Battalion in Penang. There was a Serjeant-Major in charge and he taught us a lot that was very useful. I do not know where he gained his experience.[9]

In the same draft was 2nd Lieutenant G.M Betts, whose diary entry for the day of arrival at Battalion HQ, Sunday May 21 revealed, 'Next few days undecided until the next draft comes in. Then we shall probably go to Bn. Training School for jungle warfare for a month. They don't pitch us straight into the jungle…' Second Lieutenant Betts' diary entry for Tuesday May 24 'Saw the CO … our fate has temporarily been decided. John [2nd Lt Crisp] went the same day to C. Coy. Peter [2nd Lt P.E.S. Rowledge] goes to B. Coy. as soon as transport comes in for supplies and I remain with HQ Coy. This is until the next draft comes in when we go on cadre for 3 weeks'. [The next draft arrived six days later.][10]

It was against this background that 2nd KOYLI embarked upon a long campaign that would require all its skill and patience, and would tax to the limit the vigilance of each individual soldier. The wisdom of using National

Servicemen in a war situation, when the country was theoretically at peace, would now be given a stern examination.

Fig: 14 Part of 'C' Company being transported to Alor Star, 1949   *J. Scurr*

The British Army had years of experience in policing the empire, but it had never before used conscripted soldiers for this task. Would the fighting efficiency of the Battalion be seriously impaired by the constant replacement of infantrymen as their periods of service ended? National Servicemen made up a large part of the Battalion, and their term of service, initially 18 months, was later extended to two years. Following basic training, the average two-year enlisted National Serviceman would spend approximately 18 months in Malaya, after which he would not only be an experienced infantryman, but also eligible for return to the UK. This problem was not confined to junior NCOs and private soldiers. 'Since arriving in Penang, all the officers of 'H.Q.' Company have changed.'[11] Understandably, most National Servicemen counted the days to the time when they would return to the UK, but equally, most recognised the job in hand could not be avoided. Over 50 years later Colonel C.W. Huxley, commenting on National Servicemen wrote

> My memory of them is how good they were. Often ... concerned to make the most of their two years – of which probably only 14 months would be spent with the Battalion ...some would become junior NCOs in that time, and they made the best wireless operators, medical orderlies, and even marksmen.[12]

Recalling his experience as a platoon commander, Major Crisp found, 'The arrival and departure of N.S. men gave me no concerns', and throughout the Emergency, the young soldiers of the KOYLI, encouraged by their officers and NCOs, were to perform their duties in the highest traditions of the Regiment. Indeed, after more than 50 years, the level of involvement and camaraderie of the Regiment's 'Malaya Veterans Association' bears witness to the strength of the bonds that were created at the time.[13]

Over the coming months, companies and platoons were distributed over a wide area of northern Malaya. 'At one time, one would have had to drive 590 miles to visit all companies and platoons. It will not, therefore, surprise our readers to learn that the MT has averaged 20,000 miles a week.'[14] 'A' Company was sent to Kroh, a village at an altitude of 1,000 feet and only three miles from the Thai border where, from this 'very attractive little "oasis" in the middle of the jungle', platoons carried out sweeps searching for insurgents. 'I remember on my first operation saying to the Company Serjeant Major "What do we do if we meet the enemy?" to be told, "Don't worry, Sir, it will be all right." However we learned our trade and were soon patrolling with the best.'[15] On a subsequent patrol near Klian Intan, a Chinese mining village nine miles from Kroh, Lieutenant R. Unett's 2 Platoon captured three bandits. On a later outing, however, 2 Platoon unfortunately got lost. 'I had two police guides, who, after a time said they were lost. We were in a white area [jungle about which nothing was known] with a broken line river. I decided to follow this and then a small tributary, which should lead us back to the road. We had to spend a night in the jungle very wet from following the river, but next day we reached the road where a search party, which had been looking for us, was just about to leave. We were all very relieved.'[16]

To the young soldiers newly arrived from the UK the jungles of Malaya could be both amazing, yet terrifying. One National Serviceman, Private J. Scurr, who served as a signaller with 1st KOYLI between 1950 -51, echoed the feelings of the majority when he said that, 'The principal enemy was always the jungle – dense, humid, debilitating and emanating decay and an aura of lurking death.'[17] For some soldiers who served in the Far East,

The jungle was a fascinating place. Few animals or reptiles were to be seen for they would hear us coming. The birds were all in the canopy far above us and the tall trees shut out much of the light. Reaching a river, where the sun could penetrate was very pleasant. Birds and butterflies appeared too. One creature, which we all dreaded was the ubiquitous leech. They lay in wait beside jungle trails and quickly attached themselves to you. At each halt there was a leech hunt. Burning them with a cigarette made them let go and fall off.

The rain fell each day at about 1600 hours. We all had two sets of clothing: one for wear by day, which was permanently sodden with sweat and rain; the other (dry) set we wore in our bashas at night.

The bashas were constructed using our poncho capes, saplings and leaves. The aim was to make camp and have a meal before the rain came. It died out later in the evening and our dry kit could then be put on.

Camp was made in a rough circle off any trails, but not far from water. Sentries were posted and at first light every one 'stood to'. Breakfast followed, the camp was struck, our wet clothing put on again. Then the command was given to 'saddle up', our packs were shouldered again and we were ready for off.

We carried about four days rations and were re-supplied from the air. The RAF used DC3 Dakotas; some supplies came down by parachute; others were free dropped. We had to clear a dropping zone (DZ) and mark it out with fluorescent panels. Their aim was good, but there were always a few parachutes which got stuck in the treetops.

When moving in the jungle we went in single file. First went two scouts, then the navigator, usually the commander, followed by the rest. If one met the enemy it was a case of either a charge, if he was surprised, or a flanking movement if he was in position and ready for us. But we rarely saw terrorists of the MPLA who were mainly Chinese. They concentrated on ambushes of vehicles which were easy to do on the winding roads. There was plenty of cover for the ambushers too. However they carried out some effective ambushes of soldiers and police especially if they saw our side was not on the alert.[18]

Patrolling was uncomfortable, fatiguing, and mostly dull routine; especially when patrols were completed without a sight of the enemy. However, bandits were not the only enemy to be encountered in the jungle.

The worst terrain was the swamp [where] progress through ... chest-high water was measured in yards rather than miles. Huge complexes of mangrove roots would draw you off course, and you were very vulnerable to attack. Mosquitoes were everywhere [but] the real enemy was the leech. They got in everywhere, through the eyelets of the jungle-boot (designed to let the water in and out) working their way up the body and gorging on blood. It was fatal to pull them off, leaving their fangs in the bite to fester and cause jungle sores. These can become badly infected and – as in my case – lead to hospital. Water had to be purified even in primary jungle. A nasty fever called lepto spirosis was derived from drinking water contaminated by rat's pee. Malaria was controlled by taking mepacrine (which turned the skin yellowish) and later paludrine, the pills being administered daily at a formal parade to ensure that each man took his dose. [19]

But, if the majority of patrols ended without incident, there were those occasions when actions suddenly started and patrols had to deploy, usually against an unseen enemy. Towards the end of August Lieutenant Haddon, Serjeant F. Dolby MM and a patrol from 9 Platoon discovered a 'bandit' hiding under a thick bamboo shoot near to where they had spent the night. Rifle and Sten gun fire, plus the odd grenade, eliminated what 'C' Company claimed was the first of the enemy to be killed by the Battalion. However, while this patrol had been fortunate, inevitably there would be those that were not. While on patrol with 'C' Company on 14 September, Serjeant Dolby received a shoulder wound from a shot fired by a hidden attacker. The wound was not too serious and after three weeks, the Serjeant was back with his Company.

The constant assessment of techniques led to important developments in patrol routines. While there were occasions when sweeps by a whole company were appropriate, it was believed that smaller platoon sized fighting patrols, pushing deep into the jungle and making a thorough search of an area, could be more successful. In early August Tactical HQ (Tac HQ) was formed. Under the guidance of Lieutenant Colonel Brown, Tac HQ became a leaner organization than Battalion HQ and, spared the usual burden of administration associated with the latter, devoted itself entirely to operational command. Signallers overcame the problems of wireless communication in the jungle by using a set in an Auster aircraft overhead as control. Lieutenant A.M. Davis and his Intelligence Section began to make excellent maps and improved their skill at interpreting aerial photographs. Protection for Tac HQ fell to the lot of the Buglers, and initially much of the general administration of Tac HQ became the responsibility of Bugle Major B. Harbisher MM BEM, who, with the assistance of Serjeant Haley of the Signals, kept everything 'ship-shape'.

Typical of guerrilla warfare down the ages was the insurgent's ability to strike at soft targets over a wide area. To counter this, Mobile Companies were developed, and 'B' Company thought itself fortunate to be chosen to carry out this task, every section being given its own 15 cwt truck and every officer his own jeep. In August 'B' Company left Glugor in 25 vehicles and, after spending a few days at the Caledonia Estate, moved 150 miles south to the Tapah area where it remained for three weeks carrying out several operations. The discovery of an arms dump in an area noted for the activity of its squatters, which had recently been hit by an RAF strike, was considered reasonably successful, 'though we never actually came to grips with the bandits.' The next move was to Parit on the Perak River, then to Papan, nine miles from Ipoh where Private Lyons killed the Company's first 'bandit'. The patrol was cordoning off a Chinese hut on the edge of the jungle when a man suddenly rushed out. This was no time for reflection, and in response to his training, Private Lyons fired his Bren gun with fatal results. It was later discovered the man was also armed with a loaded revolver. After a week in Papan 'B' Company moved north to Kulim in South Kedah, where the Battalion's Tac HQ was billeted. At the end of September, another move was made south to Bidor, and it was near here that the Company suffered severe casualties. On 2 October, 4 Platoon paid the price of a tragic lapse of concentration. While some men were relaxing in a jungle pool, the platoon was ambushed and in the ensuing exchange of fire two bandits were killed, but the platoon commander, Captain D.G. Lock and Lance Corporal K. Hutchinson, Privates H. Woodhouse and A. Dobson were killed and Privates Ridden, Hawksworth and Buckland were injured.[20]

On 16 October, Lieutenant R.C. Handley and 6 Platoon surprised a number of bandits in a jungle encampment six miles east of Bidor.[21]

Having gone for miles through the jungle, we suddenly came upon them. The leading scout spotted a bandit washing in a stream. As the bandit looked up, Pte Kelly gave him a full mag [sic] from his Bren gun. The next bandit we saw ran out of a nearby basha. Cpl Flint, who was just in front of me, gave him a full Sten mag…but he still managed to turn and run off into the jungle. We found his body later.[22]

The camp was being used as an armoury, and bombs, guns, and a quantity of ammunition and equipment were taken. The entire camp was subsequently destroyed and the whole operation made the headlines in the following day's edition of the *Straits Times*.

Bandits were not the only things encountered in the jungle. A patrol of 'C' Company, led by Lieutenant Haddon and including Major J.R.A. Vallance, stumbled across a sizeable elephant in the jungle. The animal, not put off by this chance meeting, peacefully ambled off into the jungle and Lieutenant Haddon continued on his way. On rounding a bend in the track, the Lieutenant discovered Private Morris shaping up to fire into the rear of the unsuspecting beast, and it required both speed and the appropriate tone of authority to prevent the Private from discharging his weapon. Unperturbed, the elephant turned to observe the commotion before peacefully continuing on its way, while the patrol made a hurried exit up an un-scaleable bank.

Later that day the same patrol was put to flight by four water buffaloes, which must have been of a particularly ferocious breed to rout such a doughty group of the KOYLI. Patrolling continued until the end of October when, 'A'. 'B', and 'C' Companies returned separately to Penang for a short period of rest and refitting.

The arrival in Malaya of the Amalgamating Cadre of 1st KOYLI on 8 October was the prelude to the amalgamation of the two KOYLI Battalions.

The cadre brought with it the 1st Battalion's Colours and a large quantity of silver and property for the Officers and Serjeants Messes. The official date of the formation of 1st KOYLI was 18 November 1948, from which time the Battalion was known as 1st KOYLI (51st-105th).

During a nine-day rest period in early November, 'B' Company was distressed to learn it was no longer to be a Mobile Company. As the calls upon the MT section increased, and the distances travelled by the Battalion's vehicles reached epic proportions, economic considerations dictated that this prodigious use of transport could no longer be afforded. When 'B' Company resumed patrolling on foot, it found a bandit camp that showed signs of recent occupation. Located deep in swampy jungle, with much of the surrounding ground waterlogged, the patrol's approach had been made by jumping from one floating log to another. Both 4 and 6 Platoons took it in turn to 'sit on the nest', until an unwary bandit returned and was promptly shot by Private Brown. Unfortunately the bandit had only been 'winged' and he crawled away into the swamp, but the following morning he was spotted by Private Denver and Lance Corporal Round who finished him off, assisted by an Indian Police Sergeant who was accompanying the patrol.

One of 'C' Company's patrols found three camps in as many days, one very large one having been built on a hill 1,779 feet high. Among the material discovered was a bag containing .303 ammunition, all the bullets having been removed from their casings, reversed, and replaced. This was an obvious attempt to manufacture a 'Dum Dum' type bullet that would inflict a far more serious wound than the usual cone shaped bullet; an illustration of the lengths to which the enemy was prepared to go in pursuit of his goals. In another incident, a grenade was thrown into a Chinese shop on Penang but failed to explode. When one of the Weapon Training staff disarmed the grenade, he 'found an almost perfectly improvised ignition set, marred only by a cut down .45 cartridge case which was a little too ancient for the job'.[23] For a short while in November, 'D' Company had a number of Dyaks operating with them. These natives of North Borneo were superb trackers and displayed a ready enthusiasm for their work, but none found an opportunity to use the wicked looking knives with which each was armed.

Luck, rather than Dyaks, played an important part in guiding a 'D' Company patrol towards a meeting with a group of terrorists in the Kulim area that later received widespread publicity. On the front page of the 16 January 1949 edition of *The Straits Times* (Singapore) was the headline 'BANDIT GIRL IN DESPERATE LAST STAND'. On 11 January, a seven-man patrol from 11 Platoon, led by Serjeant T. R. Chadwick, came out of an estate clearing above a river near the Karangan tin mine, when they saw a party of armed Chinese below them and about 40 yards away along the riverbank. Both sides quickly took cover and in the initial exchange of fire one bandit was hit, his body falling into the river and floating downstream. The firing continued for a further 15 minutes during which time another bandit was killed when he carelessly showed himself above his cover. A grenade thrown at the patrol fell short and rolled down into the river, and soon afterwards another bandit was shot dead when he attempted to escape by jumping over a fence. Only two bandits now remained, one was a girl who, although wounded, continued to fire her own revolver to enable her companion to reload his rifle. While the attention of these two was focused on the rest of the platoon, Corporal Battersby took two men around the flank. Creeping to within a few yards of them, Battersby and his companions killed both in a hail of fire. For his part in the conduct of this action, Serjeant Chadwick was awarded the Military Medal.

Just over two weeks after Serjeant Chadwick's patrol had eliminated all five of the terrorists it had encountered, another 'D' Company patrol was in action. On Thursday 27 January, a patrol from 12 Platoon surprised a number of bandits on Anak Kulim Estate, near Kulim, Kedah. The bandits ran into a house near the top of a hill and as the patrol was deploying one bandit re-emerged with a grenade in his hand. Working his way round the hill on the left flank, Private J. O'Reilly got within a few yards of the man, stood up and charged, firing his Sten gun as he went. Unfortunately, O'Reilly's gun jammed, but seeing the man was about to throw the grenade at the rest of the patrol he flung himself at him and both fell to the ground. The two men rolled down the hill and became lodged against a boulder with the live grenade between them. When the grenade exploded Private O'Reilly was severely wounded in the face and side, but this did not prevent him holding on to the bandit until 2nd Lieutenant Wigg and another member of the patrol came up and shot him. 'Private O'Reilly's action was generally considered to be the outstanding piece of bravery of the Battalion's tour in Malaya, for which he received the Distinguished Conduct Medal (DCM), the highest award in the Battalion.'[24] 'By his gallant and unselfish action Private O'Reilly threw himself to almost certain death but saved the lives of his comrades.' Although badly wounded, Private O'Reilly survived this encounter with the enemy.[25]

A number of operations were mounted in the early part of 1949, the first of which, 'Holiday', involved 'A', 'C' and 'D' companies in large sweeps along the Thai border. This operation was followed by 'Nawab', 'Raven' and 'Kolynas', each of which varied in length, the longest being ten days. Cooperating with the police, the companies were involved in jungle patrols, area sweeps, clearing out squatters (mainly Chinese) and ambushes.

One feature of all these operations was the accuracy of the re-supply drops by the RAF, although 'A' Company moaned that it had two bottles of rum broken in its first drop, and government parsimony irked the members of 'C' Company who were ordered to carry the used parachutes back to base. During 'Operation Nawab' 'C' Company estimated that platoons had walked a total of 50 miles, and even Company HQ had travelled 20 miles, although it was pointed out that the country over which the latter had moved 'was not so arduous as that which the platoons had to negotiate'.[26] The signallers accompanying each patrol had a particularly onerous task, and would certainly have preferred to tramp fewer miles. The No 68 radio weighed around 40 pounds and was particularly cumbersome when following a slippery jungle track; when steep slopes were encountered, the signallers were particularly disadvantaged by having to carry a rifle in addition to their other equipment. At times conditions in the jungle could make movement almost impossible. Later in the year, Private Bird of 'B' Company was taken ill with suspected appendicitis while on patrol and a carrying party was organised to take him back. Using a makeshift stretcher, made of poncho capes and poles, the stretcher party set off at 12:00 hrs, but by 16:00 hrs they had only managed to travel 500 yards. Such a statistic is more reminiscent of soldiering on the Western Front in the Great War than National Service in the post Second World War period.

In terms of bandits killed and captured, it must be admitted that the expenditure of effort far exceeded the results obtained, but the work was responsible for producing some of the most experienced jungle fighters in the Far East. 1st KOYLI had been actively involved in anti-terrorist patrols for a whole year, and the former members of 2nd KOYLI had been at the heart of the operations from the very first day. Despite all this effort, the editor of *The Bugle* felt the need to express the view that, 'For various reasons, not always clear to us, the British line regiments out here have not enjoyed the same press as others.' [27]

On 6 June, while based at Lubok Segintah, a rubber planter's estate in Central Kedah, 5 Platoon, led by Serjeant Sanders and Corporal Nutting, carried out a dawn raid on a suspected bandit camp. The patrol got within ten yards of the hut before a barking dog revealed their presence. As the bandits attempted to escape, four were shot and a fifth gave himself up after attempting to hide in a nearby swamp. The patrol found evidence that suggested this group had been extorting money from the local inhabitants, and when a number of Chinese came forward with fresh evidence, the whole area was cleared of bandits. While the insurgents may have returned later, the positive effect on the local population, and the boost to the morale of the Battalion, however temporary, was well worth the effort.

Once again, the Battalion's strength became a problem. 'A' and 'B' Companies were now down to two platoons, and the ration strength of 'B' Company was eventually reduced from over 100 in 1948 to less than half that number by July of 1949. At the end of this period of continuous patrolling the Battalion was given a short time for rest and refitting. When it returned to patrolling, 1st KOYLI adopted a routine whereby each company spent nine weeks on the mainland – six weeks as a jungle company, and three weeks at the training centre at Kroh – after which it was given three weeks to rest and refit at Penang.

The small state of Perlis, and its capital Kangar, lies close to the Thai border, and the ease with which insurgents crossed and re-crossed this border proved a constant irritant. It was while 'C' Company was in this area, carrying out a series of three day patrols and ambushing tracks leading over the border, that other morale boosting events occurred. An ambush by 8 Platoon, commanded by 2nd Lieutenant J.P. Thorne, succeeded in killing the sergeant of the Sintok Gang of drug smugglers and recovering his sub-machine gun and ammunition. The smugglers dropped their parcels of drugs and escaped, but a patrol from 9 Platoon, led by 2nd Lieutenant P.G.M. Walby, discovered 16 sacks of opium that was later valued at $136,000, but with an estimated street value of $500,000. This find was thought to be the second largest haul in Malayan history. Within the month, both these officers had returned to the UK to take up the university places they had gained before joining as National Servicemen, a further illustration of the manpower problems facing the Battalion.

In July 1949 Lieutenant General Sir John Harding KCB, CBE, DSO, MC succeeded General Sir Neil Ritchie KCB, KBE, DSO, MC, ADC, as C-in-C FARELF. As part of a general inspection of his command, the new C-in-C paid a visit to 'B' Company at Baling in Kedah State. It is doubtful that this one visit was responsible for the new C-in-C's subsequent condemnation of what he called 'will-o'-the-wisp patrolling and jungle bashing'. Subsequent discussions with his staff led the C-in-C to conclude that there was a need for more men, over and above the 17 battalions already operational.

During August, September and October 1949, a number of His Majesty's ships visited Penang, their captains and crews being entertained by 1st KOYLI. The first to arrive were *London, Mounts Bay* and *Belfast*, followed in October by *Constance, Cossack* and *Alert*. The most notable visit, however, was that made in September by *HMS Amethyst* when she stopped at Penang to refit before returning home. *HMS Amethyst* had been badly damaged, and some of her crew killed and wounded by Chinese Communists shore batteries as she made her remarkable escape down the Yangtse River. (*HMS London* had also suffered fatal casualties in the same incident.)

These visits by the Royal Navy were not allowed to deflect 1st KOYLI from its main task, and further anti-terrorist operations were mounted, the main ones being 'Cox and Kings' (named after the branch of Lloyd's Bank that acted as agents for the Regiment) and 'Overall'. These operations were intended to clear out the squatters from the Weng Valley; sadly, neither produced significant results. Nevertheless, better fortune attended the companies in the last two months of 1949.

On 2 November, 5 Platoon, acting on an intelligence appreciation by the Battalion Intelligence Officer (IO), Lieutenant Davis, set off on a three-day jungle patrol in the Kulim area. 'B' Company Commander, Captain (soon to be promoted Major) Sutcliffe, led the group and chose a particular sector that he suspected might contain an insurgent camp. Scouting ahead of the patrol, Captain Sutcliffe and Lance Corporal O'Brian found a bar of soap on the edge of a pond from where a track led up into dense trees that suggested a possible site for a bandit camp. Corporal Pudwell and Privates Brown and Lyness were left to cover the pond with Lyness' Bren gun while the rest of the patrol circled around the camp with the intention of pushing the bandits towards the trap that had been set near the pond. When two bandits came down to the pond to wash, the Bren gun team resisted the temptation to open fire and Lyness realised they had struck lucky.

> We now knew the Major had been right... and that we would be in action very shortly. The suspense was something I shall never forget and it lasted for quite a long time. Should we have shot them? After all, they were only 200 yards away and easy pickings for a Bren gun.
>
> It was then that the firing started and all hell broke out. Two bandits ran down the hill opposite, then turned right along the track with two 5 Platoon lads in hot pursuit, firing as they ran. Brown and I then opened fire and the two bandits fell to the ground. It was debateable who shot the bandits but the result was two bandits less.[28]

The overall result was three bandits killed, four captured and the activities of the enemy's Kedah and South Penang Propaganda Section being brought to a sudden halt.

Setting out from Kulim on 8 November, 'D' Company sent patrols over a wide area. At about 16:40 hrs on the following day, 10 Platoon, Commanded by 2nd Lieutenant P.L. Richards, was climbing a hill of lallang (elephant grass) with a few isolated rubber trees dotted about and a mound on the summit.

> As the scouts neared the top, we suddenly came under a heavy fire from the mound. Just beside me was a pile of logs which I promptly dived behind. Then I heard a voice to my rear calling: 'Help me! Help me!' It was Ward. (Private K. Ward, a National Serviceman) I crawled back and found him lying beside a rubber tree with a bullet-wound in his chest. I pulled his shirt open and reached for my field dressing. Remembering what I'd been told in training, I picked up a small stone and started to place it inside the dressing; ... At that moment, however, bullets began ricocheting off the rubber tree just above my head. They were being fired by a bandit positioned on a track over to my left. He obviously had me in his sights. I made a split-second, live-or-die decision and was back behind my pile of logs in no time. It was a case of self-

preservation, but I knew from the look of that bloody hole in his chest that Wardy was probably a goner anyway and there was nothing to be gained by having two men dead instead of one.[29]

At the head of the column, 2nd Lieutenant Richards organised his platoon, which put up a spirited defence of its position until darkness fell. At one point, Serjeant K. Holmes, who had been bringing up the rear, crawled forward and threw six grenades at the enemy to thwart an attempted flanking movement. At about 19:30 hrs the bandits (it was estimated there were about 50 of them) ceased fire and moved off taking their wounded with them but leaving two of their number dead. For their part in the action, 2nd Lieutenant Richards was awarded the Military Cross, and Serjeant Holmes the Military Medal.[30]

On the 3 December, the Battalion suffered its second highest number of casualties in a single incident since the Emergency began. Major Sutcliffe, OC 'B' Company, and a party of five soldiers in two vehicles were returning to Kroh after inspecting 5 Platoon at Klian Intan. As Major Sutcliffe's jeep rounded a hairpin bend, some 20 bandits opened fire on the two vehicles from well-concealed positions in the jungle on the high, outside part of the bend. Shouting to his driver, Private Kelly, to drive on the Major leapt out of the jeep with the intention of stopping the following armoured Dodge truck, but unfortunately its driver, Private Mills of HQ Company, failed to see him and sped past at high speed. The hail of bullets stopped both vehicles and both drivers, together with Privates Godfrey, Carter, and Fry were thrown out onto the road. Lying there badly injured, four were shot at close range by the bandits, but Private (Ginger) Fry feigned death so well it was assumed he was already dead. Fry remained motionless as the bandits removed the bandolier of ammunition from around his waist. In the meantime, Major Sutcliffe, armed only with a .38 inch pistol, the barrel of which was full of mud, made his way to the edge of the jungle where he lay flat and silent. As they were trying to find him, all the while taunting him with shouts about 'getting the Red Fox', the approach of 2nd Lieutenant C.W. Huxley's 5 Platoon frightened them off and they quickly made their way over the nearby Thai border.

Between 9 and 23 December, 'C' Company took part in an unusual patrol, 'Operation Hornet'. Venturing into the darkest corners of Upper Perak, the Company took with it elephants, complete with mahouts. The RAF dropped supplies to the patrols, although some boxes inadvertently fell into the Sungei Perak, the longest, widest, and deepest river in Malaya. Nevertheless, these were retrieved, and their precious contents of rum, cigarettes, and food were found to be intact. The elephants proved to be a most interesting diversion, and legend had it that one elephant, mistaking Private Hendry for a piece of bamboo, attempted to pick him up with its trunk. A variety of tracks were discovered, including wild elephant and tigers but, sadly, none belonged to the local bandits the patrol was hoping to find. The New Year, 1950, brought no changes to 1st KOYLI's duties. With little respite, the Battalion had been involved in security activities for two and a half years, but despite this, there was still no sign that the enemy had been defeated. 'A', 'B' and 'D' Companies began Operation 'Rabbit' in the South Kedah area on 10 January. The result of this screening operation was the detention of approximately 50 people who were to be taken to a screening point near Kulim. The Company was divided into two, with Serjeant Wilson, five men and ten Special Constables being responsible for the detainees.

> With only two miles to go down a valley to the screening point, Mr Carter and his eight men branched off to the left down a well-worn track, while Coy. HQ. and Mr Sibbald's patrol kept down the main track. About ten minutes later the sound of battle coming from Mr Carter's direction sent the main body doubling through the rubber in support.[31]

As 2nd Lieutenant J.D. Carter's eight-man patrol moved down the track they came across a man who immediately ran away. The patrol chased the man right into a camp occupied by about 20 bandits. In the ensuing action two bandits were killed (one having a reward of $15,000 on his head) and a number captured, together with a quantity of arms and ammunition. During the exchange of fire a wounded bandit, who was eventually shot by 2nd Lieutenant P.F.A. Sibbald, wounded both Privates Carey and Jones. The chief result of a second operation, 'Ferret', carried out in the same area between 24 and 29 January, was the killing by 'D' Company of an ex-captain of the MPAJA who had a five thousand dollar reward on his head.

Both 'B' and 'D' Companies were moved to Ipoh and, acting on information received from a former bandit, 'B' Company set off towards a large enemy camp deep in the jungle. The OC decided to call in an airstrike, since the approach could not be made without the enemy being warned, and RAF Tempests and Beaufighters accurately carried out the attack. Lacking previous experience of close air support, which in this case consisted of canon fire and rockets passing uncomfortable close overhead, it was three quarters of an hour before an advance was made. Although the camp was badly damaged, the enemy must have been forewarned and had escaped before the aircraft made their strike. The large scale, complicated, and highly organised operation 'Vanguard', in which 'C' Company, plus units from the Coldstream Guards and Green Howards cooperated with hundreds of police, produced scant results, although Lieutenant A. Storey of 9 Platoon did kill one bandit, and another was wounded by his batman, Private Plummer.

In April, the British Government appointed a Director of Operations whose task it was to deal with all matters civil and military. Within one week of his appointment Lieutenant General Sir Harold Briggs KCIE, CB, CBE, DSO, recently retired from the Indian Army, had formulated his eponymous plan. Working from south to north the 'Briggs Plan' called for each area to be cleared, thus isolating the Min Yuen (supporters of the MRLA), and forcing them out into the open to obtain their supplies. The army was to deploy a strike force in each area as the clear up developed and, once an area was clear, a safe system of administration was to be set up to maintain security. The army was to establish itself in populated areas from where it could dominate the nearby jungle for a distance of a five hour journey on foot, setting up ambushes on routes between terrorist camps and potential areas of supply. Starting in the southern states of Johore, Negri Sembilan and South Pahang on 1 June 1950 the plan achieved little. The lack of an adequate and efficient administrative structure, and the fact that Lieutenant General Briggs could not issue direct orders to the police or civil authorities, being the principal reasons for its initial failure.

During the month of May there occurred an incident that was to enter the collective memory of the Regiment and be talked of often in the years to follow.

It was well known that they [bandits] had camps over the Thai border which we were unable to take out, although by agreement with the Bangkok government armed police patrols were allowed to operate on their territory.

On 13th May 1950 a young police officer called Pat Evans took such a patrol over the border only to be very badly ambushed in a clearing between virgin jungle and rubber – there was little doubt their plans must have 'leaked'. Survivors returned to Kroh with the news: '100 bandits with 4 bren guns'. So, Lt John Hutton [Lt J.M.C. Hutton] of A Company decided to take out a platoon which would get lost and cross into Thailand 'by accident'. With a Malay guide the platoon attacked the bandit's position only to find empty slit trenches and piles of cartridge cases. The bodies of Pat Evans and several Malay police were recovered to the nearest motorable track with the help of Thai police who provided transport to their nearest town Betong. There the party was greeted by an embarrassed district officer who was socially well known to the Regiment and to Pat Evans himself. His guilt complex was self evident that he had no control over the presence of bandit camps on their territory. A crowd had gathered, surprised to find armed British troops among them, and a Thai police party lined the street and presented arms as the troops and casualties were driven off back to Kroh, frustrated and sad. Thus ended the Regiment's armed incursion into Thailand.[32]

The need for constant vigilance was not exclusive to active patrolling in the jungle. On the night of 24 May 1950, a number of soldiers were playing billiards in the Georgetown NAAFI when a terrorist threw a grenade through the window. As the grenade landed on the billiard table most of those present threw themselves on to the floor, but Corporal Hall of 'D' Company, 'regardless of danger, snatched up the grenade and threw it out of the window.'[33] For this act of bravery Corporal Hall was later awarded the BEM.

At the beginning of June, the Battalion was spread over a wide area from Penang, Grik and Kroh, south to Ipoh. On 10 June, Serjeant P. Hogan's 10 Platoon was scouting ahead of the rest of 'D' Company near Ampang, about three miles from Ipoh. At a fork in the track near 'Dead Man's Gully', Serjeant Hogan split the platoon sending Serjeant B. Cookson's section along the left fork while he took his section along the right, which rose slightly before descending into saucer shaped depression surrounded by jungle. Moving into this depression, Serjeant Hogan's ten-man section was hit by a hail of enemy fire from well-concealed positions. The two scouts, Privates J.E. Gough and C.M. Harrison were killed outright, as were those who followed, Privates D. Jones, W.J. Boden, R.L. Hall and J.K. Hudson. Serjeant Hogan, Lance Corporal V. Brown and Privates Daniels and Storey were all badly wounded, Storey having a kneecap blown off and Daniels having a severe injury to his right hand that later required amputation. As he lay on the ground Lance Corporal Vernon Brown saw the terrorists appear from their cover and, as one approached to collect the weapons of his dead comrades, Brown managed to raise his rifle and shoot him, at which point the rest quickly made their escape. Serjeant Hogan, although severely wounded in the back, crawled along the track and was met by members of Serjeant Cookson's section who had seen the ambush from higher ground, but had been unable to open fire for fear of hitting their own men. On hearing the firing, 12 Platoon, which was in the rear of 10 Platoon, rushed forward, but were unable to see any of the terrorists. One week later Lance Corporal Brown died of his wounds and was buried alongside his comrades on 16 June 1950.

As Serjeant Hogan's section of 'D' Company was being ambushed, the other three rifle companies were moving south to establish themselves in the Ipoh area. The move was obviously not in response to the ambush, but the deaths of their comrades did lend a measure of urgency and purpose to the forthcoming tasks. Advanced HQ and 'D' Company established themselves at Ashby Road Camp, Ipoh, while 'A' Company moved to Sungei Siput, 'B' to Batu Gajah and 'C' to Tanjong Rambutan, where they were accommodated in the Federal Lunatic Asylum! Over the next month a series of operations ranging in size from platoon to battalion strength were undertaken, all of which succeeded in subduing the bandit activity that had been increasing over a period. The RAF provided three air strikes, one of which saw Lincolns, Brigands and Tempests pound a hill near Sungei Siput where it was thought several groups of bandit were encamped; patrols later found a number of abandoned camps.

On 14 July the Battalion moved north setting up Advanced HQ at Lenggong and, over a 14-day period the companies patrolled the hill jungle on either side of the Kuala Kangsar – Grik road. Attached to the Battalion during this time was a 'fighting Troop' of 40 Commando, while to the south 2nd Malay Regiment was also under command for several days. This whole operation served to illustrate the difficulties and frustrations experienced by the Battalion while operating in the jungles of Malaya.

> At this time we ['A' Company] received information that the Malay Regiment, who were operating on the other side of the watershed, had contacted sixty bandits, who were coming our way. Unfortunately they didn't, or if they did we didn't meet.
>
> During the fortnight the Company ['B' Company] had only one minor success; a patrol... found an enemy encampment, built recently to accommodate 100. Bandits had evacuated the place approximately half-an-hour before we arrived.[34]

The 'long lost legion [1st KOYLI] rumbled home, by kind courtesy of the RASC', on 28 July. Minden Day 1950 was significant for three events, in addition to the annual celebration of the Regiment's most famous Battle Honour. Glugor Barracks, Penang was officially renamed Minden Barracks and, for the first time since June 1948, the whole of 1st KOYLI was on parade. During these two years, however, efforts had been made to keep all personnel, wherever they were based, aware of their Regimental comrades' activities with the production of a weekly Battalion newspaper, *The Minden Post*. (See appendix 6) Following a short address by Lieutenant Colonel Brown, the Battalion, led by the Band and Buglers, marched past the CO to the strains of the Regimental March. Later in the day, Serjeant Woodland of the 2nd Coldstream Guards presented the CO with a silver bugle, in token of his battalion's appreciation of the hospitality shown to it while retraining in the former Glugor Barracks. This was the second silver bugle to be presented to 1st KOYLI by a Guards Battalion that year, the 2nd Scots Guards had presented a similar bugle in May, also in recognition of the hospitality shown them whilst training at Glugor.

As part of a fact-finding tour of Malaya, the Minister for War, John Strachey, and Major General H. Redman CB, CBE, Director of Military Operations at the War Office, visited Malaya in June 1950 and stayed at Battalion HQ between 6 and 10 June. Despite the misgivings of some, John Strachey took part in an hour-long patrol, probably the only occasion on which an armed British Minister of War (he was carrying a Sten gun) has been part of an infantry patrol on active duty. The most notable visit, however, was made by the CIGS Field Marshal Sir William Slim, who was accompanied by General Sir John Harding, C-in-C FARELF, and Major General R.E. Urquhart CB, DSO, who had succeeded Major General Boucher as GOC Malaya District in February 1950. The deliberations of these high-powered visitors focused on the organisation of the internal security forces, which would have implications for the numbers of police and troops needed to combat and overcome terrorist activities.

Following the Minden Day celebrations, the Battalion settled down to two months of refitting and re-training. One negative aspect of constant 'jungle bashing' was its detrimental effect on marksmanship, and as part of the re-training each rifle company spent two weeks practising and classifying on the range. 'The two weeks spent on the Ayer Hitam ranges were the first weeks – or even days – that this Company has been able to spend on open ranges since 1948 – or before, and so the poor standard of results are more understandable.'[35] The fall in standards was common to all battalions in Malaya, and in the Malaya Shield Shoot (fired by all battalions during their re-training period) teams from the five companies of 1st KOYLI filled five of the first seven places.

On 30 September, the training came to an end and 1st KOYLI moved out of Minden Barracks, its place being taken by 1st Suffolk Regiment. During the training period, a number of cadres had been organised for NCOs, MT and Signals platoons, and a three-inch Mortar cadre. The increase in trained personnel was necessary to manage two drafts totalling 300 NCOs and men that were shortly to join the Battalion; the increased strength meant that a third rifle platoon was added to each company.[36]

Spread out in the usual places, Serdang, Kroh, Klian Intan, Kulim and Pelham Estate, the companies returned to the thankless task of patrolling. Battalion HQ and HQ Company were set up in tented accommodation at Airfield Camp, Sungei Patani, where torrential rain and an abundance of mud made life far less comfortable than it had been over the past two and a half years at Minden Barracks. In a five-week period ending 1 December 1950, the Battalion suffered three tragic accidents. On the night of 24/25 October, Private D.C. Hicks was accidentally shot and killed while taking part in a night ambush. Serjeant W.C. Baddeley was accidentally shot, 1 November, by a soldier cleaning his Bren gun, and later died of his wounds and, on 1 December, Private J.D. Gregory was accidentally shot and killed while sitting in the squad tent after playing in a game of football.

At the end of November, Lieutenant Colonel J.C. Preston DSO succeeded Lieutenant Colonel Brown as CO 1st KOYLI. As the Battalion HQ and HQ Company moved back to Minden Barracks, leaving Tac HQ in Sungei Patani, a large concentration of bandits was reported camped in the Wanga Raja area of North Perlis, just south of the Thai border. An ambitious combined operation codenamed 'Rice Bag' was planned to eliminate these terrorists. At 16:30 hrs on 15 December, 'C' Company boarded the frigate

HMS Hart and was taken to the mouth of the River Perlis from where it, and the accompanying police officers, were taken by motor launches to a rendezvous point two miles up river. The next morning at 06:30 hrs, bombs from RAF Tempests and Lincolns accurately targeted the area, a basin bounded on three sides by steep cliffs in which an estimated 300-500 bandits lived in caves. To complement the bombing, an Auster spotter aircraft directed accurate fire from *HMS Hart's* main armament of four-inch guns onto the target. Aerial photography had previously identified all possible escape routes from the basin, especially those that led to the adjacent Thai border, and these were covered by troops or police. When 'C' Company and the police entered the basin they found nothing, in fact it appeared that no one had been in the area for months! Nevertheless, the operation was not a complete disaster. It had shown that all branches of the security forces could work together closely and successfully. It also pointed to the fact that in this type of country aerial photography was far more reliable than maps when planning such operations.

During the Christmas period all the rifle companies remained operational, but none of the patrols succeeded in reducing the bandit population. It may be thought that the Battalion's increased strength should have produced better results, but a comment in the editorial of *The Bugle* clearly explains why this was not the case.

> These Company moves have in no way reduced the size of the area for which the battalion is operationally responsible. The total has now reached the astonishing figure of more than nine thousand square miles. Patrolling is thus spread over an ever widening field and goes on unceasingly day after day. Most of these patrols prove fruitless, and successes bear no relation to the effort expended.[37]

In the first month of 1951, Major Sutcliffe led 4 and 6 Platoons in an attack on a terrorist camp in the Lubok Segintah area. As the patrol moved forward through the rubber trees Major Sutcliffe spotted a number of bandits on an adjoining slope and ordered the two platoons to attack. A volley of shot met the men as they stormed the hill to close with the enemy.

> We hastened to get to cover as the Communists opened fire. We then saw Jimmy [Pte J. Whitehead] fall and realised he had been hit. One of our EY riflemen fired a grenade which hit a tree and exploded above us, showering us with shrapnel. One man was injured in the foot. We carried on and found that there must have been a rearguard left at the jungle side, as they kept firing at us. At this time, Judo Roberts and Serjeant Dee shot and killed one of the Communists who was later revealed to be an officer... A few days later, 6 Platoon was patrolling in the same area when we came

upon a clearing in the jungle which was very swampy. There were four recently killed Communists in the swamp which we believed could have been put there after the skirmish in which Jimmy Whitehead was killed. (L/Cpl Gordon Hill)[38]

Fig: 15 Travelling to Kroh before 'Operation Betong, Feb 1951   *Dr G.M. Betts*

Lieutenant Hutton's clandestine 'armed incursion' into Thailand in May 1950 was not the only one. Operation 'Betong', a ten-day patrol by 'D' Company along the Thai border which began in late February 1951 almost led to an international incident. In a letter home 2nd Lieutenant G.M. Betts wrote,

> We have been operating into Siam cooperating with the Siamese police. Officially we were not supposed to cross the national border, or if doing so sending a Malayan map reference back. I sent the correct (map) reference in Siam back to Bn. HQ. Unfortunately just at the time the CIGS was visiting. All hell broke loose'.[39]

Many years later Dr Betts recalled,

> I have rather painful memories of this patrol. I threw a phosphorus grenade on top of a basha hoping to set it alight. Unfortunately, it rolled back down the roof and landed on my shoulder still burning. It was only the quick thinking on behalf of Sjt Dunster and a medic

Braithwaite that prevented me being badly burned and even killed.[40]

Fig: 16 Preparing to leave Kroh on 'Operation Betong', Feb 1951   *Dr G.M. Betts*

Whilst everyone knew the Battalion was due to return to the UK sometime in 1951, the actual date was not known until mid May when it was announced that 1st KOYLI would depart on 6 August. Before and during the move, however, there were extensive movements of personnel that reduced the Battalion's strength on disembarkation from 880 to below 440 of all ranks.

On 25 June 1950, the North Koreans had invaded the Republic of South Korea, and thus began the first war to involve the United Nations: the British 27th Brigade joined the Americans and the South Koreans on 29 August 1950. In April 1951 seven Corporals, six Lance Corporals and 78 men of 1st KOYLI had volunteered for service with 1st King's Shropshire Light Infantry (KSLI), which was leaving for Korea to join 27th Brigade. Further reductions to 1st KOYLI were made when 230 men left for release, or on Python, while another 138 were scheduled to leave during the journey home to join 1st Oxf & Bucks LI in Cyprus. The removal of this latter group, a good example of bureaucratic ineptitude, appeared to have been made with complete disregard for the maintenance of Regimental Spirit. Despite Colonel Preston's expressions of regret and a vigorous outcry in the editorial column of the Yorkshire Post – 'Regimental Spirit disregarded' – the planned transfer of men took place.[41]

The last soldier of 1st KOYLI to be killed in action during the Malayan Emergency campaign was Private Charlie Walker of 'B' Company. About 16:00 hrs on 20 May, 5 Platoon was settling down for the night close to Kejai, near Baling Estate. A Malay arrived with a message from the local police requesting a meeting and Serjeant Dee called for six men to accompany him up the track to the police post which was about one mile away.

> Our small patrol set out with Charlie [armed with a De Lisle 45 mm silent carbine] as leading scout. We were in quite open country but there was very thick scrub to the right of us. We saw Charlie suddenly drop to the ground. He shouted: 'This is the military!' There was a reply: 'This is the police'. Charlie now rose from the ground. A sub-machine gun opened up and caught him in the chest. The rest of us dived for cover. Private Hicks landed on top of a commie and put two shots into him on the ground. All hell was being let loose. We could not see our assailants but were firing at the smoke from their weapons. Eventually, all was quiet and we had a look around. The bandit positions were heavily blooded in three places. But my best mate was dead. I was absolutely gutted.[42]

Private Walker, a National Serviceman, had never missed an operation and was due to return to the UK only three days later. Private Walker's final letter to his parents, telling them that he would be leaving Malaya onboard the troopship *Dilwara* on 24 May, arrived only days after they received the official notification of his death.

All companies of 1st KOYLI carried out their last patrols between 27-30 July and, on 30 July 1951, the Battalion officially handed over Operational Command of the States of Kedah, Perlis and Province Wellesley to 1st Battalion Manchester Regiment. Letters of thanks for the work done by the Battalion in Malaya were received from the High Commissioner, Sir Henry Gurney KCMG, the C-in-C, General Sir Charles Keighley KCB, KBE, DSO, who had replaced General Sir John Harding in May, the Director of Operations, General Sir Harold Briggs, the Commissioner of Police, Mr W.N. Gray, and the GOC Malaya, Major General R.E. Urquhart CB, DSO.[43]

On 3 August, the Senior Chaplain, Malaya, conducted a Memorial Service in St George's Church, Georgetown, for all ranks of the Regiment who had died in Malaya in the campaign against terrorism. The service was followed by a parade through the streets of Georgetown where the Resident Commissioner took the salute. On 7 August the Battalion, preceded by the Regimental Band and Bugles, and a Colour Party from 'B' Company carrying the Colours of the 2nd Battalion, marched through the streets to the quayside. Immediately after the parade 1st KOYLI embarked in *HMT Dunera* to music provided by the band of the Manchesters, which included the KOYLI Regimental March 'With Jockey to the Fair', and 'Auld Lang Syne'; as the moorings were slipped Vampire jet fighters from RAF Butterworth roared overhead in salute. So ended, for a time at least, the Regiment's long posting in the Far East, which had begun on 6 March 1922.

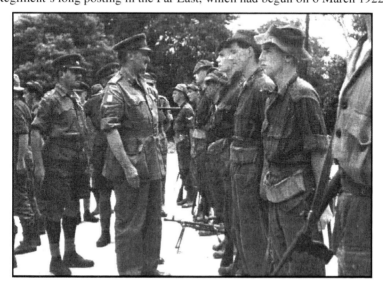

Fig: 17 Gen Sir Charles Keighley C-in-C FARELF, inspecting 11 Platoon, Kulim, June 1951   *Dr G.M. Betts*

Over the coming years, the Emergency in Malaya was to gain in intensity. The British government's response was to increase the number of battalions serving in the country to 22, and by 1956 the total number of the Security Forces had grown to 300,000. In 1948 there had been an average of 200 reported incidents per month, (which fell to around 100 in the first half of 1949), but by mid 1950 there were approximately 400 reported per month: these included attacks on police stations, ambushes on roads and railways, and an increasing intimidation of the population. The appointment of General Sir Gerald Templar GCMG, KCB, KBE, DSO, in early 1952 marked a decisive turning point. With full powers vested in one commander, the introduction of helicopters to provide greater mobility for the infantryman, and the chemical destruction of the terrorist's ability to grow their own food, much of the initiative was wrested from the enemy. By Independence Day (known as Merdeka), 31 August 1957, the number of active terrorists had fallen to approximately 1,500 and the campaign was considered won, although isolated incidents continued over the next three years.[44]

As the final edition of the Battalion's weekly newspaper, *The Minden Post* recorded, during its period of service in Malaya the Regiment had one officer and 17 other ranks killed in action, and one officer and 16 other ranks killed in accidents or died of disease. The 1st Battalion had officially killed 39 of the enemy, although reported evidence would suggest this figure is a bare minimum and many more escaped only to die later of their wounds. Members of the Battalion were awarded one OBE, one MBE, one MC, one DCM, three MMs, three BEMs, 27 Mentioned in Dispatches and five C-in-Cs Certificates.

The Depot and 4th Territorial Battalion

The 4th Battalion KOYLI (TA) was re-formed on 1 May 1947. In September 1939 the Colours of 4th KOYLI had been deposited for safekeeping with the Mayor and Corporation of Wakefield, the officers of the Colour Party being Lt M.A.C.P. Kaye and Lt A.B. Little. On 2 November 1947, the Colours were handed back to the 4th Battalion, which on this occasion was commanded by Lt Col M.A.C.P. Kaye, the Colour Party being Captain A.L.R. Hunter, Lieutenant A.R. Wilson, Company Serjeant Major L. Grist, and Serjeants McNamara and Forrester. Throughout that year there was a steady increase in numbers, and one year later the Battalion could boast one HQ Company and two rifle companies.

On Minden Day 1948, the Battalion marched to Clarence Park, Wakefield, where the Colonel of the Regiment, Major General W. Robb, inspected it. After the march past, which included members of the Regimental Association, Major General Robb presented a number of medals. Following the annual camp in September, three officers and 19 other ranks travelled to London to attend the Royal Review of the Territorial Army, which took place in Hyde Park. Despite the severe economic problems in the early days of 1949, authorisation for the establishment of a band was granted and recruiting began immediately. The 4th Battalion already possessed a complete set of instruments, together with a full complement of pre-war full dress uniforms. On 27 July 1949, the Battalion formed the Guard of Honour at the Town Hall, Wakefield, for the visit of Princess Elizabeth and the Duke of Edinburgh; the Battalion being the only unit in the West Riding that could provide a full Guard of three officers and 80 other ranks from its own personnel.

On 15 December 1949, the Regimental Depot and HQ moved from Ranby, near Retford, where it had been since November 1946, to the Cavalry Barracks, Fulford, York. In March the editor of *The Bugle*, referring to the formation of the Light Infantry Brigade, suggested that, 'they are applying a squeeze to the Regimental System...'. The physical manifestation of some of these changes could be seen in the 'Changes in

Dress' reported in the same edition. 'We have…lost our distinctive "Green on White" for cloth badges and Chevrons, [these being replaced by] shoulder titles of gold on a dark green background, badges and chevrons of green on a khaki fawn background…'[45] The writer could not have imagined the many changes the coming two decades would witness. Field Marshal Sir William Slim was appointed CIGS in 1948, and it was thanks to his efforts that steps were taken to reinstate the importance of the Regimental Depot system.

Activity at the Depot increased in June 1950 when all time-served National Servicemen from the 1st Battalion had to report for posting to their Territorial Army/Special Reserve units. (Of the first 63 only one was posted to 4th KOYLI, the others going to units nearer their homes throughout the country.) This new process had an important significance for 4th KOYLI, because from 29 March it began to receive regular batches of ex-National Service 'Z' Reservists, who would serve with the Battalion on a part-time basis for four years. Of the first 51 men to arrive at the 4th Battalion Depot, only five were former Light Infantrymen, although all but 13 of the remainder were at least infantrymen. The second half of 1950 saw a number of changes of command in the Regiment. On Minden Day, Major General William Robb handed over the Colonelcy of the Regiment to Major General Harold Redman. Major General Robb had joined the KOYLI in 1916, after being a Territorial in the Northumberland Fusiliers, the 4th Battalion of which he had commanded in 1918. At the Depot, Lieutenant Colonel J.W.R. Dugmore retired, command passing to Major R.L.N. Gowans, while in Wakefield Lieutenant Colonel Kaye handed over command of the 4th Battalion to Major J.R. Haslegrave OBE. (The official date being 14 January 1951.) When Lieutenant Colonel M.A.C.P. Kaye re-formed the 4th Battalion in May 1947, he was following the example of his father, Lieutenant Colonel H.S. Kaye DSO, MC, who had re-formed the Battalion after the First World War. In taking command of the Battalion, Major Haslegrave was also following his father's example: Lieutenant Colonel H.J. Haslegrave CMG, TD had commanded 1/4th KOYLI when it went to France in April 1915.

On 15 May 1951, the Regimental Depot moved from the Cavalry Barracks at Fulford to Queen Elizabeth Barracks, Strensall ,York, which also became the Light Infantry Brigade Depot. The number of reservists continued to rise and, at the annual 15 day camp in August 1951, which was held at Deerbolt Camp, Barnard Castle, 4th KOYLI numbered over 1,000 when it was joined by its National Service 'Z' Reservists – all 797 of them!

On its return from Malaya, the 1st Battalion docked at Southampton on 4 September 1951 and disembarked the next day. Trains transported it to Barnard Castle, from where everyone departed for four weeks leave. When the Battalion re-assembled there followed three days of ceremonial parades, the first of which was an inspection by Her Majesty Queen Elizabeth at

Strensall on 31 October. A march to York Minster on 1 November, to lay a Minden wreath in the Regimental Chapel to the memory of the 35 members of the Regiment who had lost their lives in Malaya, was followed the next day by a march through the streets of Leeds where the Lord Mayor took the salute.

On 10 November 1951, some two months after it returned to the UK, 1st KOYLI began its journey to Germany where it was to join the British Army of the Rhine (BAOR).

---

[1] Neither had any intention of taking direct military action, but Russia hoped that by offering support and encouragement to the many dissident groups (mainly communist) throughout S.E. Asia, widespread unrest would help to destabilise the Western Allies.

[2] Springhall John. *Decolonization since 1945,* Palgrave, Hants, 2001. Springhall suggests that the discovery of some local financial irregularities within the ranks of the MCP is believed to have been the initial spark.

[3] Pigott, Major General A.J.K. *Manpower Problems,* War Office, 1948 LIAP stood for 'Leave in Addition to Python'. When the Mediterranean became safe for troop movements in 1943, 'Python' was the code name given to the scheme whereby those who had served for a long time overseas could be sent home in exchange for a similar number who had been a long time in the UK. When the war in the Far East ended, Python' was continued, but with a reduced qualifying period.

[4] Scurr, J. Ed. *Malayan Tales of the YLI,* Pentland Press, Edinburgh, 1997, p 6 Williams, Pte G. 'B' Company, [formerly 2nd Durham Light Infantry]

[5] A simple red star, usually on a cap, was the identifying mark.

[6] Huxley, Col. C.W. Memoir. Regt. Archive.

[7] *The Bugle,* 1950, Vol. 42.1 p 34

[8] Ackling, Capt R. Recollections in conversation with the author.

[9] Crisp, Major J.E. Memoir. Regt Archive.

[10] Private papers of Dr G.M. Betts. Diary entries for 20/21 May 1950.

[11] *The Bugle,* 1948, Vol. 40.3 p 15

[12] Huxley, Col C.W. op cit

[13] The government carefully avoided using the word 'war' when referring to events in Malaya, the preferred term being the 'Emergency' to avoid charges of colonial oppression.

[14] *The Bugle,* 1948, Vol. 40.4 p 13

[15] Unett, Major R. Memoir. Regt Archive.

[16] *Ibid.*

[17] Scurr, J. *Jungle Campaign,* The Book Guild, Sussex 1998

[18] Unett, Major R. op cit.

[19] Huxley, Col C.W. op cit

[20] Capt D.G. Lock was on attachment from the Som.LI.

[21] The spelling use by the Regiment at this time was Bidor; the modern spelling is Bidur.

[22] Scurr, J. *Malayan Tales of the YLI.* Williams, Pte George. 'B' Company, op cit p 16.

[23] *The Bugle*, 1949, Vol. 41.1 p 23

[24] Barnes, J. Former Educ. Corps Sergeant. Sub-editor and reporter for *The Minden Post*. Correspondence with the author. February 2004

[25] *The Bugle,* 1949, Vol. 41.3 pp 2/3 Part of the citation recording the award of the DCM to Private J. O'Reilly.

[26] *Ibid,* Vol. 41.2 p 18

[27] *Ibid,* Vol. 41.2 p 8

[28] Scurr, J. *Malayan Tales of the YLI,* Lyness, Pte W, 'B' Company, op cit p 50.

[29] *Ibid,* Slade, Pte T, 'D' Company, op cit pp 56/57

[30] 2Lt P.L. Richards was on attachment from the Som.LI.

[31] *The Bugle*, 1950, Vol. 42.1 p 22

[32] Hutton, Major J.M.C. Memoir. Regt. Archive. At this time there were two officers in the Regiment named Hutton. See Author's Notes.

[33] *London Gazette*, 23 January 1951

[34] *The Bugle*, 1950, Vol. 42.3 pp 22-25

[35] *Ibid,* Vol. 42.4 p 25

[36] Were these reinforcements a direct result of the recent visit of the Minister for War, or were they in response to the invasion of South Korea by North Korea, which had taken place on 25 June 1950?

[37] *The Bugle,* 1951, Vol. 43.1 p 11

[38] Scurr, J. *Malayan Tales of the YLI.* Hill, L/Cpl G, 'B' Company, op cit pp 140/141

[39] Betts, Dr G.M. Private papers. op cit. Letter home dated 21 March 1951. 2nd Lt Betts may have been mistaken in thinking that his message had been seen by the CIGS. No record of a visit by Field Marshal Sir William Slim appears in *The Bugle* at this time.

[40] Betts, Dr G. M. Correspondence with the author, April 2004.

[41] Yorkshire Post, 13, 15 August 1951

[42] Scurr, J. *Malayan Tales of the YLI.* Sparkes, Cpl F. 'B' Company, op cit pp163/164

[43] The murder of Sir Henry Gurney led to the appointment of General Sir Gerald Templar to replace him in February 1952.

[44] The MCP leader, Chin Peng, took part in the peace talks with Thai and Malaysian officials in 1989, and sometime later moved to China until 1994 when he settled in southern Thailand as a stateless person.

[45] *The Bugle*, 1950, Vol. 42.1 pp 5/6 There is reliable photographic

evidence in the Regimental Archive to confirm that, examples of green on white chevrons, and badges of rank, were still being worn as late as 1957.

3

Germany

In March 1948, Britain, France, and the Benelux countries signed the Brussels Treaty, thereby creating the Western Union organisation. For the first time in its history, Britain agreed to commit itself to a peacetime military alliance in Europe. Initially conceived as a counter to any future threat from a resurgent Germany, the combined command, Uniforce, was to have a French land C-in-C and British air and sea C-in-Cs. While the creation of Uniforce partially removed anxiety regarding Germany, the threat from Russia increased and it soon became obvious that without the United States, Uniforce could not provide a credible deterrent to perceived Soviet ambitions. The *coup d'état* in Czechoslovakia, and the Russian blockade of Berlin in 1948, created a situation in which the use of American Strategic Air Command bombers, armed with atomic bombs, was deemed the only response capable of checking these Soviet moves. The success of this policy led to the signing of the North Atlantic Treaty in April 1949, and the creation of the military force of the North Atlantic Treaty Organisation (NATO) in September of that year. The British Army of the Rhine (BAOR) became part of NATO, and British generals were to command the Northern Army Group in Germany, Denmark, and Norway.

In the immediate post war period, the role of the BAOR changed dramatically. From being the occupying power in the country of a conquered enemy, it became, together with the American forces, the first line of defence against a potential threat from Soviet Russia's huge Red Army that occupied most of eastern Europe. In the plains of northern Germany a conventional type of warfare was anticipated, but with nuclear weapons now available to both sides, no one could predict just how any new conflict would develop.

During the Battalion's brief stay at Barnard Castle, a number of structural changes had been made to enable it to take its place alongside other NATO forces. Infantry techniques that had been vital for survival in the jungles of Malaya had to be set aside and new ones adopted for this different theatre of operations. Certain specialist skills needed to be reintroduced, and these were mainly the concern of the Support Company, which created Anti-Tank, Assault Pioneer, Mortar and Medium Machine Gun Platoons. Mortars and machine guns had formed part of the infantry's weaponry since the beginning of the century, and now the infantry's hand-held anti-tank weapons of the Second World War were augmented by the introduction of the much more powerful 17 pounder anti-tank gun. This particular gun would not have appeared out of place in a weapons display by the Royal Artillery.

Leaving Barnard Castle on 10 November 1951, 1st KOYLI travelled via the Hook of Holland to Dortmund, where it joined 5th Infantry Brigade, 2nd

Infantry Division, 1st Corps. Drafts totalling 147 helped to swell the numbers as the Battalion settled down for the first time in four years to Christmas in a cold climate. For those members of 1st KOYLI who had served in Malaya the contrast between that country and Germany could not have been more pronounced. Cordon and search operations and active patrolling in a physically hot and potentially hostile environment, where momentary carelessness could prove fatal, were replaced by training in a cold climate among the dreary mines and slag heaps of an industrialised region of northern Europe.

On 10 January 1952 the final commemoration of the Regiment's recent service in Malaya took place when the Archbishop of York conducted a service of dedication in St George's Church, Penang. During the service, the GOC Malaya, Major General Urquhart unveiled a memorial tablet listing the names of all those members of the Regiment who had died in the fight against terrorism while serving in Malaya 1947-1951.

King George VI died on 6 February 1952 and the Colonel of the Regiment immediately sent a telegram of sympathy to Her Majesty Queen Elizabeth, the Colonel-in-Chief. After the King's funeral at Windsor, the Battalion held a memorial service at the garrison church in Dortmund on 15 February.

Few relished the three-day exercises in the snow-covered German landscape during the early months of 1952. Nevertheless, following one such exercise near the Möhnesee Dam, Major A. Murray, who had served in the Glider Pilot Regiment during the war, together with Major Burrows (not KOYLI) and Captain D.D. Penfold MBE, gave talks to each of the rifle companies on the subject of the Dam Buster Raids in 1943. In January, the Anti-Tank Platoon went to Hohne for a three-day training operation, and while there paid a visit to the nearby site of the former German concentration camp at Bergen Belsen, liberated by the British Army on 15 April 1945. The memorials of the various nations made a profound impression on all who saw them.

At the beginning of March the Battalion moved to the field firing ranges at Borkenburg, southwest of Münster. The Stever Stausee (one of a number of small lakes in this area) was encircled by pinewoods and provided a much more attractive landscape than industrial Dortmund, approximately 45 miles away. The ranges, located on the edge of the woods in a somewhat desolate moorland area, proved a realistic setting for the three-day exercise, after which the platoons made the return journey on foot. Following the annual classification course, which also took place on the Borkenburg ranges, the Battalion learned that it had to send 40 regular soldiers and 150 National Servicemen to 1st DLI, which was in the process of reforming its 2nd Battalion; in return the DLI would transfer 120 National Servicemen to 1st KOYLI. While the Battalion was constantly receiving new drafts, the scribe of 'A' Company moaned that these were 'largely offset by a continual flow of National Service men who are periodically released from Her Majesty's Forces.'[1]

When 1st DCLI left Germany for the Caribbean in 1952, its pack of beagles was passed on to the Battalion. Although industrial Dortmund was by no means prime hunting country, the local landowners were fearful that their hare population would be in mortal danger from the activities of enthusiastic English huntsmen and their hounds. After a suitably generous lunch in the Officers' Mess, a group of landowners was given a demonstration of hounds at work, which they observed from the control tower of a disused airfield. 'The pack duly arrived led by the Master (Lt. C. Huxley) and his smartly dressed whips. Hounds found almost at once, chased their quarry (a local cat) across the airfield, and within 90 seconds were out of sight. The Germans were unimpressed, and shortly afterwards Anthony Eden [Foreign Secretary] agreed that British troops would not hunt. The canine population of Dortmund became heavily diluted with Beagle blood.'[2]

Winter turned into spring, and in May the rifle companies spent two weeks in Sennelager, which had been for over 80 years a training area for the German Army. Another training area included in the Battalion's itinerary was Brilon, where the companies spent an enjoyable week camping in beech woods overlooking a picturesque valley. Faced with an enemy attacking from the east, it was essential that the troops learn to cross the great rivers of Western Europe both safely and efficiently. To this end, a night crossing of the River Rhine was made, 12/13 July, with the object of establishing a bridgehead on the opposite bank. Most groups made the entire crossing in the boats provided, but there were some individuals, including 'A' and 'B' Company commanders, who somehow managed to make part of the journey clinging to the outside of their craft.

The final exercise that summer was codenamed Spearhead I, and involved another crossing of the Rhine. The Battalion assembled near the small village of Kalkar, on the western bank of the Rhine near the Dutch border, and made an assault across the river on the night of 7/8 August. The storm boat carrying Battalion HQ had only gone some 50 yards when suddenly it plunged under the water taking with it Private N. Kendall of 'A' Company and Private P.D. Everett-Proctor of the Signal Platoon; both soldiers were drowned: Lieutenant C.W. Huxley, the Signals Officer, was on the same boat.

> These were the same elderly craft that had made the same crossing in 1944. The forward planking had loosened when the loaded boat was pushed off the beach. It filled very rapidly and we were soon in mid Rhine in pitch darkness depending on life jackets. [Private] E. Proctor was carrying the batteries for the 62 set which I, as Signals Officer was wearing. Fortunately for me the cable connecting us parted when the boat sank. He was lost, I bobbed about like a cork. The upturned boat suddenly appeared. Colonel

Preston and I clung to it until rescued by – appropriately – The Life Guards who were doing search and rescue.[3]

The Battalion's role in Spearhead I was that of Brigade reserve, but this did not spare it from involvement in the action. All four companies crossed the river successfully, but soon encountered an overwhelming force of tanks. Despite fighting gallantly, only 'C' Company, 'D' Company, HQ and one of its platoons, were able to withdraw across the river, the rest were adjudged to have been wiped out. A second assault attempt on 12 August produced slightly better results with 'A' Company securing a beachhead and successfully defending it, despite Company HQ being initially located in a minefield. 'B' Company was credited with killing eight of the tanks that attacked it, but 'C' Company was over-run by tanks and, although 'D' Company advanced on the villages of Rees and Esserden, and was credited with killing twelve tanks on the way – the umpires finally declared it had been wiped out!

In September, Field Marshal Sir William Slim was appointed Governor General (designate) of Australia and stood down as CIGS. On his farewell tour the CIGS visited the depot at Strensall, but for 1st KOYLI in Germany it was the departure of General Sir John Harding that produced a spate of feverish activity. The Battalion provided the Guard of Honour for the departure of Sir John from his residence at Costedt in the morning of 24 September, and later that same day the Guard of Honour for the new C-in-C BAOR, General Sir Richard Gale.

In October, 'B' Company became wholly devoted to training recruits, NCOs, and potential NCOs, while the remainder of the Battalion concentrated on individual training and classification. On 7 November, it was announced that the Colonel of the Regiment was to become Vice Chief of the Imperial General Staff, with a promotion to Lieutenant General. For 1st KOYLI, however, of more immediate concern was the Annual Administrative Inspection that was to take place on 11/12 November, and for which everything that did not move was either scrubbed or painted. Having successfully negotiated the inspection, on 17 November Lieutenant Colonel Preston departed to become Light Infantry Brigade Colonel, command of 1st KOYLI passing to Lieutenant Colonel N.S. Pope DSO, MBE.

Coronation Year, 1953, began very cold with 13 degrees of frost, which made life rather difficult for 'D' Company as it bivouacked for three nights in woods near Hagen. This chilling experience may have prompted 18 members of 'D' Company, along with 11 other ranks from the Battalion, to volunteer to join the 1st DLI in Korea.[4] It had been known for some time that the Battalion's stay in 'the dirt, the smoke, [and] the grime of Dortmund' was coming to an end, and that it would soon leave the town that was 'far from being a good station, and from the health point of view

Fig: 18. HM Queen Elizabeth with Officers 1st KOYLI, Strensall, Oct 1951
Back Row: 2Lt R.O. Wynne, Capt G.S. Styles, Capt W.R.L. Turp, MBE, Lt D.C. Wride, 2Lt P.E.S. Rowledge, Lt J.E. Crisp,
Capt D.D. Penfold, MBE, Lt W. A.L. Mackay, Lt H.T.E.F. Green, 2Lt D.L.E. Wieler
Front Row: Major A.E. Harding, MC, Major D.G.R. Atkinson, Lt Col J.C. Preston, DSO,   Major J.R.I. Doyle,
Major G.N. Stanton, Capt E.G. Pople
Her Majesty The Queen, Col-in-Chief of the Regiment, Major Gen H. Redman, CB, CBE, Col of the Regiment

Regt Archive

leaves a lot to be desired.'[5] Everyone, except those heading for Korea, was looking forward to the next posting – Berlin.

The whole of eastern Germany was occupied by the Russians, except for Berlin, which was divided into four sectors, French, British, and American, with the Russian sector the most easterly. Berlin's position, 100 miles inside the Russian Zone, meant that those who lived in what was known as West Berlin were isolated from West Germany. If the international tension between Russia and the Western Powers had suddenly turned to outright war – even of the conventional type – the British, French and American garrisons of the city would have been immediately overrun. The August edition of *The Bugle* realistically summed up the position.

> As soldiers in Berlin our primary duty is to protect the British Zone and at the same time to maintain the confidence and morale of the Western Berliners. This means we have to put up a brave show in the shop window... [6]

The Battalion arrived at Wavell Barracks in the Spandau district of Berlin on 7 March, two days after the death of the Russian leader, Joseph Stalin. Stalin's death created uncertainty and international tension, which was not eased when Malenkov was named as his successor. Tension flared up on 10

Fig: 19 An East German watchtower overlooking the British sector of Berlin, 1953
P. Shield

March, when the Russians shot down an American plane that was flying over the US Zone, and increased two days later when a British bomber was shot down over the British Zone. With NATO looking to its defences, the Kremlin became a hot bed of intrigue as Russian leaders clamoured to fill the gaps created by Stalin's death.

The May Day celebrations in Berlin were always a potential flash point, and the Battalion was rather surprised, given the short time that it had been in the city, when it was chosen to provide the immediate support group for the German Police at the 1953 celebrations. While the whole Battalion would be available, only 'C' Company was to be deployed. Tac HQ was set up in the remains of the Kroll Opera House, while 'C' Company moved quietly into the cellars of the semi-ruined Schloss Bellvue, the former residence of a lady of the court of Frederick the Great. Although 400,000 West Berliners assembled in the Platz der Republik, the square opposite the ruined Reichstag, and listened enthusiastically to speeches by Belgian and German politicians, when the speeches ended, they quickly dispersed and within half an hour the square was empty. After spending an uncomfortable and boring day in the cellars, 'C' Company was stood down at 16:30 hrs and made its way back to Wavell Barracks.

The main event on 2 June 1953 was the Coronation of Her Majesty Queen Elizabeth II. In Berlin the day was declared a holiday for the British contingent and their families, and many listened to the coronation ceremony on the radio. In the evening, the British units in Berlin held their Coronation Parade in the 'Maifeld', a huge grass field at one end of the Olympic Stadium. The event consisted of a Royal Salute followed by the whole parade firing a *feu de joie* (a military celebration only performed on Coronation Days) and ending with a march past. Since both Heavy and Light Infantry were part of the parade, the Royal Irish Fusiliers and the Royal Scots Fusiliers trooped the colours of the Royal Irish Fusiliers in the first part of the parade, after which 1st KOYLI entered the parade area.

> As the Battalion marched past by Companies, a wave of applause followed each Company as it moved down the stands, we then halted in close column, turned about, and doubled past as a Battalion. This stole the show... The Battalion was in fine fettle.[7]

Two weeks after the Coronation Parade, tension between the Western Governments and Russia almost reached breaking point. On 16 June, 50,000 East Berlin workers rebelled against the restrictive policies insisted upon by the Russians. The riots quickly spread to the rest of East Germany and the Russians deployed two tank divisions to suppress the rioters in the city. This action immediately prompted a response from the Allied Powers who placed their garrisons in West Germany, and especially in Berlin, on alert. Reports of rioting, shooting and arson taking place in the eastern sector poured in, and to protect the British sector 'B' Company 1st KOYLI was despatched into the city itself.

> The Company Commander went with the CO to the Brandenburg Gate and studied from close range a Russian T34 tank which was supported by several half-tracks. It sat squat and ugly in the middle of the thoroughfare, like a particularly unprepossessing toad, its gun pointed straight at us.[8]

That night, 16 June, guests from both the American and French units in Berlin attended dinner in the officer's mess. Lieutenant A.R. Tinson had a vivid memory of the evening's events.

> Towards the end of dinner Lt Philip Davenport who was the Orderly Officer, and as usual manning the telephone in battalion HQ in battle dress, entered the dining room and spoke to the Commanding Officer, Lieutenant Colonel N S Pope, DSO, MBE. Colonel Nic nodded and we continued with dinner, wondering at this unusual event. After the port went round Colonel Nic rapped on the table (also unusual as we never had speeches) and said, 'Gentlemen, we must break up this gathering as we have been stood to for war!' There was a mad rush; our guests to the telephones to call their units, and the rest of us to change into battle dress, and in my case to stuff more kit into my haversack than ever before or since. Then we took off for the barrack blocks to get our soldiers ready. [9]

The dinner ended sometime before 22.00 hrs, the time at which all British soldiers had to be back in their barracks. There had been a pay parade earlier in the day, which resulted in some soldiers returning at the last moment somewhat worse for wear. 'I remember holding one of my soldiers under a cold shower trying to get him sober enough to load Bren magazines. None-the-less, the battalion was ready to move, magazines and trucks loaded, before three am.'[10]

During the night, the whole G 1098 (equipment and ammunition kept ready in all respects should mobilisation be ordered) was loaded on to transport, full scales of ammunition were issued and all necessary preparations were made for war. Few in the Battalion could have had any illusions as to the outcome if the order came for them to go into action within the next few hours, and that included Private P. Mckenna (ACC attached) who remembered, 'When the riots started in East Berlin and we were stood to all night that was a bit scary.' In the early hours of the morning, the Company Commanders made a reconnaissance of the positions to be occupied by the Battalion. Fortunately, the West Berliners refused to join in and by the morning of 17 June the rioting in the eastern sector appeared to have died down. Private Mckenna recalled that, 'we were still stood to when all the civilian staff came into work the next morning, my future wife as she was then, thought we were moving out and leaving them.'[11] For the East Germans, Russian retribution was swift and decisive. In quelling the riots, 21 people were killed with hundreds more wounded, and in the following days 1,300 Germans were sentenced to varying terms of imprisonment. The 1st Battalion's editorial in the November issue of *The Bugle* began

The future historian of the KOYLI whose job it is to record the post-war years of the Regiment will probably dismiss the 1st Battalion's stay in Berlin with a sentence or at most a paragraph. [12]

How quickly the writer had managed to put out of his mind the events of the previous three months.

One important duty of any British Battalion stationed in Berlin was to guard the seven remaining Germans who had been convicted of war crimes at the Nuremberg Trials and were still incarcerated in Spandau Prison. Guarding Spandau was done on a monthly basis by each of the occupying powers, and on one occasion when taking over from the Americans the KOYLI guard included Private B. Haigh, a National Serviceman from Leeds. While there were many important tasks for the guard detachment, other day-to-day activities also needed attention. Private Haigh, a recently qualified joiner, recalled, 'I had to do a tour of the look out posts, towers, and remove the scratch marks which the Yanks had left on the timber for example like "Joe Smith Philadelphia".' [13] Fortunately, for Joe Smith, none of the prisoners escaped while he concentrated on his carving. On New Years Day 1954, 'A' Company was scheduled to take over as guard company, but the KOYLI was not impressed by the American's disregard of military protocol. At the handing over ceremony the Americans, who always used a Demonstration Platoon, in contrast to 1st KOYLI who mounted the actual guard, marched off before the KOYLI's first relief guard had reached the guardhouse. Consequently, the ceremony, which was carried out in sub-zero temperatures, was completed in about three minutes.

Fig: 20 Lt Gen Sir Richard Gale, C-in-C BAOR, Lt Col Nic Pope and Major Healing observe 2Lt J.S. Cowley's Anti-Tank Gun Platoon at work in Berlin, 1953
Col J.S. Cowley

The start of a new year brought with it real winter weather, and the exceptionally cold nights caused particular problems for the MT Platoon who had to resort to draining vehicle radiators, even though the latter were filled with anti-freeze. In January the Foreign Ministers of the Four Powers held a conference in Berlin that passed off without disturbing the whole Battalion, although the Foreign Secretary, Mr Anthony Eden, did dine in the Officers' Mess one evening, and enjoyed a drink in the Serjeants' Mess on another occasion. Guards, ceremonies, and training continued, and on 9 May yet another distinguished visitor, the Lord Mayor of Leeds, paid a two-day visit to the Battalion.

In early August, after a tour of 18 months in Berlin, 1st KOYLI prepared to move back to the UK. The delights of a capital city had made a welcome change for everyone, but the uniqueness of the situation, and the isolation from the rest of the army, meant that it was not an ideal posting for a full three-year tour of duty. Berlin imposed its own demands and limitations on its resident defenders and their families. Travelling into and out of the city from the Western zones required a special pass, and military personnel travelling by train completed the journey to and from Helmstedt in carriages with darkened windows. Within the city there was little room for large scale training exercises, but there was a great demand for parades and ceremonial and, as one of the representatives of the British Army, the Battalion was duty bound to maintain a high standard of turn out and drill, which it did at all times.

Fig:21 Sjt L. Raveney's MMG Platoon being inspected by GOC Northern Command, Lt Gen Sir Geoffrey Evans, and Lt Col Pope, Strensall, 1954
Regt Archive

Rumours regarding the next foreign posting were finally settled when the Battalion was warned for the Canal Zone in Egypt, a location not much favoured by anyone. Kenya, where civil unrest had increased with the growth of Mau Mau terrorism, offered much better prospects, and when news was received of a change of destination from the Canal Zone to Kenya, it met with all-round approval: the Battalion was to take over from 1st Buffs and form part of 39th Infantry Brigade. The December 1952 edition of *The Bugle* had contained an article entitled, 'The Mau Mau in Kenya' in which a brief description of the growth of the terrorist Mau Mau movement, together with some of the measures being put in place to counter this threat thus providing the reader with an inkling of what the future might hold.

The journey home from Berlin was uneventful, except for an extremely rough North Sea crossing, and 1st KOYLI arrived at Strensall at 16:00 hrs on 24 August. After three days settling in, most of the Battalion left for 28 days of well-earned leave.

The Depot and 4th Territorial Battalion

During November 1951, the Regimental Depot was firmly established in Queen Elizabeth Barracks, Strensall, and by the end of the month it had also become the Light Infantry Brigade Depot. Following the outbreak of the Korean War in June 1950, National Service was increased from 18 months to two years. The first Basic Training Intake, No 51.21, passed out on 12 December 1951 and was followed by a steady stream of recruits, both regular and National Servicemen, who were sent to all the battalions of the Light Infantry. When, half way through the training of the second intake, 'B' Company was told that 25 of the intake would have to go to 1st KSLI in Korea, eleven volunteered immediately and the remainder were drawn out of a hat.

Throughout 1952 the Depot put each intake of recruits through the standard six-week period of training, until 20 November when the course was increased to ten weeks. Two features of the year were the increasing numbers of regular recruits passing through the Depot, and the arrival in June of the first 'Z' Reservists for service with the 4th Battalion.

Inevitably, the 4th Battalion grew as more ex-National Servicemen were attached for their period of reserve training. The increase in men and equipment meant the Battalion now had an anti-tank platoon, whose members were extra keen to show their skill with the 17 pounder anti-tank gun. The highlight of the year, as ever, was the annual camp, which in 1952 took place at Bodney North Camp in Norfolk. Since the Battalion was in camp on Minden Day the traditional Parade took place. When the Battalion was drawn up in line, the Hon. Colonel – Colonel T. Chadwick, MC TD DL JP – gave the command 'General Salute – Present Arms' after which the Battalion was inspected by Colonel of the Regiment, Major General H. Redman.

Coronation Year, 1953, began with the Depot's 'C' Company voicing a serious complaint before it was disbanded.

> Our great fight all along has been to obtain sufficient instructors who know their job, as well as obtaining the maximum time for training. The order of priority, I fear, has, on occasions, given more weight to the political as opposed to fighting aspects. When "Z" Reservists came through Strensall on their way to and from the Army, it is the National Serviceman, due for Korea, who had to give up his training for a few days. Latterly another big difficulty has been ammunition, but that was due to the men in Korea, quite rightly, getting priority.[14]

The principal event of the year was, of course, the Coronation of Her Majesty Queen Elizabeth II. A detachment from the 1st Battalion, commanded by Major W.L. Slingsby, and another from the 4th Battalion, commanded by Major G.C.W. Harland MC, were in the Coronation procession. Colonel J.C. Preston DSO, as Colonel of the Light Infantry Brigade, commanded the Light Infantry Street Lining Party, which had a portion of the route in East Carriage Drive near the Dorchester Hotel. Included in this group were two small detachments, one from the Regimental Depot commanded by Lieutenant C.W. Huxley, and another from the 4th Battalion commanded by Lieutenant E. Beckwith.

Having been promoted to the rank of Lieutenant General in November 1952, and appointed Vice Chief of the Imperial General Staff, the Colonel of the Regiment was further honoured in the Coronation Honours List, 2 June 1953, when he was promoted KCB.

The year also marked the 150th Anniversary of the formation of the Light Brigade by Sir John Moore. To commemorate the event the Massed Bands and Bugles of the Light Infantry Brigade carried out the ceremony of Sounding 'Retreat' at Aldershot, Sandhurst, Maidstone, Hythe, Folkestone and Shorncliffe during the period 7-25 June; at the Hythe ceremony, 22 June, the salute was taken by General Sir Charles Deedes. Lieutenant General Sir Harold Redman took the salute at the final ceremony, which took place on Sir John Moore's Plain at Shorncliffe on 25 June. The ceremony took place in the presence of the newly appointed CIGS, General Sir John Harding, himself a Light Infantryman and Colonel of the Somerset Light Infantry. A Civic Lunch given by the Mayor of Folkestone followed the ceremony, after which the CIGS laid a wreath at the Memorial to Sir John Moore at Sandgate.

In August 1953, the Territorials held a Divisional Camp on Salisbury Plain. The location was a fitting one on this occasion for the numbers were bolstered by the attendance of 1,000 'Z' Reservists. Later in the year 4th KOYLI' s numbers were further increased when it absorbed a further 60 'Z' Reservists.

On 13 January 1954 command of 4th KOYLI passed from Lieutenant Colonel Haslegrave to Lieutenant Colonel H.E. Barker TD, who had served with the 5th Battalion for ten years before the war, with the RA during the war, and finally rejoined the TA in 1947. The first problem facing the new CO was the possibility of a cut of 20% in his permanent military and civilian staff!

By the middle of 1954, there had been a huge increase in the numbers of each intake at the Depot – from the usual 20-30 to over 80. Those recruits who arrived at the height of summer may have felt themselves hard done by, for 'B' Company's notes revealed a distressing situation.

> Where is our coal ration and woollen underwear, and why can't umbrellas be issued to soldiers? These are the most pressing needs of the Basic Training Intake in this merry month of July 1954. We have never known a Summer so cold ... [15]

If the recruits were cold in their barracks, the 40 officers and 825 other ranks of the 4th Battalion at their annual camp on Fylingdales Moor, near Scarborough, were even greater victims of the unseasonable weather. Nevertheless, despite the unusual amount of rain, the camp proved to be a success.

---

[1] *The Bugle*, 1952, Vol. 44.3 p 11
[2] Huxley, Col C.W. Memoir. Regt. Archive.
[3] *Ibid*, A Royal Engineer officer, in charge of all the boats, was aboard the HQ boat because the engine had been playing up. He too was drowned in the incident.
[4] *The Bugle*, 1953, Vol. 45.1 p 19
[5] *Ibid*, Vol. 45.1 p 16
[6] *Ibid*, Vol. 45.3 p 25
[7] *Ibid*, Vol. 45.3 p 26
[8] *Ibid*, Vol. 45.3 p 31
[9] Tinson, Lt Col A.R. Memoir. Regt. Archive.
     After a lapse of more than 50 years, recalling the exact words used by Colonel Pope on this momentous occasion cannot be easy. Also present at the dinner was Colonel J.S. Cowley, whose recollection is slightly different. 'After receiving the message, the Colonel left the table asking us to continue. When he returned he calmly announced, "Gentlemen, we must prepare for war. I will hold an O Group at midnight".' Some 15 years later, Lt Col P.G. Fleming, who was not present at the dinner, but returned to the Battalion with his wife and daughter through the Russian Zone the following morning, was introduced to an American Colonel

who recognised his collar-dogs and exclaimed 'Hey, are you in the KOYLI?' Being complimented on recognising the regimental badge he answered, 'Gee, I'll never forget your regiment.' He then gave his account of the events that evening and ended by saying, 'I gotta tell you, that was one helluva way to end the evening'.

[10]   *Ibid*

[11]   McKenna, Pte. P. Memoir. Regt. Archive.

[12]   *The Bugle,* 1953, Vol. 45.4 p 21

[13]   Haigh, Pte. B. Memoir. Regt. Archive.

[14]   *The Bugle*, 1953, Vol. 45.1 p 11

[15]   *The Bugle*, 1954, Vol. 46.3 p 20

4

Kenya and Aden

An increase in the number of acts of sabotage and assassinations, attributed by the Kenyan authorities to Mau Mau terrorists, prompted the newly appointed Governor of Kenya, Sir Evelyn Baring, to declare a State of Emergency on 20 October 1952. Unlike Southern Rhodesia (Zimbabwe), Kenya had no form of self-government but was a colony under the supervision of the Colonial Office. Accounting for a mere 4% of the population, European white settlers, together with the small Asian community, were the main source of the country's economic success. Unlike many other parts of the continent, Kenya's growing prosperity had resulted in approximately half of all wage-earning Africans being employed in non-agricultural activities. The White Highlands, a vast tract of land covering some 16,700 square miles in the heart of the country, was reserved exclusively for European settlers, many of whom had arrived at the end of the Second World War. The increased level of investment by these settlers, together with their use of modern farming methods and technology, had contributed to making this area one of the most productive in the whole of Kenya.

The Bantu tribes, of which the largest is the Kikuyu, form the country's main ethnic group; the other tribal groups, the Nilotes and the Cushitic, accounting for only one third of the total population.[1] The main grievance of the Kikuyu was its exclusion from the White Highlands, and it was from this tribe that the Mau Mau recruited most of its supporters. When the government introduced measures to improve the land by reforming poor agricultural methods, the Kikuyu felt them to be a severe threat to their mainly peasant culture. Some doubt surrounds just what Mau Mau represented: a tribal led peasant revolt, a disorganised nationalist movement, or some combination of the two. What is not in doubt is the revulsion felt by those in the UK on reading lurid press accounts of bloodthirsty oath taking, and the horrifying deaths of black and white Kenyans hacked to pieces by panga wielding Mau Mau. Whilst there were, without doubt, many individual cases of indiscriminate murder, and indeed mass-murders of a most horrific nature, when the emergency was over figures showed that the Mau Mau had paid a heavy price for their insurrection.

A single act of murder is often the spark that ignites the powder keg of civil disorder, and in Kenya it was the murder of Senior Chief Waruhiuwa Kungu of Kiambu, a Kikuyu and strong supporter of the government. On the day following the Governor's declaration of a State of Emergency,

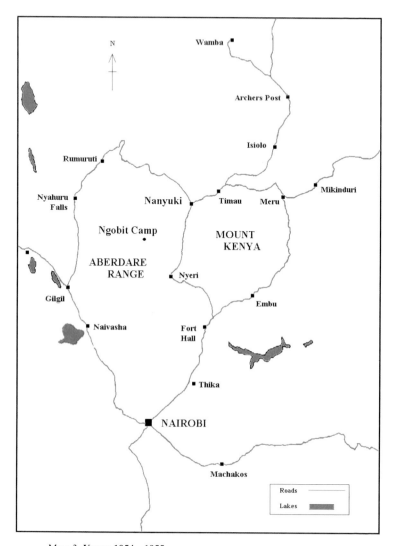

Map: 3. **Kenya 1954 – 1955.**
The 1st KOYLI's main area of operation was to the west of Mount Kenya
in the Aberdare Range.

'Operation Jock Scott' saw the arrest of 130 suspected Mau Mau leaders. Among those arrested was Jomo Kenyatta, the leader of the Kenya African Union (KAU), who most white settlers believed to be the overall leader of the Mau Mau movement.

Both sides began to build up their forces. Within hours of the declaration of the Emergency the 1st Lancashire Fusiliers were airlifted from the Suez Canal Zone to join the three battalions of the King's African Rifles (KAR) already in Kenya. (Other battalions of the KAR were assisting with the continuing Malayan Emergency.) By mid-1953, it was thought the number of Mau Mau in organised gangs was approaching 15,000. The self-styled 'General China' commanded one group in the forests on the slopes of Mount Kenya; Dedan Kimathi commanded another in the Aberdare Mountains, while a third, in the area around Nairobi, was commanded by Stanley Matheuge.[2] Many Kikuyu remained loyal to the government, as did most of the other tribes in Kenya who were opposed to Kikuyu domination. Only about 1,500 Mau Mau had serviceable guns, the majority having pangas, but some did have home-made guns that proved to be more lethal to the user than the intended victim.

In the early stages of the campaign the 'hearts and minds policy', which Sir Gerald Templer had recently introduced so successfully in Malaya, was not introduced in Kenya. An increasing number of attacks were launched on guard posts and villages thought to be loyal to the government, but it was not until the appointment of General Sir George Erskine in May 1953 that some of the important anti-terrorist lessons learned in Malaya were finally implemented.

In April 1954, a cordon of troops and police was placed around the capital Nairobi and some 20,000 Africans, mainly Kikuyu, were arrested. It was thought the movement would be weakened if individual Mau Mau members could be persuaded to break the promises they had made in the secret oath taking ceremonies. As a consequence, these suspects were detained in camps and subjected to anti-Mau Mau propaganda, rehabilitation programmes and compulsory work projects. (Throughout the Emergency some 80,000 men were detained for varying periods of time in such camps.) The Malayan policy of 'villagization', the creation of fortified villages overlooked by watchtowers and protected by spiked ditches, was introduced to try to isolate those Mau Mau in the forests from their supplies of food and possible recruits. Mau Mau camps in the forest were bombed and machine-gunned by the RAF, and army patrols were sent in to increase the offensive pressure. In November 1954, 1st KOYLI, who had first hand experience of this type of specialised jungle patrol work, was despatched to Kenya from its Depot at Strensall Barracks, York.

An advance party of three officers and 55 other ranks of 1st KOYLI flew out to Kenya on 5 November to join almost half the Battalion's officers who were already in Kenya making preparations for its reception; the main body sailed from Liverpool in the *S.S. Georgic* on 9 November. The 1st KOYLI disembarked at the port of Mombasa on 26 November, from where it went by train to Nanyuki, which was reached in the evening of 28 November. The three weeks that were spent under canvas at Nanyuki coincided with the short rainy season, and mud became a regular feature of life. The centre of Nanyuki is just over one mile north of the equator, but being 7,000 feet above sea level, the training and acclimatisation schedule sometimes proved more than a little strenuous, especially for those who enjoyed the occasional 'Clipper' cigarette. In mid December, the Companies moved out to their locations in the foothills of the Aberdare Mountains, some 40 miles south west of Nanyuki, to acclimatise for the forthcoming operations.

The tasks of patrolling, sweeping and ambushing, that had become the familiar stuff of everyday life in Malaya, were revived, but in a somewhat different setting. The Aberdare Mountains of Kenya rise to an average height of 11,000 feet and, while the days are very hot, at altitudes above 7,000 feet the nights are very cold. Elevation determines the vegetation with grasslands covering the base, dense forests of natural wood (large cedars and bamboo) growing on the slopes between 6,000 and 10,000 feet, and above this heathers in the area often referred to as the moorland; beyond this lay the African Alpine region.

On one of the first patrols in a particularly steep river gorge, 'C' Company's 7 Platoon spotted a Mau Mau, but a jammed Sten gun meant the man escaped. At the end of the acclimatisation period, the soldiers had sampled the countryside, built their own 'bashas', cooked their own food, and were ready to return to Nanyuki for the Christmas festivities.

In the first three months of 1955, a number of large-scale operations disrupted and scattered the main Mau Mau gangs, forcing them to disperse into the forests. The first of these, Operation 'Hammer', began on 9 January and lasted 14 days. It was a combined operation in the Aberdare region involving most of the security forces in the area and all 1st KOYLI's companies, each company dividing its three platoons into three patrols. The sweep element of the operation aimed to clear any Mau Mau from the moorlands, forcing them down through the forests to the camp area, at about 7,000 feet, where the stops were placed. (Some of the troops in the stop line patrolled while others remained in ambush positions.) During one operation, the Battalion sustained a casualty from a source often referred to as 'friendly fire'. Second Lieutenant J.A. Hare's platoon placed a night-time cordon around a native village that was suspected of providing the Mau Mau with food and information. 'As there was a curfew in place at the time, anyone who moved was assumed to be enemy. During the night, Second Lieutenant Hare attempted to re-position one of his men and was caught in a burst from his patrol's Bren gun, losing his right eye in the process. [3] Despite the elaborate preparations, for most of the operation little or nothing was seen of the Mau Mau, although 'C' Company did claim first blood, having shot a Mau Mau 'in the rear portion of his anatomy.'

During Operation 'Hammer', Lieutenant Colonel Pope established his tactical headquarters on the Fletcher farm just on the northern edge of the Aberdare Forest. This being essentially a company operation, the CO decided that he would interfere as little as possible and took the opportunity to indulge his passion for fishing. Mau Mau activity in the area over the past four years had prevented any fishing in the trout streams coming down the Aberdares with the result that they were literally swarming with brown trout.

> Guarded by buglers, his daily fishing trips always managed to feed Tac HQ with delicious fat fresh trout. He always insisted on using a fly, never a spoon, which he regarded as unsportsmanlike. At least one of his company commanders (and I strongly suspect the rest!) forbore from informing him that he too was feeding his company from the same source, but by using a grenade instead of a fly rod. It seemed sensible not to incur Colonel Nic's wrath and a possible court martial for 'conduct unbecoming'.[4]

If the Mau Mau had posed little threat to the patrols, the same could not be said for the local fauna. Numerous accounts of chance encounters with elephants, rhinoceros and buffaloes litter the company notes of *The Bugle,* and tales of un-climbable trees being scaled with ease in a frantic effort to escape these animals grew by the day. Corporal Hall's patrol from the Anti-Tank Platoon was typical. 'His worthy patrol became airborne at the sight of a chugging rhino and in spite of their heavy packs were soon on the branches of the nearest trees.'[5] It was estimated that each patrol could expect to encounter elephant, rhino or buffalo on at least nine occasions each day, and the advice from the local Kenya Regiment sergeants was to stand still: when the myopic beast charged, it was possible, given a strong nerve, to jump clear. (This advice did not apply to buffalo.) If, however, the RAF had been bombing and an animal had been wounded, the consequences could be quite serious. On one occasion whilst moving along a narrow trail, Captain J.R. Turpin (known to one and all as 'Dick') encountered a rhino that perceived him to be something of a threat.

> Dick was capable of a fair turn of speed (especially give the incentive) but the rhino was faster: he caught up with Dick, nudged him with his shoulder – fortunately not his horn – and propelled him over the first stand of bamboo on the edge of the track. Dick landed on his head, badly scratched down his front from the bamboo and thorns, but otherwise fortunately not hurt.[6]

Immediately following 'Hammer', 'C' Company took part in a screening operation named 'Scaramouche'. Designed to sweep the Nanyuki area and destroy one of the terrorists' main bases, the operation gathered in a significant number of Mau Mau suspects.

The East African School of Jungle Warfare had adapted some of the skills of jungle patrolling previously developed in Malaya. The use of existing tracks made by man or animals was to be encouraged (elephants, buffalo and rhino were capable of producing very well defined tracks), but resting or camping needed to be done away from these tracks. The need to move quietly was stressed, and patrols were encouraged to avoid, if possible, cutting paths with machetes that would give away their presence. Track discipline was important and patrols were instructed not to leave such things as cigarette ends (and certainly not cigarette or sweet packets) on the track. Careful observation of existing tracks could reveal signs of who, or what, had passed that way recently, and particular signs used exclusively by the Mau Mau needed to be learned. All this, and much more, was essential if the patrols were to have any chance of locating the Mau Mau gangs.

Fig: 22 The Anti-Tank Platoon's camp cookhouse during Op. 'Searchlight II' in the Aberdares, Aug 1955   *Sir David Goodall*

Practising 'snap firing' was part of basic training. After being told not to fire at the first of six targets to be exposed, most recruits instinctively fire first and think afterwards. In anti-terrorist operations target identification can be problematical, especially when it is almost impossible to distinguish friend from foe. A tip off to the Kenya Police that a gang of Mau Mau was hiding in a forested area near their camp at Deighton Downs sent 50 men of 'D'Company at breakneck speed to investigate. A cordon was quickly thrown around the area and a patrol sent in to flush out the terrorists. Private

P. Kirton was soon to be faced with a difficult decision. A shout from another member of the cordon alerted Private Kirton to the fact that a Kikuyu was advancing towards him with a large spear aimed directly at him. Orders had been given for the cordon to shoot any terrorist that emerged from the forest.

> My colleague was now shouting frantically, 'shoot him, shoot him'. By this time he was about forty yards from me so, uncertain what to do, I stupidly shouted to him, 'Are you a Mau Mau?' 'Mingy Mau Mau' he shouted back, which meant plenty Mau Mau. I was still uncertain and colleagues from both sides were now shouting at me to shoot him. When he was approximately twenty yards from me I cocked my rifle and came up into the aim. His reaction startled me as he immediately let the spear fall and dropped to his knees sobbing uncontrollably.[7]

A Kenyan police inspector later told Private Kirton, 'I'm glad you didn't shoot him; he is the guy who informed us of the Mau Mau'. The man had been told to stay in a certain area for his own safety but had wandered away. It nearly cost him his life.

Operations over the previous two years had had a decisive effect on the situation in Kenya. Whilst the current ones were important, the darkest days of the Emergency had passed. Obviously there was no room for complacency, but there was, however, a feeling that these were clearing up operations rather than confronting a desperate situation.

> The emergency has changed for the better but we all regret we were not out here in the 'Good Old Days' when Mau Mau were Mau Mau and success came easily. Now, except for one or two gangs our opponents have one idea only and that is to avoid trouble at all costs. They run, and, at the first sight of troops, run very fast. Patrols and ambushes are generally a long, tedious and unrewarding business. [8]

Operation 'First Flute' followed 'Hammer'. While two battalions kept up the pressure on the terrorists in the Aberdare region, eight battalions, under the nominal command of Major General W.R.N. Hinde (Brigadier Lord Thurlow was in actual command of the operation, Major General Hinde being in England at the time) were to carry out this second large-scale offensive against the terrorists in the Mt Kenya area. The overall plan of the operation, which was to last over four weeks and cover an area of over 400 square miles on the western slopes of Mt Kenya, was similar to operation 'Hammer': clear the moorlands, then concentrate on the forests and end with ambushes and searches on the edge of the forests.

Each Company began by cutting tracks through the thick forest to enable troops and supplies to be moved up the mountain, the task proving so difficult for 'D' Company, who were making two tracks, that spotter planes had to be used to help the cutting parties keep their direction. 'D' Company notes recorded,

> After the track cutting was completed the Company prepared for the long trek up the mountain, moving off on the 18th February. Each man carried, in addition to his personal kit and rations for three days, a portion of the equipment necessary to maintain a Company in the field, ie, wireless sets and batteries, stretchers, cooking utensils, etc. Loaded to the full, Platoons moved off up the track, and after a long and arduous trek in which three members of Company HQ fell by the wayside from sheer exhaustion, the Company arrived at the forest base on the edge of the moorland.[9]

'C' Company had been designated a Tracker Company and reorganised its platoons and sections into three Tracker Teams, each with its own reinforcement section. Fortunately for these teams, they were not required to carve their way up the mountainside but were allowed to use HQ Company's track, which had been cut by a native labour force. HQ Company provided some of the stops, but the specialist platoons of the Support Company had most reason to moan.

> For five weeks we sat in the same positions manning the Battalion stop line. At first the Platoon had to patrol forward during the day, then lay ambushes during the night, which was interesting, but at the end of five weeks without any results they were ready for a change.[10]

Re-supplying the troops along the tracks proved to be a slow and laborious process, although 'B' Company's mule train did manage daily journeys to and from the moorland zone; but beyond this, the going was difficult. Parachute drops, courtesy of the RAF, had been organised but, unlike the Aberdares, here the RAF had to contend with a cloud problem. At one Dropping Zone (DZ) Company Serjeant Major Kitching and Serjeant Beetham, 'D' Company, were placed in mortal danger when preparing for a drop. Ration boxes suddenly rained down on them from above when an over zealous pilot released the whole consignment a full hour before it was expected. The Company was much more appreciative of the Kenya Police Air Wing which dropped vital supplies of cigarettes, newspapers etc.

While 'A' Company spent 21 days patrolling in the forests, 'B' Company's patrols operated up to 12,000 feet in the moorland, and 'D' Company had patrols moving up to the snowline, the highest point reached being 15,100 feet. Most of the patrols maintained a pattern of three days out before returning to their base to rest and re-supply. Despite all the time and effort expended, and GHQ's assumption that there were approximately 2,000 terrorists in the operational area, once again no Mau Mau were seen, although Serjeant Davey's 6 Platoon did find a cave that may have housed 100 Mau Mau over a year before. Indeed, 'B' Company notes made the point, 'It is believed that at least in our Brigade area there are no large gangs, as there are on the other side of Mt Kenya, at Embu and Meru.' [11]

With the end of Operation 'First Flute' the Battalion returned to Nanyuki. In early April, after refitting and a few days rest, the rifle companies once again set out on their quest to find the Mau Mau. 'A' and 'C' Companies moved into the Aberdares, 'B' Company's search was located quite close to Nanyuki, and 'D' moved into nearby farming country. During this operation, 'C' Company had the opportunity to assess the new Belgian Fabrique Nationale d'Armes de Guerre (FN) self-loading rifle, which they found to be an excellent weapon. The FN rifle, which eventually replaced the Lee Enfield .303 No 5 rifle, was a 7.62mm self-loading assault rifle designed for use by NATO troops in northern Europe.

Fig: 23 2Lt David Goodall's patrol – Op. 'Torchlight I' in the Aberdares
L:R. Rear: Pte Sayer, 2Lt Goodall, L/Cpl Thomson, Joshua (Kikuyu Tracker)
Front: Pte O'Toole, Pte Wales, Pte Moffat, Aug 1955   *Sir David Goodall*

The Support Company was given a short respite from acting as a rifle company when it was sent to assist the Royal Engineers with the construction of Ngobit Camp (A most unfortunate name, especially for a Yorkshire Regiment.) Largely designed by Lieutenant Colonel Pope, the camp was set up halfway between Mt Kenya and the Aberdares, and was one of the few in Kenya to be purpose built as a battalion base. It benefited from a sports ground, officers and serjeants' messes, a NAAFI canteen, a cinema/theatre and a small airfield. The muddy waters of the Uaso Nyiro meandered past on their way to nowhere in particular, the river failing to reach the sea and ending ignominiously in a swamp. Water was extracted from the river and, after being allowed to settle in tanks, was purified and chlorinated to the MO's satisfaction before being issued for drinking, cooking and washing. (There were times, however, when its use had to be restricted to drinking and cooking only.)

The move to Ngobit at the beginning of April preceded Operation 'Hungerstrike', which was scheduled to begin about the middle of the month. In the Mt Kenya area the Mau Mau had been getting supplies of cattle and pigs from surrounding farms, and 'Hungerstrike' was an attempt to prevent this. Each Company HQ plus one platoon was established in its own farmhouse, the other platoons being located in nearby farms. Long hours were spent monitoring herds of cattle, and their herd boys, in an effort to prevent losses of stock, or quantities of food being left for collection by the Mau Mau. Some losses were inevitable as the terrorists became increasingly desperate for food, and one night twelve cattle were spirited away just 200 yards from 'A' Company HQ. But while the work was tedious the companies were persuaded that preventing losses of cattle and foodstuffs meant success in the overall campaign.

Operation 'Gimlet' placed 'C' Company under the command of 70th Brigade, its Tracker Teams being ordered to clear the forests of the

Aberdares that bordered on the Kikuyu reserve. On 2 June, 'A' Company was put under the command of 39th Brigade for use on the eastern side of Mt Kenya in the Meru area. As part of one of the Meru operations a troop of 3.7 guns of 156th HAA Battery was used 'to induce as many surrenders as possible.' The MG and Mortar Platoons were also involved with 'A' Company for some of the time, and the use of their specialised armaments undoubtedly contributed to the success of the operation. 'They can certainly claim to have caused more than one terrorist to give himself up,'[12]

Fig: 25 Cpl Atkinson (standing) and his team prepare for a Mortar shoot at Hall's Farm, Kenya, 1955.   *Sir David Goodall*

The operations between January and June 1955, which involved some 10,000 troops dispersing an estimated 4,000 terrorists, proved so successful that it was decided to become more aggressive and again harass the gangs in their forest hideouts by intensifying the patrols, sweeps and searches. The government offer of surrender terms to those terrorists still out in the forests expired on 10 July, but many of the hard-core Mau Mau rejected them. Once the amnesty had been withdrawn, those terrorists who refused to surrender were placed under extreme pressure and it became the Battalion's job to seek them out and destroy them. There were some successes, but for the majority of the patrols it was hard and often unrewarding work. In a letter home, 2nd Lieutenant A.D.S. Goodall, who had joined the Battalion in early August and was placed in-charge of the Anti-Tank Platoon (which at this time was operating as a rifle platoon), described one such patrol that he undertook in mid-August.

> I am writing this from somewhere in the Aberdare forests – I can't tell you where it is, not for security reasons, but because it simply isn't anywhere near anywhere. We have been out here nearly four days – so far absolutely nothing has happened: here, high up in a forest clearing with green grass and familiar looking trees around us it is hard to believe we are in Africa at all; but with each morning fresh and sunny like an early summers day at home its impossible to believe that the tracks which run in the forest in all directions round our camp are of buffalo, wild boar, elephant or rhino.
>
> Yesterday a patrol came in and reported that an old Mau Mau Aide had been found in the forest on one of the few streams with water in them, with the remains of a dead body lying across the stream. I went out with a patrol to inspect this grisly sight – it lay in the densest part of the forest at the bottom of a narrow valley from which the sky was completely invisible, and to reach it we had to cover the last part of the journey by actually wading up the stream. The corpse – if that is not too grand a name for a few rags and a heap of evil smelling bones – was two months old and of a man who had probably been shot up by the security forces and died in the hide. His companions had dragged it across the stream and left it to foul the water.[13]

Ten days later, 2nd Lieutenant Goodall was again out on patrol, but in somewhat different conditions.

> Back in the forest again, this time much further in and much higher up. We're again in a small clearing, but overhung this time by enormous forest trees which make everything dark and damp. Outside my tent on the right the ground falls away down into a low

valley filled with tall trees and feathery bamboo. Altogether our new position has none of the gentle deceptively English appearance of the last one. We arrived in pouring rain after a very tiresome journey in which the lorries persistently got stuck on the villainous tracks, and although yesterday and today there were no more rainstorms it has never been warm since. Last night was quite a wild one – the wind wailing in the treetops, a pale moon, and a glowing fire to keep the sentries warm.[14]

In July, Lieutenant Colonel Pope returned to the UK to become Chief Instructor at Warminster, which meant that he had to forego landing his 500th African trout, a decision that must have come as a welcome relief to the local trout population; command of 1st KOYLI passed to Lieutenant Colonel C.J. Deedes OBE, MC. On 1 September, the Battalion was officially informed that it would be leaving Kenya in November, its destination being Aden or Cyprus, or possibly Dover. Patrolling and ambushing continued until 15 October, when the Battalion became non-operational.

During its time in Kenya 1st KOYLI was responsible for eliminating over 30 Mau Mau terrorists. For their part, throughout the Emergency the Mau Mau had murdered almost 2,000, their chief victims being those Kikuyu who remained loyal to the government. The type of offensive patrolling carried out by the Battalion was to continue until the Emergency was finally declared over in November 1959. In the same year there was a change of Governor and Colonial Secretary and, following a conference on the future of Kenya, held in London in January 1960, majority rule was agreed. Jomo Kenyatta was released from prison in 1961, and when KANU won a decisive victory in the elections of 1963, he was elected the country's first president.

Fig: 24 Capt Dick Unett, Lt John Cowley, Capt Tom Cairns (MO) at about 15,500 ft on Mount Kenya, 1955
Col. J.S. Cowley

On 6 October, the Battalion had its first live show in Kenya, when Terry Thomas and Lorrae Desmond, plus a 'bewildering magician', visited Ngobit to entertain them. At the end of the show Lieutenant Colonel Deedes thanked the performers and announced that the long awaited signal giving the Battalion's next posting had arrived. The alternatives had been either Aden or Cyprus, but as the CO explained to the accompaniment of applause, cheers, and whistles – it was to be BOTH! The Battalion was to leave for Aden to relieve 1st Seaforth Highlanders, but, since Aden could only accommodate 700 men, 'D' Company would remain on board the *Dilwara* and sail on to Cyprus.

In the early hours of 7 November 1955, 1st KOYLI boarded a very long train at Naro Moru that struggled hard, despite the power of its two locomotives, to reach Nairobi by lunchtime. Before leaving Nairobi station for Kilindini, the C-in-C East Africa, Lieutenant General G.W. Lathbury, had this to say, 'There is no doubt that the British Army is generally liked and respected in Kenya and it is the high standard of regiments like yours which have made it so.'[15] The sea journey to Aden was, according to *The Bugle*, 'the calmest, sunniest days ever experienced in a troopship.'

Aden

The RAF station at Khormaksar was the Battalion's destination in Aden.[16] There was no permanent accommodation for 1st KOYLI but, this being the cool season, the Battalion was to live in tents close to the RAF base. Though the tents were a little old, it was thought that life, though a little dusty, would not be too uncomfortable. Mess accommodation was shared with the corresponding ranks of the RAF, as were the social facilities of cinema, swimming pool and library, all proving to be superior to those available in Kenya. The officer in Command Land Forces Aden was none other than Brigadier W.S.F. Hickie, who had commanded 2nd KOYLI in India and Malaya.

In late 1955, Aden was a relatively peaceful posting, even though the whole of the Middle East was entering a state of extreme uncertainty. In Egypt the *coup d'état* in July 1952 was organised by a Revolutionary Command Council of eleven officers under the control of Colonel Gamal Abdel Nasser, which ousted King Farouk and replaced him with a puppet head of state, Major General Mohammed Naguib.[17] The subsequent rise of Nasser was viewed with great concern by the British government, and when news of his secret purchase of arms from the communist government of Czechoslovakia was confirmed, it was feared that Russian influence in the area might increase. Between March and October 1955, Turkey, Iraq, Iran and Pakistan were persuaded to join with Britain in the Baghdad Pact, an organisation that it was hoped would be strong enough to discourage further Soviet ambition in the Middle East. Nasser's antagonism towards Britain

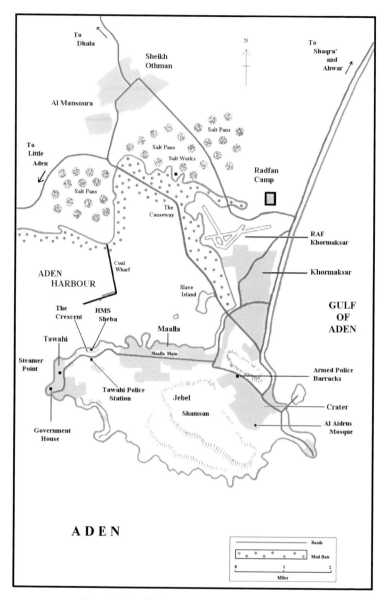

Map: 4. **Aden 1955 - 1956**
The town of Aden and the immediate surroundings.

and the West was obvious, and Cairo Radio constantly broadcast his message of revolutionary nationalism to the whole of the Arab world. The opening of a £50,000,000 oil refinery in 1953, and the development of the Abyan irrigation scheme, which facilitated the growth of cotton, had much improved the economic prosperity of Aden.

First occupied by the British in 1839, Aden had been ruled as a Crown Colony since 1937. The Protectorate was divided into two main areas. The western, with nineteen small sheikdoms, had a border with the Arab state of Yemen, with whom there were frequent disputes and incursions. The more peaceful eastern area had two rulers and a border with the 'Empty Quarter' of Arabia.

Defence of the colony had been in the hands of the Aden Protectorate Levies, an Arab force officered by the RAF Regiment, but increasing signs of Arab nationalism, and growing anti-British feeling in the whole of the Middle East, had created problems with the Levies who had, since June, become 'disaffected'. The problem with the Levies had resulted in a battalion of the 1st Seaforth Highlanders and a Squadron of the Life Guards being sent to the Protectorate. A Planning Team from GHQ Middle East Land Forces was working on the problem of accommodation for 1st KOYLI, but prospects of their producing an early solution, or the Battalion being allowed to continue its journey to Cyprus, were not good.

Shortly after arriving in Aden, the Bugle Platoon was swiftly transported to Ethiopia where it was scheduled to play for the British Trade Fair Celebrations. The platoon sounded the Retreat at the Trade Fair, and before Emperor Haile Selassie in the grounds of his palace in Addis Ababa. After the ceremony, the Emperor, accompanied by the Battalion's 2nd i/c, Lieutenant Colonel S.H. Kent, inspected the Buglers on parade.[18]

Meanwhile, in Aden, Lieutenant Colonel Deedes faced a number of problems, not least of which was the exact role to be played by the Battalion, and its relationship with the RAF. Since the RAF Regiment was theoretically responsible for security in the Protectorate, the presence of a battalion of infantry acted as a constant reminder of their perceived inability to deal adequately with the problem. There was also some uncertainty of just how long the Battalion was to stay in Aden. The attached RAOC, RASC, REME personnel had all been assured they were attached for two or three weeks, but the RASC had already been there seven months and saw no immediate prospect of relief; the Seaforths, expecting a two weeks stay, had been marooned for six months.

Captain N.C. Rowe, KSLI, had severe misgivings about his future. On being posted to 1st KOYLI in Cyprus, Captain Rowe had contacted the Regimental Depot and been informed that 1st KOYLI was not in Cyprus but in Aden.

> I rang the War Office branch responsible for postings and told
> them what the Depot had told me. I was informed in no uncertain

terms that the War Office knew where the battalion was and that I should go to join them in Cyprus. So I flew out to Cyprus and then had to wait in a Transit camp for several days before I could get a flight down to Aden.[19]

Officially, Aden was a station where Khaki Drill (KD) uniform was to be worn, but 1st KOYLI, having arrived from Kenya, was dressed in Olive Green (OG) and the QM stores at Aden was unable to provide a change. If the Battalion was to be stationed in Aden during the summer months, it was a matter of vital importance that it was not housed in 'ancient fly-ridden tents', and it needed to be dressed appropriately to withstand the severe heat.[20]

Fig: 26 Dhala Camp, 80 miles north of Aden.   *P. Sheild*

Within days of arriving the Battalion commenced training. There was a small training area at Little Aden on the peninsular some twenty miles from Aden town, and it was here that 2nd Lieutenant Goodall began training his men for 'rearguard actions in defence of a mobile column.' The Battalion's main training area was to be just outside Dhala, an Arab town some 80 miles, and 8 hours, north of Aden near the border with the Yemen. Each of the three rifle companies spent some time at Dhala, and for most men the time spent at altitude in Kenya provided them with more than enough stamina as they clambered up the rocky hillsides that surrounded the town and camp area. At Christmas, the whole of the Battalion was together in Aden, with the exception of 'C' Company, which remained at Dhala until after New Year's Day. Unfortunately, two members of the Battalion, Serjeant N.S. Morris and Private P.M. Callaghan, were killed in a mortar accident in the Dhala area on the penultimate day of the year.[21]

Fig: 27 Dhala market – L:R Capt Mike Tibbets (MO), Capt Tim Green,
2Lt Dan Dyas   *Sir David Goodall*

In early January, a ten-day operation to relieve a police garrison at Khora,
said by the Governor to call for a whole battalion, was cancelled after the
task was satisfactorily accomplished by a lone District Officer and 17 Arab
policemen. Instead of receiving the generous thanks of the authorities for
having saved some 25,000 man-hours and considerable expense to the
Exchequer, the Governor placed the District Officer under arrest!

The story of Operation 'Flagday' would have been all too familiar to any
soldier who had seen service on the Northwest Frontier of India in the 19th
Century. The Regent of Ahwar, a town 150 miles east of Aden along the
coast of the Eastern Protectorate, had been murdered in December 1955 in a
dispute over water. In February 1956, the new Regent was to be installed,
and it was 1st KOYLI's task to ensure the proceedings took place safely,
and, a suitable fine was collected from the tribe to which the murderers
belonged. The convoy of jeeps, lorries and armoured cars took three days to
transport 300 Light Infantrymen, plus numerous specialists and their
equipment, along the primitive roads, tracks and, for part of the journey,
over sandy beaches, to Ahwar where they made camp. At first, the Political
Officer was uncertain of the details of the fine, but after some haggling with
the murderers it was agreed at 13 rifles, £2,000 and three houses.

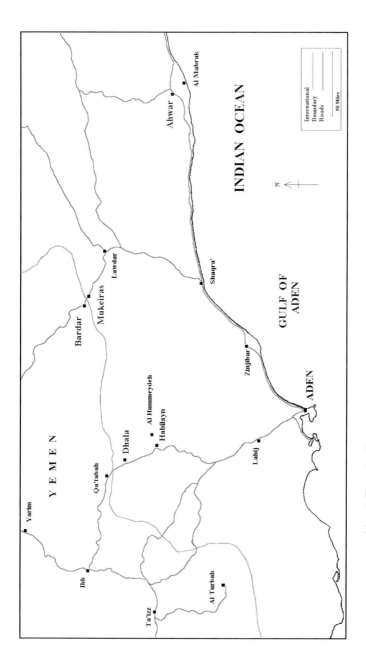

Map: 5. **The Aden Protectorate 1955 - 1956**
1st KOYLI initial HQ was at RAF Khormaksar, but companies trained at Dhala, and forays were made to parts of the western sheikdoms.

Fig: 28 Op. 'Flagday'. On the way to show the Flag, and collect the money,
L:R. Pte Lawson, Pte Johnson, 2Lt David Goodall, 1956
Sir David Goodall

The camp [named Leicester Square] is a fifty-yard square in the
middle of the desert which stretches away to the north: to the slag
heap foothills of the interior. Eight miles to the south over soft
sand dunes lies the sea with a hard sandy beach that might be the
envy of Blackpool. Half a mile to the west, bounding the horizon,
stretches Ahwar itself, in the distance looking like a group of sky-
scrapers; in fact a long straggling township of tall narrow houses
built of mud bricks and ending in whitewashed castellations. All

Fig: 29 Op. 'Flagday' 2Lt Brian Dale and Sjt Ashcroft making camp on the
first day, 1956   *Sir David Goodall*

round the poor live in huts made out of dead brushwood. The stench is overpowering; and everywhere the dust blows all day, a sort of blizzard drifting powdered sand everywhere. It sounds hellish; but, though we all grumble it is in fact all quite enjoyable. There has not really been a lot to do: we put on a demonstration of what we could do in the way of fire power: took our enemies up in trucks to the top of one of the local hills: brought jet fighters in to dive bomb a target: produced first the Armoured Cars, then two jeeploads of MMG (Medium Machine Guns), then the 3" Mortars to do their stuff; finally, two companies of Light Infantrymen came swinging round the corner: in a series of drill movements to lay down and open fire: then got up and put in a most convincing bayonet charge. The Arab was impressed: not, apparently, by the weapons; but by "the bearing and discipline of the soldiers." He paid the fine, contrary to all expectations, without a murmur; we then went out and completed the punishment by blowing up three of his forts – they dissolved magnificently in a towering column of smoke and sand while black and turbaned tribesmen with silver-hilted daggers in their belts and ancient French rifles on their shoulders stood around and watched with every mark of polite and detached interest.[22]

Fig: 30 Three houses in Ahwar were blown up as part of the fine, 1956.
Sir David Goodall

Retribution having been meted out, the forces of 'Pax Britannica' packed up their tents and returned to their base, sound in the knowledge that they had achieved their objective.

One question that kept recurring in the collective mind of 1st KOYLI was 'When are we leaving Aden?' The fierce heat of summer was only a matter of weeks away, and the prospect of having to consume large quantities of sand each mealtime was being viewed with some apprehension. Major Saltonstall's description of the sand in 'Operation Flagday' clearly illustrated the problem.

> It isn't the nice, clean, coarse-grained sand of English beaches. It is dirty yellow-grey dust, the consistency of face powder but gritty to the teeth. Why, you may ask, mention the teeth? Because we ate it … in our compo because it got there and there is no way of keeping it out. It gets … in your hair, your watch, your fountain pen and your ears. In future wars we will defend our country in the streets and the hills but please send someone else to the beaches. [23]

The arrival of *HMT Cheshire* towards the end of February brought the prospect of relief. The *Cheshire* was en route to Mombasa and rumour had it that when she returned she was to take 1st KOYLI to Cyprus. Confirmation of the move was not immediately forthcoming from any quarter, but on Sunday 4 March orders were issued for the Battalion to sail in the *Cheshire* the following Thursday! For a battalion of infantry that was still operational, four days in which to pack before embarkation called for feverish activity. Nevertheless, the task was accomplished. The advance party left Aden by air for Nicosia at 06:00 hrs, 8 March: the baggage was on the quayside; the heavy baggage was already aboard lighters in the middle of the harbour, and parties of soldiers had gone off to the ship. The Adjutant, alone in his empty and deserted office, was preparing to leave when the one remaining telephone rang. The embarkation had been postponed for at least 48 hours, and 1st KOYLI was to 'Stand To' at an hours notice ready to quell riots!

Hearing that the Battalion was about to leave the Protectorate, the local Arab stevedores had gone on strike. Faced with the prospect of losing the Battalion at the very moment when serious trouble was about to break out, the Governor had halted the embarkation and ordered three mobile columns, each of company strength, to assemble immediately. At this point, the traditional Light Infantry method of communication was employed. Much to the surprise of 2nd Lieutenant Goodall 'The Bugler sounded 'Light Division Assembly' - a call which I imagine has not been heard since the Peninsular – and then, 'All Officers at the double.'[24] Second Lieutenant Goodall may not have been the only officer to be surprised for this call had only recently been re-introduced for all Light Infantry Regiments.[25]

Whether the Battalion's furious activity at the docks had any influence on the stevedore's actions is uncertain, but the immediate danger passed without incident. On Friday word came that the *Cheshire* was being held and the Battalion was to embark on Saturday morning, but at midnight a further message cancelled this movement. During Saturday the baggage was retrieved from the docks and the Battalion settled down to await re-embarkation for a period that was variously estimated at between ten days and six weeks. An unconfirmed report suggested the stevedores had planned to strike when the Battalion was safely at sea, but their calculations had gone awry and they struck 24 hours too soon. The strike continued on the Sunday and the Commissioner of Police organised an elaborate set of precautions to deal with any disturbances, but they proved unnecessary and the strikers quietly returned to work.

There followed an uneasy peace during which time 'A' Company was ordered to 'Stand To' to fly to the Persian Gulf if needed. A dispute about pay caused dissatisfaction among the labourers at the oil refinery, which resulted in a number of incidents of rioting in Little Aden. A strike by civilian petrol-bowser drivers could have presented problems, but Lieutenant Tinson's MT section drivers were used to secure the safe delivery of essential fuel supplies. On one occasion the Deputy Police Commissioner was badly injured in the eye when rioters began throwing stones, but the appearance of 'A' and 'C' Companies preparing to take up their Internal Security Box Formation was sufficient to defuse the situation. The oil company, British Petroleum, provided air-conditioned accommodation, a swimming pool, and many other extras for the company that was stationed on site, thus making this a very popular assignment.

> Near the camp we had an interesting example of the civil unrest campaign. A young Arab shorted out the electric power cables to the local oil company installation by throwing a metal chain across them. Unfortunately for him he forgot to let go in time.[26]

A final departure date was confirmed and, on 17 April 1956, the advance party again flew to Nicosia. Over the next ten days, Hermes and York aircraft brought members of the relieving battalion of the 1st Gloucestershire Regiment to Aden, and returned to Cyprus carrying 1st KOYLI.

The Depot and 4th Territorial Battalion

When 1st KOYLI departed for Kenya, those National Servicemen whose remaining period of service was too short for them to accompany the Battalion abroad were left behind at Strensall. These men were known as 'the ineligibles'; apparently, no substitute for this inelegant title could be found. One National Serviceman, who was to leave later in the year, did not qualify for this semi-official sobriquet. Serjeant W.T. Charlton, Weapons Training Serjeant of the NCOs Cadre at the Regimental Depot, had the distinction of having risen to the rank of Serjeant within the two years of his conscripted service. (He was not the only National Serviceman to achieve this rank.) About the time that Serjeant Charlton returned to civilian life, his soldiering days done, an older and very distinguished soldier of the Regiment prepared to end his days in uniform. Colonel Tom Chadwick MC TD DL JP, handed over the Honorary Colonelcy of 4th KOYLI in April 1955 to Colonel M.A.C.P. Kaye, who had commanded the 4th Battalion when it was reformed in 1947. Sadly, Colonel Chadwick, who had won his MC on 10 October 1917 during the Battle of Poelcappelle in the Ypres Salient while serving with 1/4th KOYLI, was to die only four months later.

The year 1955 had great significance for the King's Own Yorkshire Light Infantry for it marked the two hundredth anniversary of the raising of the Regiment in Leeds. It was decided that the most appropriate day on which to celebrate this event would be 1 August, Minden Day. Preparations for important celebrations are always at the mercy of a number of variables, not least of which is the English weather. In this instance the weather was fine, but the demands of the War Office meant that one of the principals would be absent. It was probably in keeping with the Regiment's long and distinguished history that, in its Bicentenary Year, 1st Battalion, (51st/105th) KOYLI, was in a far off land attending to the business of its Sovereign, as it had done consistently for two hundred years.

On Friday 10 June, Her Majesty The Queen Mother attended a Dinner given by the Officers of the Regiment at the Skinners' Company Hall in the City of London. On 1 August the celebrations began with a service at York Minster that was attended by Her Majesty The Queen Mother, Lieutenant General Sir Harold Redman, the Lord Lieutenant of the North Riding, the Lord Mayor of York and nearly 200 officers of the Regiment, their wives, numerous distinguished guests and a congregation of over 900. Before entering the Minster, Her Majesty inspected a Guard of Honour formed by 50 recruits who had just completed their training; she then spoke to members of the Regimental Association including Captain F.W. Holmes VC, Serjeant L. Calvert VC MM, and the oldest veteran present, Private W. Stuthard who had joined the Regiment in 1886. Following the service in the Minster, Her Majesty travelled to Strensall for lunch, after which she met many members of the Regiment and their wives and families as she walked around the marquees that had been erected on the cricket ground. Between 500 and 600 attended the all ranks' Minden Ball that night, and soon after midnight some of the KOYLI performers from the Northern Command Tattoo, which was taking place in York at the time, arrived in their uniforms of former days.

The first week's battle simulation exercise at the 4th Battalion's summer camp in the Bicentenary year was noted for its excessive realism. Brigade HQ had to order the 4th Battalion's Support Company to stop firing live ammunition from its 17 pounder anti-tank guns and medium machine guns. This excess of zeal was not, however, responsible for the subsequent curtailing of the 'Z' Reservist's training commitment, which resulted in a 60% reduction in the Battalion's strength. The effect of this change to the terms of service of the National Servicemen eventually resulted in reducing to 350 the numbers attending the following year's annual camp, and of these 200 were National Servicemen.

---

[1] At this time Kenya's tribal groups were made up of – Bantu 66%Kikuyu, largest tribe forming 20% of the total population – Central highlands.
Nilotes 25% The most well known tribe being the Masai – Western plateau.
Cushitic 4% Arid regions of the north and northeast.
Whites/Asians 5%

[2] Kimathi was not captured until 17 October 1956 when, after a clash with the security forces, he was found by an African policeman hiding at the edge of the forest. He was tried for murder, found guilty and hanged in 1957.

[3] Cowley, Col. J.S, Memoir. Regt. Archive.

[4] Lees, Col. B. M. Memoir. Regt Archive.

[5] *The Bugle,* 1955, Vol. 47.1 p 25

[6] Lees, Col. B.M. Memoir. Regt. Archive.
On a similar occasion, Colonel Lees was leading his patrol when he was confronted by a buffalo, which suddenly appeared 20 yards ahead. Following the received wisdom, Colonel Lees stood still, and after a short while risked looking behind. The Kenya Regiment sergeant, who should have been behind him, and the rest of the platoon, were nowhere to be seen. 'I don't think that I have ever felt so isolated. I continued to stand there and the buffalo did move off. The rest of the patrol, including our big game expert, then materialised from the bush.'

[7] Kirton P. *Normanton Grit, Grime and Courage,* Pub. by the author. York 2001 pp 239-242

[8] *The Bugle,* 1955, Vol. 47.2 p 19

[9] *Ibid.* Vol. 47.2 p 23

[10] *Ibid.* Vol. 47.2 p 27

[11] *Ibid.* Vol. 47.2 p 21

[12] *Ibid.* Vol. 47.3 p 23

[13] Goodall, Sir David, Memoir. Regt. Archive.

[14] *Ibid.*

[15] *The Bugle,* 1956, Vol. 48.1 p 7

[16] Khormaksar (current spelling – Khaur Maksar) is now an international airport.

[17] Encyclopaedia Brittanica, Millenium Edition. General Naguib was deposed and arrested in the spring of 1954, after which, Nasser proclaimed himself prime minister.

[18] The Buglers made such an impression on the Emperor that, when the Bandmaster, WOI H. Balshaw, retired from the Army, he returned to Ethiopia at the request of the Emperor.

[19] Rowe, Capt. N.C. (KSLI att.) Memoir. Regt. Archive.
Capt. Rowe remembered that the War Office had once before lost (or rather mislaid) a battalion. The South Staffordshire Regiment, when stationed in the West Indies, was 'forgotten', and when re-discovered the men's uniforms had disintegrated forcing them to wear improvised ones made of sacking.

[20] Lees, Col. B.M. Memoir. Regt. Archive.
'In fact Colonel John Deedes appreciated, sensibly, that Jungle Green offered better camouflage in the mountains of the Western Aden Protectorate than KD, which tended to shine. Likewise, jungle boots were better than ammunition boots for scrambling up the rocks during picketing. Unfortunately, they wore out quickly on the sharp rocks and could not be replaced.'

[21] Sjt. N.S. Morris and Pte P.M. Callaghan were buried in the civilian cemetery in Ma'ala instead of the military cemetery in Silent Valley. On a visit to Aden in 1977, Colonel Lees found that during the Communist period the graves had been desecrated, but when he revisited, after the fall of the Communists, they had been restored.

[22] Goodall, Sir David, op cit

[23] *The Bugle,* 1956, Vol. 48.2 p 54

[24] Goodall, Sir David, op cit

[25] The bugle call appeared in *The Bugle,* 1955, Vol 47.1 p 4. See Appendix 10.

[26] Rowe, Capt. N.C. op cit

5

Cyprus

Cyprus had been leased from the Sultan of Turkey in 1878 but, when Turkey entered the war on the side of Germany in 1914, the island was annexed to the British Empire and became a Crown Colony in 1925. The majority of the population belong to one of two main culture groups, those who speak Greek (80%) and those who speak Turkish (20%). A small minority of Greek Cypriots had been seeking ENOSIS (union with Greece) since the early 1930s, but the Turkish Cypriots were fiercely opposed to this, fearing they would become second-class citizens if the island was ruled by Greece. The lack of a university on the island meant that students had to go either to Greece or Turkey to further their education, an experience that all too often reinforced any xenophobic tendencies they may have harboured.

Britain, having left its bases in Palestine (1948) and the Suez Canal Zone (1954), was determined to maintain control of the three 'fortress colonies' of Gibraltar, Malta and Cyprus.[1] Cyprus had become crucial to British military strategic planning in the Middle East, and by 1954 the island had become the base for the HQ of Middle East Land Forces (MELF). With two large RAF bases, plus secret intelligence gathering facilities to monitor Russian activity throughout the Middle East, the importance of Cyprus to British interests in the region was beyond dispute.

Negotiations between the British government and representatives of the Greek and Turkish communities in June 1954 failed to reach a solution to the problem of ENOSIS. During a debate in July 1954, Colonial Office Minister Henry Hopkinson told the House of Commons that because of its 'particular circumstances' the island could 'never expect to be fully independent'. This led the Greek prime minister to raise the issue of Cyprus at the United Nations and, following the rejection by the Greek Cypriots of new constitutional proposals, tension on the island increased. Archbishop Makarios, the nationalist leader of the Greek Cypriots, called for EOKA, the terrorist wing of the ENOSIS movement, to resort to armed struggle, and within a short time Colonel George Grivas, a retired officer of the Greek army, had made a clandestine arrival on the island.[2] The terrorist campaign in Cyprus began on 1 April 1955, when bombs went off in Nicosia and an attempt was made on the life of the Governor, Sir Robert Armitage. Field Marshal Sir John Harding replaced Sir Robert Armitage as Governor on 3 October 1955.[3] The new Governor immediately adopted the 'Briggs Plan', already used so successfully in Malaya and Kenya, whereby the Army, Police, Administration, and the Intelligence agencies were drawn together into one cohesive anti-terrorist organisation.

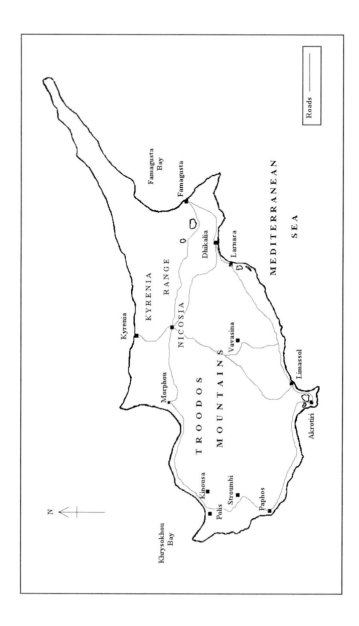

Map: 6. **Cyprus 1955 - 1964**
Numerous roads criss-cross the whole island. Remote tracks in the Troodos and Kyrenia areas were frequently used by EOKA.

Cyprus had been one of the two possible destinations for 1st KOYLI when its Kenya tour had been completed. In the event, it was only 'D' Company that made the journey and it disembarked at the port of Famagusta on 20 November 1955. It seemed that, having served under Field Marshal Harding in Germany, Malaya and Kenya – wherever Sir John went, the KOYLI was sure to go. Once again, as in Malaya, 1st KOYLI was to begin a tour at the very moment when a protracted period of civil unrest and acts of terrorism was about to begin. Six days after 'D' Company arrived on the island, the Governor declared a State of Emergency that was to last for the next four years.

'D' Company, and its baggage, was transported 110 miles to Limni Mine Camp near the small town of Polis on the northwest coast of the island, where it relieved 'B' Company, 1st Royal Scots Regiment. Its arrival coincided with a violent storm of thunder, lightning, wind, rain and hail, but in the Royal Scots' Officer's Mess, the substitution of a large glass of whisky for the expected cup of afternoon tea was much appreciated. Within days the Company was about its work of guarding four police posts and the magazines of the local mines at Limni and Kinousa with their dangerous explosive contents. On each of the first three nights the terrorists welcomed the KOYLI guard at the Polis police station by throwing a bomb at the station – none of which caused casualties, but a later attack on the magazine at the Kinousa Mine resulted in Private Hoult being wounded by Sten gun fire.

Fig: 31 FM Sir John Harding, Governor of Cyprus, with Lt Col John Deedes during a visit to 1st KOYLI at Limni, 1956.   *Col J.S. Cowley*

Christmas passed without incident. Much of the festive fare was provided by the generosity of the Royal Scots, and the Cyprus Copper and Sulphur Mining Company on whose land 'D' Company was camped. On 28 January, a bomb thrown into the perimeter of Lyso police station exploded near the guard tent. Lance Corporal C. Russell was seriously wounded in the blast and died in hospital the following day. A decision to reduce the numerous static guard duties, which had made it hard to react to the terrorists hit and run tactics, resulted in two platoons being made available for offensive patrols. The Company felt this development would meet the offensive type operational requirements of 40 Royal Marine Commando when it arrived to replaced the Royal Scots on 24 January.

It was almost six months before the main body of 1st KOYLI was released from its duties in Aden, and it arrived in Cyprus over a ten-day period commencing 18 April 1956. While 'A', 'B' and HQ Companies made the journey by air 'C' Company escorted the Battalion's baggage on its sea voyage. On arrival, 'C' Company experienced a number of problems in gaining entry to the island. Included in the baggage were a number of swords, used when mounting ceremonial guard duties, but it was illegal to import knives over a certain length into Cyprus. 'However, we eventually managed to convince the Cypriot officials that, if we could be trusted with some 600 lethal firearms, we should be trusted with a few ceremonial swords.'[4] Although great care was taken unloading the Battalion's flagpole, an item much cherished by successive RSMs, the same could not be said of the Battalion's safe, which was dropped on to the dockside, thus jamming the door and creating another 'dubious import' by the KOYLI. 'D' Company's campsite at Limni was expanded to accommodate two more companies, but when 'C' Company arrived the lack of space resulted in it being sent south to Stoumi. The 1st KOYLI formed part of 3 Royal Marine Commando Brigade, covering the western end of the island, and was to operate in the northwest coastal area; 40 Commando was already performing a similar task in the southwest coastal area.

Arriving with the advance party, 2nd Lieutenant Goodall, the Battalion's Intelligence Officer, began assembling information about the area, its population, the local terrorists, their methods of operating, and the difficulties facing the security forces. It was estimated that EOKA never had more than about 300 dedicated active terrorists on the island, but it was also known that almost the whole of the Greek Cypriot population was sympathetic to the cause, this included government officials, and policemen. Attempts to 'win hearts and minds' were frustrated by the lack of interpreters. Second Lieutenant Goodall's intelligence summary referred to this problem, and some years later, he recalled that

> A major handicap for British units operating in western Cyprus when we were at Limni was the problem of language. According to my recollection, it is a melancholy fact...that in the entire Brigade

area there was only one British officer or official (apart from the District Commissioner) who could speak modern Greek, which (to put it mildly) severely limited the ability of our patrols' road block contingents to communicate with the local population or obtain useful information from them. The lack of interpreters was also a factor in alienating the local population from the Security Forces, especially during the (understandably very unpopular) cordon-and-search operations against villages.[5]

Although there were fewer active EOKA terrorists in Cyprus than Mau Mau in Kenya, they were much more familiar with, and expert in, the use of high explosives, electronic detonators, and modern automatic weapons. Locating Mau Mau terrorists in the vast open spaces of Kenya had proved extremely difficult and contacts had been few, but almost every Greek Cypriot village was a possible terrorist refuge and the chances of confrontation were much greater. EOKA terrorists also proved to be more sophisticated than their Mau Mau counterparts in luring the security forces into ambushes and carrying out hit and run attacks.

On 9 March, following the breakdown of talks between the British Government and the Greek Cypriot leaders, Archbishop Makarios had been arrested and deported to the Seychelles. While there was no great increase in the number of incidents following this development, there was a failed attempt on the life of the Governor.[6] In the first six months following its arrival on the island, 1st KOYLI was subjected to numerous planned hostile acts that had varying degrees of success for the terrorists. The wounding of Private Hoult and the death of Lance Corporal Russell were only the first of the 1st Battalion's casualties.[7] When the police station at Limni Mine came under fire on the night of 27 May, 2nd Lieutenant J.W. Olink took 2 Platoon to assist, but as they approached, they came under fire from a deliberately planned ambush position and two soldiers were wounded. Private J. Ashe died of his wounds the following day, and Private Elliott's wounds were so serious that he was later evacuated to the UK. Second Lieutenant J.J.O. Clennell of 'B' Company was to fall victim to the terrorist's cunning when in late September he rushed into a field to remove an EOKA flag. Unfortunately, the flag was booby-trapped and in the ensuing explosion, 2nd Lieutenant Clennell lost an eye.

Initially the whole of 1st KOYLI took up similar static guarding and patrol programmes to those that had occupied 'D' Company over the previous months. It was not long, however, before major operations were organised under the command of 16th Parachute Brigade, which was acting as Island Reserve Brigade.

In May, Operations 'Pepperpot' and 'Lucky Alphonse' were aimed at the hard-core gangs of terrorists and involved the Battalion in sweeping searches of the Paphos Forest and the Troodos Mountains. In the second of these operations, Tac HQ and the Support Company actually spent 16 days buried away in the forest and enjoyed the cool climate of life at 4,000 feet.

Fig: 32 A well-armed signaller in the Troodos mountains, 1956   *Regt Archive*

It was during a search of ruined buildings in a gully that Private Richardson of Lieutenant J.A. Charlesworth's 2 Platoon caught a wanted EOKA terrorist named Nicos Xenophontos. A large haul of clothing, medical supplies, food and weapons was found in what appeared to be a bomb-making factory complete with lathes and a variety of modern tools. At his trial in Nicosia, Xenophontos, who had a price of £5,000 on his head, was found guilty of murder and sentenced to death, but was later reprieved.

The prospect of spending the summer of 1956 in the picturesque northwest of the island was dashed with the early return of the 1st Royal Warwicks to the UK. The 1st KOYLI moved to Nicosia to replace the Royal Warwicks on 28/29 June, and there joined forces with the 1st South Staffords, each battalion spending one month as Internal Security Battalion and the next as Area Reserve. The 1st KOYLI HQ was set up at the Cyprus Broadcasting Station (CBS) Camp, so named for its close proximity to the broadcasting station. At least two companies were committed to static guard duties at the central prison, the detention camp for political suspects, the secretariat and the broadcasting station.

The tented accommodation at CBS Camp left much to be desired. The primitive electrical system, intended to provide one light bulb per tent, often proved inadequate when radios, irons, or other electrical accessories were connected. Should an electrical fire be the cause of a tent burning down, the soldier responsible was required to make financial restitution, the formula used to calculate the amount to be paid being based on a tent life of 20 years. The frequency with which tents burst into flames brought about a court of enquiry, which, on finding that one particular tent was 30 years old, concluded that the soldier in question should pay only half its original cost. A reservist 'Brigade Ordnance Officer', whose reservist liability time was all but expired, solved the problem of the tents at the time of the Suez Crisis. Following a session of 'generous hospitality', his signature ensured a steady flow of new tents to replace the ancient ones.

An exceptionally hot summer meant that guard duties in Nicosia were performed in temperatures that frequently reached 100 degrees. Guarding the suspects at the detention centre was reminiscent of wartime POW camps complete with watchtowers and the searching of visitors. However, by general agreement, the worst duty was guarding the central prison, which housed convicted murderers awaiting execution and those found guilty of terrorist activities. On one occasion when three terrorists were hanged, the attempted riot staged by the other prisoners was ably kept under control by 2nd Lieutenant Pigott and his platoon. 'In Nicosia we are more policemen and less soldiers than ever.'[8] Town patrols proved to be a more rewarding experience, especially for those who rode in the two Champ vehicles that toured the streets ready to respond to any emergency.

One effective piece of psychological warfare adopted by the security forces was the publication of a list of photographs of 'Wanted Terrorists'. The photographs were published in a document that could be folded between cardboard covers and was small enough to fit into a tunic pocket. Every few months the list was re-issued, but with a very large 'X' over the photographs of those terrorists who had been eliminated.

Fig: 33 CSM F.H. Dolby leading a mobile night curfew patrol in Nicosia, 1956
Regt Archive

For a six-week period from 3 August to 13 September, 'There was hardly a dull moment...and except for the truce period we had our fair share of murders, attempted murders, time-bombs, ordinary bombs, kidnappings, abductions – in fact, the lot.'[9] On 17 September, the static duties were handed over to Oxf & Bucks LI, and 'B' and 'D' Companies moved out of Nicosia to more rural accommodation south and west of the city, leaving 'A' Company as reserve.

A significant drop in 1st KOYLI's manpower meant that it could no longer maintain four rifle companies with the result that, when the Battalion left Limni, 'C' Company became a training company. It quickly set about the task of organising courses in the use of the new FN rifle that was to be introduced to the Battalion and eventually to all infantry battalions on the island. ('C' Company had already used the new rifle in Kenya.) Within the context of the Battalion's task in Cyprus, the new weapon was seen as 'an ideal weapon for our present job,' although it was felt that 'it is not very satisfactory for smart Light Infantry drill.'[10]

For the first time since its departure for Kenya, it became possible for families to join the Battalion, but given the nature of emergency operations this could occasionally create difficulties. In Nicosia the families were in an enclave some distance away from the camp and, since many of the Regular NCOs were married, inevitably some emergencies had to start without them; this required creative solutions to the problem of command.

> In 'A' Company a Cpl then acted as CSM while the Company Storeman acted as CQMS. One platoon Sjt was a Cpl, the other two L/Cpls. The Rifle Sections were commanded by L/Cpls or Ptes. I always insisted that if no NCO was available, the senior Private soldier took over. The National Servicemen responded well to this as they soon realised that, in a few weeks or months they would be the longest serving soldier taking command. At one time we had to hand over a post to a Guards battalion. When I showed the Guards Company Commander that it was commanded by a Private Soldier he was appalled and said he would have to have a Serjeant doing the job. Interesting that a Guards Major equates a Regular Guards Serjeant with a Light Infantry National Service Private![11]

Other events in the Middle East were now to play their part. In June 1956, Colonel Nasser was elected President of Egypt, and in the following month he nationalised the Suez Canal, which had previously been jointly owned by Britain and France, with Britain being the majority shareholder. Diplomatic efforts to persuade the new president to reverse his decision failed, and preparations for military action followed. Cyprus, as the main HQ of Britain's Middle East Land Forces, would obviously be very much involved in any military action in Egypt, and as the build up of British and French troops progressed, the opportunities for EOKA terrorists to create serious difficulties increased. To forestall any such activity, plans were laid to take the fight to the terrorists in their hideouts.

In September, while 'A' and 'C' Companies remained in Nicosia, 'B' and 'D' Companies took part in operations around the city with the object of dominating the area where it was believed a significant number of terrorists lived and operated. Frequent cordon and searches, roadblocks, and ambushes were carried out in an effort to hound the terrorists. 'We used to have a 'Q' car for reconnaissance purposes. I don't believe KOYLI officers with regimental ties driving around in it fooled anyone. We hoped the EOKA might be induced to move out of the area we had recce'd so ostentatiously into the next door area where we could then catch them on the real cordon and search.'[12] Such operations were seen by some 'locals' as an ideal opportunity to make a profit, although they were not always successful.

Fig: 34 'D' Coy removing a barbed wire barricade in Nicosia, August 1956.
Col J.S. Cowley

> Some Greek Cypriots complained internationally about the 'unnecessary damage' caused by British soldiers on cordon and searches. An international commission (basically Red Cross) was sent to investigate. However, they went the wrong way round the circuit and, as a result, arrived at a house where the Greek Cypriot owner was happily destroying his own furniture. From then on complaints of damage were not taken seriously.[13]

If the terrorists and their sympathisers failed to appreciate this type of operation, it did provide lots of activity for the KOYLI, even if there were moments of danger. One enthusiast who found this life full of interest was Captain C.W. Huxley. As he later recalled,

> It was a good role – a lot of snap cordon and search operations in the nearby villages, quick follow-up patrols on rumours of Grivas or one of his henchmen being seen, and a permanent stand by

company at Nicosia police station ready to rush into Ledra Street. They were good days. Lots of activity, and a battalion at the top of its form under John. [Lt Col Deedes] [14]

In early October, 'A' and 'B' Companies took part in the very successful Operation 'Sparrow Hawk' in the Kyrenia Mountains, where the experience gained in the mountains of Kenya proved invaluable. Later that month, between Larnaca and Famagusta, the Battalion assisted in the elimination of three gangs of 'hard core' terrorists and the capture of a quantity of ammunition. At the end of October, preparations for the Suez Operation required the Parachute Brigade be withdrawn from its role as Island Reserve, a move that increased the workload of 'A' and 'B' Companies as they searched for Colonel Grivas in the forest area around Paphos.

The need to be constantly vigilant, and suspicious of anything that appeared unusual, was well illustrated by an incident that occurred on a routine vehicle patrol. On a hillside above a road on which the patrol was travelling, a flock of sheep was grazing peacefully with the shepherd sitting on the grass below them. The officer halted the patrol and got out of his vehicle, at which point the shepherd ran off. What had caused the officer to halt the patrol, and why had the shepherd made off? From his observation of local customs, the officer knew that shepherds in Cyprus always sat above their flocks, but in this case, it was impossible because the cable connecting the firing mechanism to the explosive charge in the culvert under the road was too short.

When carrying out Operation 'Quicksilver' in early November, Privates Kingdon, Rushman and Squires of 'A' Company discovered a quantity of arms, ammunition and two bombs hidden in the cavity of a wall on a terraced hillside. Part of 'B' Company's role in the same operation involved them in the gruesome task of digging in a graveyard at dead of night in a search for concealed arms. On this occasion, none was found. During operation 'Golden Rain', Support Company HQ had based itself on top of a flat roofed house. In the early hours of the morning the owner roused everyone with the news that a 'happy event' was imminent, at which the Company signallers attempted to call for help. The arrival of two REME fitters, complete with spanners and jacks, was not reassuring, but all was saved when a helicopter appeared carrying members of the RAMC.

A Brigade operation in the Troodos Mountains required each of the three battalions to establish Observation Posts (OPs) on selected hills in the area. The observers were taken to the tops of these hills by Sycamore helicopters of No 284 Squadron based at Nicosia airport. Helicopter development had gathered pace after World War II and British forces had demonstrated the aircraft's capabilities in the later stages of the Malayan Emergency Campaign, and the Americans had used them extensively during the Korean War. Initially they were used for observation and rescue, the first operational helicopter in Cyprus being used for air/sea rescue, but they were increasingly used in cooperation with the infantry.

In Cyprus, each Sycamore helicopter was capable of carrying approximately 600 lbs, the equivalent of three soldiers with all their arms and equipment. Three methods of leaving the helicopter were practised: getting out when the aircraft had landed, jumping out while it hovered about six to eight feet above the ground, climbing down a rope from the aircraft as it hovered some 30 feet above the ground, the time taken to debouch varying from two minutes by rope to 45 seconds by jumping. A number of casualties resulted from the earliest efforts to master these techniques, one of the more colourful attempts being made by Private Hind.

> Pte Hind began his decent from 15 feet when the rope anchor worked loose and he fell this distance, clinging tightly to the rope – A dull thud, a cloud of dust, Hind, bren gun on back and green beret in hand, emerges saying 'That was ******* lucky it wasn't from 30 feet!!' Incident closed! Hind has now left us for civil life and we all wish him well in the future.[15]

Others were not so lucky. During another practice exercise, Private Rhodes broke both wrists and Private Miller cracked his spine and had to be evacuated to the UK.

Rumours of a move to 'the delightful mountain resort of Platres' for the last few months of the tour were dashed in February 1957; varying excuses being proposed for the change in plan. *The Bugle* made the point that to say the Battalion was based at Nicosia was not strictly accurate because 72 of the first 113 days of 1957 had been spent on operations, mainly in the Troodos Mountains and Paphos Forest areas.[16] Operations 'Black Mac', 'Brown Jack' and 'Red Knight' took place in wet and cold conditions that were in stark contrast to the exceedingly hot days in Nicosia during the height of the previous summer. Operation 'Closed Shop' in Ledra Street in early January was followed later that month by a cordon and search operation within the walls of Nicosia. The main object of all this furious activity was to capture Grivas and those close to him. Two of his most important lieutenants, Drakos and Afxentiou, had been eliminated, and another, Georgadjis had recently been recaptured.[17] This increased activity by the security forces placed a great strain on those terrorists who remained active.

Transporting troops to all parts of the island kept the Battalion's MT Platoon very busy. On arrival in Cyprus, the platoon had not been equipped with the latest modes of military transport, some vehicles even showed signs of having seen service against Rommel's Afrika Corps. One incident could have qualified for inclusion in a Disney cartoon, the driver, however, may not have been particularly amused.

Our vehicles were ex-2nd World War and often very ancient. On an operation in a mountain village with a curving, narrow street I saw the Company ['A'] 15 cwt truck passing with the driver waving a stick at me. A closer look revealed that the gear lever had come out in his hand. How he managed not to have an accident I shall never understand. [18]

In May 1957, the MT Platoon was able to report, 'At long last we have got rid of our clapped-out vehicles, or most of them, and are now running on rather more reliable wheels; those of Bedford RL 3-tonners and Austin 1-tonners.'[19] However, the roads of Cyprus could prove a challenge to any vehicle, or driver and during an operation near Vavitsinia, the Support Company's HQ (admin) 3-tonner disappeared over a precipice, completing three somersaults during its decent. 'On hearing the news, the CSM's reaction was only what could be expected. His face fell as he exclaimed, "Oh my God, the BEER!" Fortunately the driver escaped injury – and also the beer!' [20]

One of the longest operations was 'Lucky Mac', which took place between 18 March and 3 June, when companies were again employed in searching the Troodos Mountains and Paphos Forest. During this operation, Privates Sharratt and Hubbard of 'B' Company joined members of 40 Commando's climbing team in searching sheer cliffs for terrorist hideouts, and a number of soldiers became acquainted with a form of transport more often seen on holiday beaches in the UK – donkeys: the two used by 'B' Company being nicknamed 'Grivas' and 'Drakos'. The length of this operation had decided consequences for many soldiers in the field.

> During Luck Mac we lived throughout on composite rations (the dreaded compo) which were notoriously inadequate in both taste and choice. Over a long period they also proved unhealthy: soldiers started to develop boils, to such an extent that the Director of Medical Services insisted that there should be a fresh ration supplement to provide the necessary extra vitamins. Everyone rubbed their hands at the prospect of fresh bread (instead of hard tack), fruit and even – so we speculated – fresh meat. The keenly awaited arrival of the QM with the promised rations was greeted with joy, which soon turned to dismay as the supplement proved to be sacks of onions – undoubtedly nutritious but not what we had hoped for.[21]

Operation 'Lucky Mac' began four days after Grivas had published a pamphlet in which he said that, 'in order to facilitate the resumption of negotiations between Britain and the real representative of the Cypriot people, Archbishop Makarios, EOKA declares that it is ready to order the suspension of operations at once, if ethnarch Makarios is released.'[22] When

Makarios was released in March 1957, the number of incidents diminished and the emergency was, for all practical purposes, over.

One activity that signalled the easing of tension was the use made of Pinewood Valley Hotel. When 'B' Company first entered this unused hotel in the Troodos Mountains, it had to undertake a mammoth task cleaning the place to make it serviceable, but 4 and 5 Platoons did sterling work and soon it was habitable. Each company had a spell at Pinewood from where they carried out limited operations and, as circumstances changed, the pressure began to ease. During their time at Pinewood, both 'A' and 'D' Companies had periods guarding the Monastery at Kykko in an area that had been notorious for its terrorist activity. Those who visited the monastery and sampled Father Erasmus' 'Kykko Gin' found it to have a close affinity with methylated spirits.

Following 'Lucky Mac' came the 'Tricycle' series of operations during which a lorry carrying members of 6 Platoon left the road and fell 150 feet down a very steep slope. Amazingly there were no serious injuries. The speed with which RAF helicopters removed the injured to hospital greatly impressed all those involved, and the numerous favourable comments related to helicopters illustrated the increasing dependence of the infantry on these aircraft. The 'Tricycle' operations, which continued throughout July and August, involved a return to the forest area where opportunities to carry out training in ambush and patrolling techniques were combined with the overall purpose of maintaining a high profile military presence.

By the end of August both sides had accepted the truce that had tentatively begun in March. For the Battalion, the focus of training shifted from Internal Security duties towards the more conventional role that would be required when it eventually returned to Germany. New section and platoon tactics had been devised and these needed to be practised, together with infantry/tank cooperation, and aspects of the more sinister atomic warfare. One training exercise, 'Kestrel', involved a brigade seaborne landing on the northwest coast of Cyprus in which a platoon of 'B' Company attempted to prevent a landing by 1st Royal Berkshires (in the event unsuccessfully), while the whole of 'A' Company provided a more serious defence from a feature 1,500 feet above the beach.

Following the traditional Minden Day parade, the Battalion and the families attended a party on the beach near Kyrenia, the only absentee being 'A' Company, which was away at Pinewood. The day was also significant in that it marked the departure of Lieutenant Colonel Deedes, who handed over command of the Battalion to his 2nd i/c, Lieutenant Colonel S.H. Kent OBE. Lieutenant Colonel Deedes (shortly to be promoted Colonel) was to take up an appointment in the MT Directorate of the War Office.

In mid September, the Colonel of the Regiment, Lieutenant General Sir Harold Redman, Governor of Gibraltar, visited the Battalion. Lieutenant General Redman arrived on the island accompanied by the Under Secretary of State for War, Mr Julian Amery, who was on a routine visit to the British

Forces in Cyprus. Over the next few days, the Colonel of the Regiment managed to visit almost every company and platoon in the numerous training areas throughout the island. After seeing a great deal of the island, and especially the conditions in the mountains, the Colonel of the Regiment was able to appreciate the difficulties the Battalion had experienced in its search for EOKA terrorists. In his departing message he referred to the outstanding service the Battalion had given during the emergency and he passed on the thanks of the Governor, Field Marshal Sir John Harding.

With the departure of Lieutenant General Redman, all attention was concentrated on the forthcoming return to the UK. There were, however, two engagements the Battalion had to complete before it left Cyprus. On 4 November, 1st KOYLI provided the Guard of Honour at Government House for the departure of Field Marshal Sir John Harding and, on Remembrance Sunday, the CO, Lieutenant Colonel Kent, laid a wreath on the Cross of Sacrifice at Wayne's Keep Cemetery. During the course of this ceremony, individual wreaths were laid on the graves of Serjeant Wade, Lance Corporal Russell and Private Ashe who had been killed in Cyprus. A wreath was also placed on the grave of Mrs M. Lee, wife of Serjeant J. Lee of 'D' Company, who had recently died in the British Military Hospital, Nicosia. Another wreath was laid in remembrance of Private D. Townend, MT Platoon, who had died in September in hospital in the UK from burns he received when the engine of the vehicle he was servicing burst into flames.

This three-year tour of duty by 1st KOYLI had been spent mainly under canvas. The temperate climate of the Aberdare Mountains of Kenya had been followed by the heat, sand, and dust of Aden, and finally the Battalion experienced the Mediterranean climate of Cyprus with temperatures ranging from the fierce heat of summer in Nicosia to the freezing cold of winter in the Troodos Mountains. Rarely can the KOYLI have experienced such a range of conditions within the space of one tour.

The Depot and 4th Territorial Battalion

After the previous years memorable celebrations marking the 200th anniversary of the raising of the Regiment, 1956 began in a quieter mood. But, further celebrations were not long in coming and on 29 April, Captain J.M.C. Hutton and five soldiers drawn from three Light Infantry Regiments (KOYLI, DCLI, Oxf & Bucks LI) joined one officer and six Other Ranks from 29th 'Corunna' Battery RA on board HMS Corunna, which was anchored at Tower Pier, London. Sir John Moore, founder of the Light Infantry Brigade, was killed at the Battle of Corunna, and the soldiers represented regiments that had been present at the battle. All were guests of the Captain of HMS Corunna, which was to pay the first visit of the first ship of her name to the Spanish port of La Corunna, a town with enormous significance for the Light Infantry.

Leaving Portland on 1 May, it took *HMS Corunna* two and a half days to reach Lisbon, where Lieutenant General Sir Harold Redman joined it. A large crowd of Spaniards greeted the ship when it reached La Corunna on 7 May, and Brigadier C. Goulburn, Military Attache, Madrid, and Mr Guyatt, British Consul, joined the party, together with Lady Redman. Following a short ceremony wreaths were laid at the tomb of Sir John Moore by General Martinez for the Spanish Army, Lieutenant General Redman for the Light Infantry and the Captain of *HMS Corunna*, Commodore Lewin. Over the next two days the party toured the site of the battle, which began at 2pm on 16 January 1809. During the five-day stay the members of the party were official guests at a huge passing out parade of 3,500 recruits for the Spanish army who, 'marched with a great swagger, but the precision of their drill does not attempt the same standard that we know.'[23] *HMS Corunna* arrived in Chatham on 14 May flying her 'Paying off' pennant, denoting the last voyage of her current commission.[24]

In February 1952, the Prime Minister, Winston Churchill, announced that Britain had its own nuclear device, and by 1954, the RAF's Canberra bombers were armed with atomic bombs. In the first months of 1956, the NCOs of 4th KOYLI had been asked to focus on the implications for the TA in the event of a nuclear war. In a lecture given to the NCOs at the Wakefield drill hall, Commander Bailey, RN, spoke of the tasks that would need to be faced should a hydrogen bomb be dropped on Leeds or Sheffield. Commander Bailey suggested that trying to return to some form of normal life would be all but impossible, and that attempting to ensure the very survival of humanity, given the appalling devastation following a nuclear explosion, would be the main priority.

In August 1956, Lieutenant Colonel S.H. Kent and Captain J.M.C. Hutton travelled to Maralinga in South Australia to witness the first in a series of four atomic test explosions. The test witnessed by Lieutenant Colonel Kent and Captain Hutton was of a 20 kiloton bomb, the same size as the bomb exploded over Hiroshima, 6 August 1945. An hour or so after the explosion,

> We could see a circular area of devastation in the bush as though someone had neatly shaved a tonsure on a man's head. The tower was quite, quite gone. ... Where there had been small trees, shrubs and flowers was sheer desert. For quite a distance there was no sign even of tree stumps. ... At ground zero there was a wide shallow area, grey-green in colour, where the soil had melted in the heat, and solidified in a glass like substance. It was alarming, but true, and we have read about these things before.[25]

Meanwhile, back in Yorkshire, the 4th KOYLI's journey to the 1956 annual camp was made in thirty vehicles estimated to be of 1940's vintage and drawn from the RAOC depot. Attempts to encourage the National Servicemen attending the camp to sign on in the TA met with dismal results; but on reflection, 15 days on Fylingdale Moor, with rain every day, may just have tipped the balance to provide this negative result.

On 31 October, 4th KOYLI was transferred from 50th (Northumbrian) Division to 49th (West Riding) Division in which it had served with great distinction during two world wars. In January 1957, Lieutenant Colonel M.P. Robinson TD succeeded Lieutenant Colonel Barker as CO 4th KOYLI. Lieutenant Colonel Robinson served in the RA during WW II, transferred to the KOYLI in 1944, and was then seconded to the King's African Rifles. He returned to 4th KOYLI when it reformed in 1947 and was to assume command at an important time, not only for the TA, or the army, but for the whole of the armed forces.

The outcome of the recent Suez Crisis had serious repercussions for Britain and its worldwide commitments. In January 1957, the new Prime Minister, Harold Macmillan, appointed Duncan Sandys as Minister for Defence. A complete overhaul of Britain's global strategy, plus financial pressure on sterling, required Sandys to look for substantial cuts in defence spending, which could mean only one thing – a major reduction in Britain's armed forces. The cuts, however, were to be far greater than any of the Service Chiefs anticipated. The government's Defence White Paper of 1957 sought to reduce conventional armed forces (especially the army) from the present 700,000 to 375,000 by 1962. The overall effect of this was to place a greater reliance on thermo-nuclear weapons and the missile systems that were to deliver them.

One of the most significant proposals in the white paper, especially for the army, was the ending of National Service. Although this was not to come about for another three years, it was seen that an immediate saving could be made if National Servicemen were no longer required to carry out part-time training. This had a major effect on the 4th Battalion, and indeed on the whole of the TA, especially when there were no National Servicemen at the annual camp. The three battalions of 146th Infantry Brigade, together with the Brigade HQ were so small in number that it was decided they could all be accommodated in the huts at Proteus Camp, Ollerton, Nottinghamshire, for the period of their annual camp.

For the KOYLI the most important aspect of the defence white paper was the fact that the Regiment had escaped the axe. Thanks largely to the foresight of General Sir Charles Deedes and the other Colonels of the Light Infantry Regiments who had formed the Light Infantry Club in the 1930s close regimental ties had been forged. The unanimity of purpose and approach must have gone some way towards ensuring that, with the exception of the amalgamation of the DCLI with Som. LI, on this occasion at least the Light Infantry Regiments were spared the wholesale amalgamations that were inflicted on 30 Infantry Regiments of the Line.[26]

[1] Although Britain had agreed to withdraw from Suez in 1954, the evacuation of the Canal Zone was not completed until 13 June 1956.

[2] *Encyclopedia Britannica, Millenium Ed.* EOKA – Ethniki Organosis Kipriakou Agonos Grivas was a Cypriot who had served with the Greek army.

[3] Sir John resigned as CIGS, 25 September 1955, and took up his appointment as Governor of Cyprus on 3 October.

[4] Rowe, Capt N.C. op cit

[5] Goodall, Sir David, Memoir, Regt. Archive.

[6] *Ibid,* During the first three months of 1956, there had been a steady increase in the number of main incidents in the Battalion's area. January – 3, February – 6, March – 11.

[7] Serjeant L. Wade DCM, who had recently been Mentioned in Despatches for his work in Kenya, died of gunshot wounds on 27 March 1956.

[8] *The Bugle,* 1956, Vol. 48.3 p 96 'B' Company notes.

[9] *Ibid,* Vol. 48.4 p 135

[10] *Ibid,* Vol. 48.4 p 139 ('C' Company notes) and p 136 (1st Battalion editor's notes) The rifle's overall length, and the calibre of its bullets, while contributing to greater accuracy, would later prove to be a disadvantage in the confined conditions experienced by jungle patrols, especially when the Battalion operated in Borneo.

[11] Rowe, Capt. N.C. op cit

[12] *Ibid,*

[13] *Ibid,*

[14] Huxley, Col. C.W. op cit.

[15] *The Bugle,* 1957, Vol 49.1 p 27

[16] *Ibid,* 1957, Vol. 49.2 p 63

[17] Afxentiou had been the EOKA leader in the Paphos Forest area.

[18] Rowe, Capt. N.C. op cit

[19] *The Bugle,* 1957, Vol. 49.2 p 70

[20] *Ibid,* 1957, Vol. 49.2 p 67

[21] Lees, Col B.M. Memoir. Regt. Archive.

[22] Springhall, John, *Decolonisation Since 1945,* op cit

[23] *Ibid,* 1956, Vol. 48.3 p 84

[24] In 1982 Admiral Lewin was Chief of the Defence Staff and played a significant part in planning the successful outcome to the Falklands War.

[25] *The Bugle,* 1956, Vol. 48.4 pp 126/127, Kent, Lt Col. S.H. *Australia and the Atom Bomb.*

[26] The DCLI and the Som. LI were amalgamated on 1 October 1959.

6

Germany

The 1st KOYLI's journey from the port of Limassol in Cyprus to Southampton was made in *HMT Dilwara*. The *Dilwara* called at Malta where Major J.M. Dickenson TD, who had been chosen to represent the Regiment at the opening of the Medjez-el-Bab War Memorial, disembarked. The Regiment has only one name on the memorial, but in the nearby cemetery are the graves of 38 men of 2/4th KOYLI killed in the North African Campaign. The *Dilwara* also stopped at Gibraltar, where the Colonel of the Regiment took the opportunity to deliver a short address to the Battalion over the ship's public address system. The Regiment's connections with Gibraltar are many, but this visit recalled an incident over 50 years earlier. On 22 February 1905, the 1st KOYLI disembarked from their transporter, also named the *Dilwara,* at the beginning of an 18 months tour of duty on The Rock. Just over two weeks later, 11 March 1905, the *Dilwara* returned to Gibraltar carrying 2nd KOYLI on its way home to England from Crete and Malta. Although the *Dilwara's* stay in Gibraltar on that occasion was also only a few hours, it was the first time the two KOYLI battalions had met since they formed one Regiment in 1881.

This latest edition of the *Dilwara* arrived at Southampton at 22:00 hrs, 21 November 1957, to be greeted by friends and relatives including the Deputy Colonel of the Regiment, the Commanding Officer (fresh from his quick visit to Germany), and the Officer Commanding the Depot. The following day two special trains sped the Battalion to York where, thanks to the efficiency of the advance party, the men were quickly processed into, and out of, Strensall on their way to a well deserved leave.

At the end of the year the Battalion reassembled and prepared for a programme of marches through the Freedom towns and cities of Yorkshire. At each of the five venues, Doncaster – 22 January, Batley – 25 January, Leeds – 28 January, Dewsbury – 1 February and Wakefield – 4 February, 200 men paraded in No 1 Dress with ceremonial accoutrements of white belts and rifle slings. Preceded by the Regimental Band and Buglers, the detachments exercised the Regiment's right to march through the streets with bayonets fixed and Colours flying. On each occasion, the detachments re-assembled after lunch and the Band and Bugles sounded 'Retreat' before returning to Strensall. Despite the winter weather, the Regiment was greeted with great enthusiasm and the bonds linking it with the cities and towns were immeasurably strengthened.

While these marches were taking place, an advance party was working in Sennelager preparing for the move to Germany that had been scheduled for the end of February 1958. A sign of the many changes afoot, only one of many that were occurring at this time, concerned the aspirations of Captain

A.R. Tinson. (promoted Capt. 8 February 1958) 'Lt Tinson has disappeared to some unlikely place in Wiltshire to learn how to fly light aircraft ... [he] is hoping to get a Pilot's Licence and join the newly formed Army Flying Wing'.[1] The increasing use of helicopters for troop transport, and small fixed wing aircraft for reconnaissance work, had resulted in the Army deciding to have its own aircraft, thereby providing a greater degree of independence from the RAF.

Before the programme of ceremonial marches in Yorkshire had been completed, the majority of 1st KOYLI left Strensall on the morning of 26 February 1958 for Harwich and the sea crossing to the Hook of Holland. Another train journey brought the Battalion to Sennelager, where an efficient transport service distributed the personnel to Dempsey Barracks, a former German Cavalry Barracks built before the Second World War. The All Arms Training Centre, plus its accompanying ranges and field firing areas, were also at Sennelager, and the Battalion's close neighbours were the 4th Guards Brigade Field Regiment, Field Squadron, and the 17/21 Lancers.

Soldiering at this time could, and very often did, provide contrasting environments and roles, and in the case of 1st KOYLI these were brought sharply into focus as it settled into its new programme of training. Over the previous three years its role as an anti-terrorist force assisting the local police, and patrolling in jungles, deserts, or narrow streets, had been undertaken in the heat of Kenya, Aden, and Cyprus. In the cold winter months in Germany, its new role was once more that of a conventional infantry battalion in northern Europe, preparing to fight a defensive war with an increasingly significant nuclear component.

The dead hand of politics, however, was never far away and, at the end of March, the Battalion took part in a demonstration at 4th Guards Brigade HQ at Hubbelrath. The purpose of the demonstration was to show the visiting Minister of Defence, Mr Duncan Sandys, the increased effectiveness of a battalion at higher establishment when compared with an average battalion in BAOR. The government's reliance on the deterrent effect of nuclear weapons was specifically designed to produce substantial cuts in defence spending, but it was hoped that the politicians would see there was a point at which a severe reduction in numbers would become counterproductive.

For 'A', 'B' and 'D' Companies, a three week period of training in tents at the Battalion's Training Camp at Haltern, north west of Sennelager, gave a welcome relief from barrack fatigues. 'A' Company, however, marched the 87 miles to Haltern as part of a training programme that aimed to enter three teams of eleven men from the company in the Nijmegen Marches. The Marches, organised by the Netherlands League for Physical Culture, consisted of four marches on consecutive days of either 40 km carrying weapons and equipment weighing 22 lbs, or 50 km without weapons and equipment. (The Regiment chose the former, as did all the other military teams.) In a field of 13,000 marchers (2,000 of them British troops), the three teams from 'A' Company were hard pressed to feature among the stars in an event that most of the entrants had been working towards for many months.

After five months at Sennelager there was an unexpected development when the Battalion was moved to Hilden near Dusseldorf. The need to provide a more satisfactory distribution of married accommodation throughout BAOR was given as the primary reason for the move, which resulted in the Battalion being closer to Brigade HQ. The barracks at Hilden, previously occupied by HQ 4 Division, had the advantages of sports grounds, a swimming pool, squash, and tennis courts, an excellent cinema, a canteen and reading rooms. One decided advantage of Hilden was its proximity to Dusseldorf, 'which was full of restaurants, night life and jazz clubs. The Dusseldorf Karnival just before Lent, was always huge fun and provided entertainment for all ranks.'[2]

The remainder of the year was given over to training with the main exercises involving work with some 200 tanks. Not all the companies were thus occupied. Unfortunately, 'C' Company, now known as the Training Wing, stayed in Hilden and carried on with its new and very important role. All the companies spent some time at the nearby Winter Training Centre at Winterberg where a thick covering of snow fell on 1 December, much to the delight of the Battalion's skiers and tobogganers.

The following year, 1959, was to be a year crammed with important events for the Regiment. The 150th anniversary of the death of Sir John Moore at Corunna occurred on 16 January and special services were held at Shorncliffe, and his birthplace, Glasgow. A short service was conducted at the Regimental Chapel in York Minster, at which a detachment from the Depot, together with representatives of the Light Infantry Brigade and each of the Light Infantry Regiments, was present. The Commanding Officer of the Regimental Depot, Major J.S. Wood, laid a wreath on the Peninsular War Memorial, which contains a tablet to the memory of Sir John Moore, and the Buglers sounded 'The Last Post' and 'Reveille'.

While visiting Germany to inspect those units of which he was Colonel-in-Chief, His Royal Highness The Duke of Gloucester paid a visit to 1st KOYLI on 24 March. Even though this was only a one-day visit, His Royal Highness managed to see a wide range of activities including the Mortar Platoon, the Training Wing, a driving display, the Band and Bugles rehearsing the Retreat Ceremony for a forthcoming event, and finally 'A' and 'D' Companies enjoying some recreational activities in the gymnasium.

The tenth anniversary of the founding of NATO took place on 4 April 1959. The 1st KOYLI (plus one company of the DCLI) had the honour to be chosen to represent the British Army in a ceremonial parade of all the representatives of NATO at Mainz. Once again European spectators were treated to the sight of a British Light Infantry Battalion, in No 1 dress, white rifle slings, belts and gloves, led by the Regimental Band and Buglers marching at the traditional Light Infantry pace and performing a rapid succession of drill movements.

A week of training with the tanks of 17/21 Lancers at Vögelsang in June was some relief from the heavy programme of parades and ceremonial. During the exercise, the companies made a number of attacks on the former Siegfried Line, but one of the most significant happenings involved Private Ramsey of 'D' Company. Private Ramsey, 'with the aid of a traversing tank turret, succeeded in adapting his self-loading rifle so that it would fire round corners – an essentially simple modification that might well be passed on to Hythe.'[3]

The Minden Bi-Centenary Dinner was held at the Guildhall in London on 27 July 1959. Present were the three Royal Colonels, Her Majesty The Queen Mother, Her Royal Highness Princess Margaret, and Her Royal Highness the Duchess of Gloucester, together with Lieutenant General Sir Harold Redman, the Colonels of the Minden Regiments and, of course, the Lord Mayor of London. The 600 dinner guests in the New Livery Hall represented past and present members of the six Minden Regiments and the two Minden Batteries; there were exactly 80 officers of the KOYLI present. On Minden Day, 1st KOYLI celebrated the 200th anniversary of the battle with a ceremonial parade in front of the C-in-C British Army of the Rhine, General Sir Dudley Ward. The traditional ceremony of the Troop was carried out, and on this occasion the Commanding Officer, Lieutenant Colonel S.H. Kent, and the Adjutant, Captain P.F.A. Sibbald were both mounted, their horses wearing the Regimental brow bands and plumes that had been carefully preserved since the beginning of the war in 1939.

During all these ceremonies, one group had a more punishing schedule than most. The Band, as usual, had been involved in numerous engagements throughout the year, but on Minden Day their commitments were particularly heavy. Following the main parade in the morning, the Band sped off to the Officers Mess to play during a cocktail party that lasted until 13:30 hrs. After a quick meal it was on parade again for the beating of Retreat that was performed at 16:00 hrs, and the nine members of the Dance Band had little time before they reassembled in the Serjeants' Mess at 21;00 hrs for the traditional Minden Ball which eventually finished at 04:15 hrs on the Sunday morning. At 10:30 hrs the Band was seated in church for the service, which was followed by a march past.

Within 72 hours of the end of the Minden Parade, the Battalion resumed its routine activities. Travelling approximately 320 miles to Putlos, north of Hamburg on the Baltic coast of Schleswig-Holstein, the Battalion spent one week training and the next enjoying numerous recreational activities before embarking on a concentrated period of training exercises. Moving to Sennelager, there followed a week of 'Night into Day' exercises with the tanks of 17/21 Lancers, travelling in Armoured Personnel Carriers (APCs), and being covered in dust and grime, the result of a particularly hot summer. The Brigade training ended at Brilon where,

The highlight of one exercise was the Yorkshire cunning which resulted in bouncing a bridge across a river, developing a night attack from an unsuspected flank and rapidly building a bridge from hewn-down forest pines. [4]

Tuesday, 6 October 1959 brought about a change of great significance for all Light Infantry Regiments. Amalgamation Day created the Light Infantry Brigade, a reorganisation that required all Light Infantry Regiments to wear the same cap badge, although, until further notice, each regiment was allowed to keep its own collar dogs. For two Light Infantry regiments, the Duke of Cornwall's and Somerset Light Infantry, this was the second change in six days; the two regiments had amalgamated to form the Somerset and Cornwall Light Infantry on 1 October.

On being promoted to Brigade Commander of 128th Brigade (TA), Lieutenant Colonel Kent handed over command of 1st KOYLI to Lieutenant Colonel S.N. Floyer-Acland, who joined the Battalion from the Somerset and Cornwall Light Infantry.[5] During the traditional dining out of the departing Commanding Officer an old Regimental custom was revived. The 1881 Cardwell reforms had introduced territorial titles in place of regimental numbers, a change that generated much resentment throughout the British Army. To commemorate this event the officers of 51st Light Infantry had presented the Regiment with a magnificent silver gun carriage upon which was mounted a silver coffin that carried the inscription, 'In Memoriam, 51st Light Infantry, obiit 30th June 1881, RIP'. Until the opening of the Second World War, it had been the custom that newly joined officers took snuff from the silver coffin and on this occasion, since the custom had lapsed for many years, there were a number of unsuspecting victims, which included the new Commanding Officer. At this 'mass snuff taking' all went well, but on a later occasion, when the ladies had been invited to dine in the Officers' Mess, one unfortunate subaltern accidentally overturned the carriage and the scattered snuff brought on a prolonged bout of coughing and sneezing from all those seated nearby.

The Forecast of Events for 1960 was much smaller than for the previous year, and with outside temperatures in January reaching –5°F, the skiing enthusiasts contemplated with eager anticipation the forthcoming visit to the Winter Training Camp at Winterberg. In February Lieutenant M.J.A. Wilson represented the Battalion in a similar exercise to that which Corporal B. Spence had attended in March 1959. On that occasion, Corporal Spence, a competent skier from 1st KOYLI Anti-Tank Platoon, had represented the KOYLI in Norway on a joint exercise with Norwegian troops. He joined a company of 10 Officers and 43 Other Ranks from BAOR who spent almost the whole of the month close to the Arctic Circle training in winter warfare and survival techniques. One of the most important lessons to be learned from these activities was that in arctic warfare the main struggle was against the climate itself, a lesson that

Russian armies had been aware of for centuries. In March 'A' and 'D' companies spent time in the Schwerte area while 'B' Company and the Support Company enjoyed a spell in the Harz Mountains, all four companies spending some time living outdoors in winter conditions.

To complement the usual training sessions that were scheduled for the summer months, a new concept was introduced in 1960 – Adventure Training. Lieutenant C.L'e. Backhouse, together with Corporals Clifton, Flint, and Lance Corporal Mellor, joined 21 soldiers from 4th Guards Brigade Group for a three-week period at Isefjaer Fjiord near Kristiansand, Norway, where they spent time sailing, canoeing and climbing. Another lucky group, consisting of 2nd Lieutenant C.D. Hunter, Serjeants Bisby and Foott and Corporal Bray, spent a week in Kiel harbour learning how to sail the *Pelican*, a four and a half ton thirty metre yacht. In June the whole of the Mortar Platoon, complete with rations, sleeping bags, Bergan packs, ropes, and two three-inch mortars, were sent to Oberstdorf in Bavaria. The object of the exercise was simply to practice deploying mortars in mountainous areas, but somewhat surprisingly, when it was time to return to Hilden, most of the platoon agreed that given a chance to repeat the exercise they would do so. The Anti-Tank Platoon, complete with all necessary equipment, departed for Munich from where they were to return to Hilden on bicycles. Unfortunately, the start of their return journey was delayed by a violent thunderstorm that raged through the first night and most of the following day. Visiting Oberammergau, camping on the shores of Lake Constance, and passing through the Black Forest, it took the men nine days and eight and a half hours to complete the 573 miles back to Hilden.

The Battalion strength was now made up of 500 regulars (the full BAOR establishment being 570) and fewer than 30 National Servicemen. Those recruits who had recently joined were the first to have been trained exclusively on the Self Loading Rifle, but this fact alone cannot have accounted for the very satisfactory classification results that showed 29% of men entitled to Marksmen's Badges and a further 34% classed as First Class Shots.

In late August, the Battalion again made its way by train to the Baltic coast of Schleswig Holstein to take part in the largest NATO exercises ever held up to that time. Of the three exercises, 'King Cobra' 3-6 September, 'Black Mamba' 11-13 September, and 'Holdfast' 20-24 September, the latter was to be the most memorable.

> During the exercise ['Holdfast'] each rifle company had at least one "pure infantry" action, at least one action using APCs and tanks, at least one carried into action on the tanks, and at least one battle into which they were flown by helicopter'. [6]

The Battalion was part of Orange Corps, a force consisting of 4th Division, a parachute brigade group from England, an SAS regiment, and RAF support.

Attacking from the east, the group's objective was to capture the Kiel Canal, some 50 miles to the northwest, which was defended by a German Corps and a company of the Danish Army. No one seriously thought any unit would ever reach the canal itself, but 'B' Company, KOYLI, and 'C' Squadron of the "Skins" (5th Royal Inniskilling Dragoon Guards) made fantastic progress. In the morning mist the German forward positions guarding the Kiel Canal were bypassed, and on reaching the canal Second Lieutenant D.R. Thomas' 4 Platoon successfully ambushed a company of the Royal Danish Life Guard that had arrived from Denmark just 10 minutes before.[7] 'B' Company's progress was so good that 'A' Company was flown forward some 20 miles, and 'D' Company set out on a wide encircling route.

> Thus the whole Battalion group, complete with CO's Rover Group, were soon established in a "Tobruk" perimeter on the Kiel Canal, a good twenty miles behind the enemy lines and ahead of the remainder of the Brigade Group – and of their own main Command Post and echelon! [8]

The Regimental Band had the honour of being the musical component of the International Guard of Honour at the ceremony to welcome the new C-in-C NATO, General Bruce Clarke of the American Air Force, on 12 December. In a letter sent to Lieutenant Colonel Floyer-Acland by the C-in-C Northern Army Group, General Sir James Cassels said, 'The Band played excellently, and its drill and turnout was very good.'[9]

Fig: 35 Honour Guard for the Under Secretary of State for Defence, Christopher Soames. Hilden, 1961.   *Capt. R. Ackling*

The newly appointed Colonel of the Regiment, Lieutenant General Sir Roger Bower KCB, KBE, visited 1st KOYLI in early December, and in his address to the Battalion said that wherever it might go in the future he would visit them. It was known that 1st KOYLI would leave BAOR sometime during 1961 and speculation, as usual, covered almost every possibility. For many members of the Battalion, who were shivering in yet another cold German winter, it came as a great relief when, on 6 January 1961, the Battalion was informed that its next posting was to Fort George, near Malacca in Malaya.

This welcome piece of news had important repercussions for the reorganisation that was taking place at this time. Extra drivers were being trained to drive the one-ton Armoured Personnel Carriers (APCs) that were intended to make the whole Battalion mobile. The projected move to Malaya had the effect of reducing the total number of these vehicles to five, the Battalion being issued with a fleet of three-ton lorries for troop carrying. Other changes made at this time were the introduction of company MT sections, the disbandment of the Support Company, the formation of Support Platoons in each company and the formation of a Reconnaissance Platoon.

As winter gave way to spring, the usual pattern of training began again. In May there occurred one of those tragic accidents that will always accompany the wholehearted involvement of young men in strenuous and challenging activities. On 12 May, 2nd Lieutenant J.S. Beaumont, Private J. Smith and Private A. Reynolds were drowned when their canoe overturned during a squall at the British Leave Centre at Isefjaer in Norway.

The rifle companies returned to the Sennelager training area in May, where a greater emphasis was placed on the type of skills that would be needed in Malaya later in the year. During the evening of 2 June 1961, the Battalion was asked to provide help for the town of Hilden, which was in danger of being flooded when the nearby Trozhilden Dam burst its banks. During that weekend, men of 'A' Company filled over 2,000 sandbags to stem the flow of water; constructed emergency footpaths, and built various sandbag dams in the town. As the CO was visiting the Battalion's flood HQ at the Fire Station, Lieutenant J.J.R. Wingfield and his men were busy constructing a sandbag wall to protect the local bank. Suddenly, six well-armed German policemen appeared, cordoned off the bank, and one of them kicked down the door and rushed inside. Since no one was found inside, and the alarm was ringing, it was assumed that the thieves had made off. Lieutenant Wingfield immediately volunteered his unarmed men to cordon off half the town while the police searched for the armed robbers. Fortunately, there were no armed robbers; the alarm had been short-circuited by the rising floodwaters.

Fig: 36 The last National Servicemen leave the Regiment, Hilden, 10 July, 1961.
Regt Archive

On Monday 10 July 1961, 1st KOYLI said goodbye to the last draft of National Servicemen. The eight soldiers were given a sending off party at which there were representatives of the television and press. (It would be almost a year later, 18 May 1962, before the last National Serviceman, Pte Woodfine, was discharged from the Regiment.) Unfortunately, the Commanding Officer could not be present, but his second-in-command, Major H.C.I. Rome, read his message to them. Lieutenant Colonel Floyer-Acland paid tribute to the valuable contribution that hundreds of National Servicemen had made to the working, sporting, and social life of the Regiment.

> We are naturally pleased and proud that, from today, we are an all-regular battalion, full of regular soldiers. But, at the same time, we cannot help feeling sad that the last of our "amateur" comrades are leaving us...all of us thank all of you and wish you every good fortune in the future. [10]

National Servicemen had indeed played an important part in the history of the Regiment, and served their country well during a period of great uncertainty. While Britain had theoretically been at peace since the end of the Second World War, there were many memorials that carried the names of National Servicemen who had lost their lives in Malaya, Kenya, Aden, Cyprus and Germany whilst serving their country.[11]

The final exercise in Germany, 'Last Straw', took place between 20-23 June in the high pastures and mountainous forests of the Rothaargebirge to the south of Winterberg. Exercises in laying ambushes, searching camps, reconnoitring bandit camps, cordon and searches were all familiar to those who had experienced soldiering in Malaya during the 'Emergency'; but for many this type of work, in preparation for real jungle conditions, was quite new.

Following the final field exercise, there was a period of intense drilling in preparation for the visit of the Colonel-in-Chief to the Battalion at Pontefract on 28 October. When 1st KOYLI moved back to the UK in late August, it was the first battalion to be air-trooped from BAOR and, on 14 August, 'A' Company flew out of Dusseldorf aboard a Hastings transport appropriately named 'City of Bradford'. Despite strenuous efforts to persuade the War Office to fly the Battalion to Manchester, or Yeadon (now known as Leeds-Bradford airport), the final destination was Manston in Kent, which, complained the 1st Battalion's Bugle editor, 'is just about as far from Pontefract as it is from Dusseldorf!'[12]

Returning to the Regimental Depot at Pontefract Barracks after six weeks leave, the Battalion quickly established itself and resumed its preparations for the important visit of the Colonel-in-Chief. On 28 October 1961, the Colonel of the Regiment, Lieutenant General Sir Roger Bower, the Commanding Officer of 1st KOYLI, Lieutenant Colonel S.N. Floyer-Acland, and all ranks of the 1st Battalion were joined by a host of honoured guests. Present were, Lord Scarborough KG, GCSI, GCVO, TD, Lord Lieutenant of the West Riding of Yorkshire, the C-in-C Northern Command, Lieutenant General Sir Michael West KCB, DSO, the Lord Mayor of Leeds, the Mayors of the Freedom towns, and members of the Regimental Association, chief among whom were Major W. Edwards VC and Ex-Serjeant L. Calvert VC. It had been almost ten years to the day since Her Majesty had last visited the 1st Battalion, and in her address she made reference to the activities and achievements of the intervening years. After drawing attention to the recent re-organisation of the Light Infantry, and the need for a steady flow of recruits to ensure the continuation of the Regiment, Her Majesty The Queen Mother said,

> This Battalion will shortly be leaving for Malaya to join the 28th Commonwealth Brigade Group. You will be much in my thoughts, and I know that the reputation of the Regiment will be safe in your hands. [13]

Four days later, 1 November, there was a rather different ceremonial performed when Lieutenant Colonel Floyer-Acland was hauled away in the traditional fashion after completing his tour with the Battalion, command passing to Lieutenant Colonel H.C.I. Rome.

An advance party of four officers and 16 NCOs left Pontefract for Singapore on 8 November to attend a training course at the Jungle Warfare Training School. The original date for the departure of 1st KOYLI to Malaya had been 20 December, but common sense prevailed and this date was changed to 30 December, which allowed many to enjoy a rare Christmas at home. The departure of 1st KOYLI from its Depot at the end of December 1961 had an echo of a bygone age. 'The Battalion marched from the barracks to Pontefract Railway Station, with personal luggage going by transport. This must have been one of the last occasions when a move to the Far East started on foot'.[14]

The Depot and 4th Territorial Battalion

The effects of the 1957 Defence White Paper began to appear in 1958 when new proposals were made that would re-organise the infantry into brigades of three or four regiments. To keep its identity, it was necessary for the Light Infantry to field only four regiments, hence the amalgamation of the DCLI with the Som LI, 1 October 1959. Another result of the re-organisation was to be the closing down of all the Light Infantry regimental depots except one: the KSLI Depot at Copthorne Barracks, Shrewsbury, would become the new Light Infantry Brigade Depot.

On 31 March 1958, the KOYLI's regular strength stood at 345, but projected figures showed that, if steps were not taken to increase numbers by the time National Service ended in 1960, the future of the Regiment could be in jeopardy with amalgamation, or even disbandment, being the ultimate price of failure. It was calculated that the Regiment needed to have over 600 regular soldiers when National Service ended and, to ensure this, a vigorous programme of recruitment was needed.

The Adjutant of the Depot at this time was Capt P.G. Fleming who, together with Regimental Serjeant Major H. Hardy and his successor Regimental Serjeant Major L. Grist, set about the task of recruiting. Competition in Yorkshire had always been fierce with six line regiments, the Coldstream Guards, two cavalry regiments and, of course, the Royal Navy and the RAF all eager to recruit. Covert wheeling and dealing with the local recruiting offices in Doncaster and Barnsley took place, plus imaginative offers like – 'Learn to Drive in the KOYLI'.[15] Appeals for active cooperation were made to the Regimental Association, self-preservation being the motivation used to illustrate the point. The cunning ploy of having two tables on pay parade meant that the National Servicemen could not avoid being made aware that regular soldiers were getting up to eight times more than their own meagre twenty-six shillings, minus stoppages. In 1958, the Depot Commander, Major J.S. Wood, ended the practice of employing regular recruits, awaiting training, on fatigues. Instead, supervised 'learning by playing' with weapons, and four-day treks to the North Yorkshire moors and the dales of the West Riding not only gave them confidence, but gave them something to tell their friends when they went home on weekend pass.[16] All this effort had the desired effect. Over 200 recruits had joined at the end of the first year's campaign, and by the end of the second year, this figure had risen to 533. As we have seen, when the last National Servicemen left 1st KOYLI on 10 July 1961 the Regiment became an all-regular battalion, the first of any English, Scottish or Welsh regiment since 1939. By the end of 1958, 4th KOYLI had increased its strength from 197 to 236, which made it the strongest battalion in the Brigade. With the ending of National Service, and for the first time since 1939, TA battalions began to train recruits who had no previous military service experience.[17]

On 2 April 1959, the Light Infantry HQ moved from Strensall to its new home in Shrewsbury, but the training of recruits continued at Strensall until the necessary alterations and improvements could be made at Copthorne. In May, the training platoons of the Light Infantry, and the KOYLI Regimental Depot, moved back to Pontefract, from where the Regiment had departed to Strensall in 1939 as part of its mobilisation plan. Change was not confined to names and locations. From now onwards all Light Infantry recruits passing out at Pontefract doubled past the saluting base with rifles at the high port, the balance of the new FN self-loading rifle being such that it was not possible to carry it at the trail.

> Details of instructions such as "catch the rifle at the point of balance" will no longer be heard on the barrack square, nor indeed will many familiar words of command, for we understand the "Shoulder", "Present" and "High Port" are about the only arms drill movements that are left.[18]

Shortly after the move to Pontefract a 48 hours Initiative Scheme was included in the training programme for new recruits. Intended to develop their ability to plan ahead, read maps, and generally use their imagination, each recruit was given five shillings and expected to travel as far as possible and return to the Depot within 48 hours. By August Privates Rayne and Bapty held the record by travelling 1,332 miles in 33 hours and 25 minutes. Almost twelve months later the Depot News had to confess, 'Our old initiative exercises have been discontinued and new types of adventure training exercises designed. If these fail to attract as much publicity, there is little doubt they are of greater value.'[19] Whether the publicity had been good or bad was not forthcoming.

On 6 June 1959, 4th KOYLI celebrated the centenary of the raising in Wakefield of its forebear, the 9th West Riding Yorkshire Rifle Volunteers. In July the Battalion was proud that it could muster its recruiting target of 400 officers and men at the annual camp at Plasterdown Camp near Tavistock, Devon, and it vowed to reach 500 before the end of the year.

At a short parade on Amalgamation Day, Tuesday 6 October, the Regimental cap badge, the smallest in the British Army, was exchanged for the new Light Infantry badge, the old ones being handed over to Major A.C. Elcomb, Adjutant of 4th KOYLI, for safe keeping.

The Regiment, along with the York and Lancaster Regiment, was honoured when Pontefract conferred upon it the Freedom of the Borough at a ceremony in front of the Town Hall on 11 October. The Colonel of the Regiment, Lieutenant General Sir Harold Redman received the Freedom Scroll from the Mayor, Councillor John Walton JP, who later took the salute as a detachment from 4th KOYLI marched past on parade.

Lieutenant Colonel Robinson completed his tour of command with 4th KOYLI on 14 January 1960 and was succeeded by Lieutenant Colonel W.H. Lossock. At the beginning of 1960, 4th KOYLI was awaiting a decision on its future, and that of the TA in general. Despite the very active recruiting campaign, no one was certain whether the Battalion would survive the government's latest cutting and amalgamating exercises. Early training for 4th KOYLI officers and NCOs in 1960 continued to reflect the ever-present threat of a nuclear conflict. Concentrating on the problems of the civil authorities in the period immediately following a nuclear attack, there were a number of study sessions with the Wakefield division of the Civil Defence, together with the city's Police Force and Fire Brigade. In June, the Battalion, now 500 strong, was at the All Arms Training Centre at Otterburn for the annual camp where the highlight was a 24-hour 'Tough Training Exercise'.

On Minden Day 1960, Lieutenant General Sir Harold Redman completed his ten years as Colonel of the Regiment, the Colonelcy passing to Lieutenant General Sir Roger Bower KCB KBE. On 10 October, Sir Roger, who had recently been appointed the 92nd Lieutenant of Her Majesty's Tower of London, was involved in the installation of Field Marshal The Earl Alexander of Tunis KG, PC, GCB, OM, GCMG, CSI, DSO, MC, DCL, LLD, as the 150th Constable of the Tower. The ceremony had been arranged by another former KOYLI officer, Brigadier L.F.E. Wieler CB, CBE, JP, the Major and Resident Governor of the Tower. To complete the KOYLI's connection with these proceedings, the music for the occasion was provided by the band of the Irish Guards under their Director of Music, Major C.H. Jaegar, who had joined the KOYLI Band as a boy recruit in 1927.[20]

The 1st KOYLI had emerged unscathed from the latest amalgamations of regular battalions, and in 1961, the Regiment was again spared when it was learned that 4th KOYLI would retain its own identity. The Battalion was to remain in 146th Brigade, whose Brigade HQ would be transferred to York. The new Brigade Commander was to be Brigadier C.J. Deedes who, together with his deputy, Colonel M.A.C.P. Kaye, would need no introduction to 4th KOYLI. A certain measure of reorganisation of the

Fig: 37 HM the QM with Officers 1st KOYLI, Pontefract, 28 Oct 1961.
Back Row: Lt J.J.R. Wingfield, Lt J.E. Kendall, Lt C.L.'e Backhouse, 2Lt R.J. Preston, 2Lt R.J.R. Taylorson, Lt L. Dickinson RAEC,
          2Lt T.N. Barker, 2Lt C.C.W. Hickie, 2Lt D.R. Mills, Lt A. Makepeace-Warne
Second Row: Lt D.J. Dinwiddie, Capt R.St.C. Preston, Capt B.M. Wilson, Capt H. Chadwick, MBE, MM, Capt A.R. Tinson,
          Capt J.S. Cowley, Capt D.L.E. Wieler, Lt J.B. Charlesworth, Capt N.R.M. Petrie, Lt T.N. Bates
Front Row: Major C. Landells, RAPC, Major M.R. Wade, Major T.A. McCuthie, MC,
          Lt Col S.N. Floyer-Acland,   Major H.C.I. Rome, Major J.M.C. Hutton, Major S.D. Butterell
HRH The Queen Mother, Col-in-Chief of the Regiment, Lt Gen Sir Roger Bower, KCB, KBE, Col of the Regiment

Regt Archive

structure of the Battalion was also made together with a reassessment of its establishment.

The wartime role of the TA depended upon the nature of any future conflict. An all out nuclear war would require it to cooperate very closely

with the Civil Powers to ensure the survival of the nation. However, a conventional war, or one that involved the tactical use of battlefield nuclear weapons, would require the TA to act as the first line reinforcement of the regular army. The question was, which role would it be given, and, if it were the latter, would sufficient resources be allotted to allow it to undertake the necessary training? Meanwhile, 4th KOYLI received a particularly good report from the Commandant of the Army School of Civil Defence on its work at that year's annual camp held at Millom.

Fig: 38 Parading 4th KOYLI's new Colours, 3 Aug 1962.   *Regt Archive*

Known throughout the Regiment as 'Uncle', the death of the former Colonel of the Regiment, Major General W. Robb, on 27 March 1961 at the age of 73, came as a profound shock to everyone. An even greater shock was felt, however, when shortly afterwards it was learned the Mrs Nancy Robb, affectionately known as 'Auntie', had also died. She had survived her husband a mere five weeks.[21]

Plans for the future training of the Light Infantry had to be amended later in 1961 when it was learned that necessary changes being undertaken at Copthorne Barracks were behind schedule. From January 1962, the RHQ would be formed at Pontefract where the training of all Light Infantry Regiments would take place.

---

[1] *The Bugle*, 1958, Vol. 50.1 pp 19-20 HQ Company and MT Section notes.

[2] Preston, Brig. R. St C. Memoir, Regt. Archive.

[3] *The Bugle*, 1959, Vol. 51.3 p 96 'D' Company notes. Hythe had been the centre for the British Army's School of Musketry, now the Small Arms School.

[4] *Ibid*, Vol. 51.4 p 135

[5] Floyer-Acland, Lt Col. S.N. was to have the distinction of being the only C.O. of 1ˢᵗ KOYLI, during the period 1945-1968, not to have been commissioned into the Regiment.

[6] *The Bugle*, 1960, Vol. 52.4 p 169

[7] A cousin of Major General A. Makepeace-Warne was a conscript in the Danish company and complained to him that, the British soldiers had thrown sugar beet at the Danish defenders. Memoir. Regt Archive.

[8] *Ibid*, 1960, Vol. 52.4 p 170

[9] *The Bugle*, 1961, Vol. 53.1 p 30

[10] *Ibid*, 1961, Vol. 53.3 p 123

[11] Even though the Regiment did not serve in Korea, some members of the Regiment were killed in that campaign while on attachment to other units.

[12] *The Bugle*, 1961, Vol. 53.4 p 183

[13] *Ibid*, Vol. 53.4 p 169

[14] Preston, Brig. R. St C. Memoir, Regt. Archive.

[15] The brain-child of RSM H. Hardy, the scheme depended on an agreement between the Adjutant of the Depot and 1ˢᵗ KOYLI that a battalion 'driving club' would be formed as a spare-time activity. The club was to purchase 'old-bangers' and teach those interested to drive and service them. The scheme could not be implemented immediately; but, in 1962, Capt H. Hardy, by then QM(Tech) of 1ˢᵗ KOYLI, formed the club in Terendak, thereby fulfilling the promise to those recruited in and after 1958 (all of them 6 or 9 year men).

[16] Fleming, Lt Col P.G. Memoir, Conversation with the author.
During the recruiting campaign, a skilled bugler, Pte A. Fothergill (later to become RSM Forthergill) was enlisted. Pte Fothergill came from a long line of regimental buglers, which it was believed stretched back to a representative who served with the 51ˢᵗ at Waterloo. At a recruiting display in York, Pte Fothergill stood atop Cliffords Tower in the city and played bugle calls requested by the public. 'Cookhouse' and 'Defaulters' were said to have been the most requested.

[17] Fleming, Lt Col. P.G. *The Second Raising of the Regiment*, Memoir. Regt. Archive.

[18] *The Bugle*, 1959, Vol. 51.1 p 2

[19] *The Bugle*, 1960, Vol. 52.2 p 39

[20] Major Jaeger had been introduced to the Regiment as a boy in 1927 by another KOYLI Bandmaster, Capt Charles Raison.

[21] Major-General Robb had served throughout the First World War as a territorial officer in the Northumberland Fusiliers, and had commanded that regiment's 4ᵗʰ Battalion in 1918. After the war he was given a regular commission into The King's Own Yorkshire Light Infantry.

7

Malaya and Borneo

On the penultimate day of 1961, the Band of 1st KOYLI played on deck as *HMT Nevasa* left Southampton on the first leg of its journey to Malaya. The *Nevasa* was scheduled to make brief stops at Gibraltar, Aden, and Colombo, but local political tension in Colombo made it necessary to cancel that particular visit.[1] This slight alteration resulted in the Battalion arriving in Singapore on 20 January 1962, one day earlier than expected. Following disembarkation, a train journey north took the Battalion to Tampin station, from where it moved into the newly built Terendak Camp.[2]

The 1st KOYLI quickly settled into the Imjin Lines at Terendak Camp where its neighbours were 1st New Zealand Regiment and 2nd Royal Australian Regiment, all three forming 28th Commonwealth Brigade, part of 17th Gurkha Infantry Division under the command of Major General Walter Walker. (The Commonwealth Brigade was the direct descendant of the Commonwealth Division that had fought with great distinction during the Korean War.)

Despite the Regiment's excellent recruiting record over the previous years, the use of large numbers of men in a variety of administrative roles resulted in the rifle companies being sadly under strength. Within three weeks of their arrival, the three companies were sent to the Gemas and Segamat areas where they took part in a ten-day Brigade exercise 'Charity Angel'. With each man carrying equipment weighing between 55-70 lbs, the Battalion marched through rubber estates, mainly at night, and arrived at its destination on time and unseen. From here, twin and single engined Pioneer aircraft transported it to 'the sharp end'. Jungle training included roping out of Royal Naval S55 helicopters and marking out Dropping Zones for supplies; the main problems being the difficulty of marking out a clearly visible DZ, using only a machete, and retrieving supplies from containers that dangled from parachutes many feet off the ground. For those new to living and fighting in the jungle, which was by far the majority, these first experiences made a great impression. Despite being the only Malayan jungle that he had seen, Private Gascoigne, 'A' Company, was convinced that this particular jungle 'was a virtually impregnable mass that when you chopped through, it seemed to grow behind you.' Gascoigne maintained that progress was particularly slow because,

> Only one man could chop at a time, the others had to march behind in single file, it was bad up front, we had our jungle greens on and boots that were made of canvas plus a heavy pack and rifle and

124

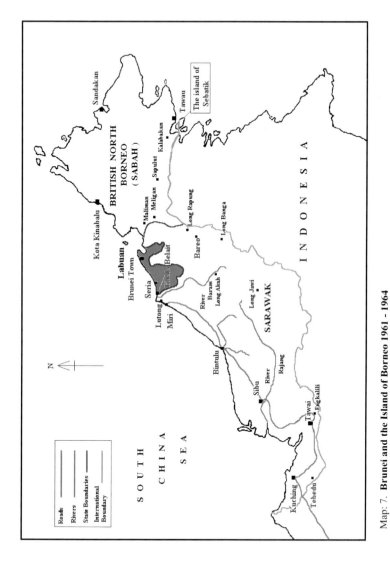

Map: 7. **Brunei and the Island of Borneo 1961 - 1964**
With few roads, rivers provided the principal means of transportation. For 1st KOYLI, helicopters became an important means of moving troops over this difficult jungle terrain.

food in the packs change of clothes etc. In the jungle of this type there were palm fronds that had hard long thorns that were hooked and it tore at your skin, there were thick vines and large ants, red ants that bit your skin, centipedes over a foot long, if you were bit by them you were paralysed over an area of several inches around the bite, the size of them made your flesh creep. [3]

Insects, heat, high humidity, and thick undergrowth had always presented problems for soldiers on active service in the jungle. Following the first Malayan Emergency, improved techniques, and the use of helicopter transport and re-supply from the air, had increased the infantry's effectiveness. Once the initial exercise had been completed, there followed section, platoon and company training, but the ability to mobilise quickly is a major requirement of any form of rapid reaction force and this too required constant practice.

Since those busy days we have relaxed not at all, in fact our work has considerably increased in tempo. To give an example we have practised mobilization three times and have thus thrice been through what some call Wally's high flying eight-hour cycle. [4]

An exercise of a very different nature took place in Singapore in mid-May. Exercise 'Rabbit Punch' required 200 men from 'B' and 'D' companies to make themselves as objectionable as possible to units of the Singapore Police, the Singapore Infantry Regiment, and several battalions of Gurkhas. In the event of civil unrest in Singapore, the local government policy was to avoid using European troops, except as a last resort. The 1,000 combined European 'rioters' were drawn from the Queens Own Highlanders, 1st Royal Green Jackets and 1st KOYLI. After plotting some suitably fiendish schemes, Major M.R. Wade had to hand over command of 'D' Company to Captain D.L.E. Wieler who, together with Lieutenant C.L'e. Backhouse and 2nd Lieutenant R. J. Preston, led their motley crews into the fray. On the first day two men of 'D' Company received hefty whacks from the batons of the police and had to be admitted to hospital for an overnight stay. The following morning saw much internecine conflict in the ranks of the rioters. 'The Police, on arrival, couldn't make head or tail of this, and never made any attempt to part us. Then in came the Gurkhas ... [but] the approach roads were so blocked with spectator and umpire transport that the Gurkhas couldn't get up the road.' [5] At the MacRitchie Reservoir mock antisocial behaviour by 'B' Company and others was contained by the police who, with the aid of their dogs, managed to confine the 900 miscreants to the top of the reservoir dam. At the end of the whole exercise the rioters were awarded a 24 hour paid holiday in Singapore before returning to Terendak.

Exercise 'Trumpeter' was a Battalion exercise to simulate a realistic operation anywhere in the jungles of South East Asia. Leaving Terendak in the early hours of Whit-Sunday, the Battalion travelled by train for a four-day stay at Nee Soon transit camp near Singapore, where the men listened to lectures, swam, and drank lots of coffee. A return train journey marked the start of the active part of the exercise, which involved helicopter drops and long approach marches.

> Each man had to carry, in addition to clothing and sleeping bag, one week's scale of ammunition and one week's supply of 24 hours ration packs. Some solved the weight problem by having a huge meal before the exercise started, with the result that many ran out before the end of the week. Those with a few bags of rice and tea left suddenly became very popular with the hungry – but to no avail.[6]

The main objective was to search out the enemy, then attack and destroy him, an operation that was all too familiar to those who could remember the days of the first Malayan Emergency. On this occasion, when the enemy was finally located he was not in a village, or purpose built and visible strongpoint, but in camouflaged trenches that were almost impossible to see in the thick undergrowth. 'Suddenly the blast of a rifle aimed in your direction would indicate the position of some gleeful little Gurkha thoroughly enjoying the whole business.' [7]

The second half of the year was spent in a variety of ways with training exercises in the jungle taking second place to a host of sporting activities. A tour of duty on the Thailand Border, across which communist terrorists had frequently escaped to safety during the original Emergency, was planned for later in the year. On 28 December, and within 72 hours of the departure time for this tour, the Battalion was informed that it had been called off. No reason was forthcoming, but it was strongly suspected that 1st KOYLI was to be used to relieve one of the battalions already operating in Brunei. A long wait of nearly two weeks ended with a signal that warned the Battalion it was to begin a three-month period of duty in Brunei, starting in the first week of February 1963.

In the years following the first Emergency, Britain developed a twin strategy for the area, which, it was hoped, would lead to political and economic stability. To satisfy the political aspirations of the Malays living on the peninsula, the Chinese, especially the entrepreneurs living on the island of Singapore, and the peoples of the three British territories in Borneo – Sarawak, Brunei and North Borneo, it was proposed that they form the Federation of Malaysia. The proposal was accepted and the Federation of Malaysia was established on 16 September 1963. During the nine months before the Federation was established, and for three years afterwards, East Malaysia was to be subjected to terrorist attacks and a threat of outright war by its neighbour Indonesia.

The second part of Britain's strategy for the region was a military one. Britain's three Service Chiefs for the whole of South East Asia had their HQs on the island of Singapore. (The army HQ for Far East Land Forces was known as FARELF.) The Chief of the Defence Staff, Admiral of the Fleet Earl Mountbatten, wished to see command vested in a single Supreme Commander, in much the same way that he had overseen land, sea, and air operations throughout South East Asia during the Second World War. The idea was greeted with little enthusiasm by any of the three services, and especially not by the service chiefs themselves. They rightly concluded that in the event of war, or any form of emergency, their individual roles would be diminished to that of merely providing administrative support to a C-in-C and his Director of Operations. In face of this opposition the plan was nevertheless adopted, and the first Commander-in-Chief, Admiral Sir David Luce, took up his appointment in November 1962.

> The rebellion that took the Far East Command by surprise was not one of the communist-inspired insurrections which they had expected. It was primarily a domestic revolution aimed at political and social reform in the Sultanate of Brunei but, far from wishing to replace the Sultan with a left-wing junta, it aimed to re-create the empire of Brunei which ruled much of Borneo and adjacent islands in the sixteenth century. The rebels did enjoy some external help but it was not from communists nor from the Chinese. Indeed, fear of Chinese domination made the rebels as hostile to the idea of Malaysia as the Indonesians. [8]

Some vague warning of possible trouble in Brunei had been given to Admiral Luce on 23 November and, in the light of this, he called for the existing Brunei contingency plan to be amended. The rebellion began in the early hours of 8 December and, on being informed, Admiral Luce ordered the plan known as 'Ale Yellow' to be implemented immediately: two infantry companies were to be placed on 48 hours standby. Some nine hours after he had issued this order, Admiral Luce received further intelligence that persuaded him to order the 'Ale Red' alert. Two companies of $1/2^{nd}$ Gurkhas were immediately airlifted to Brunei town where the rebels had attacked police stations, the Sultan's Istana, the Prime Minister's house, and the power station. The two companies of $1/2^{nd}$ Gurkhas moved into the town and fought a series of sharp actions in which they had two soldiers killed and six wounded. These local actions were both swift and decisive, but the rebels still posed a significant threat to the whole of the territory. The situation demanded that reinforcements be sent immediately and, by 10 December, $1/2^{nd}$ Gurkhas had been brought up to battalion strength and was joined by the Queen's Own Highlanders. When Major General Walter

Walker took over command as Commander British Forces Borneo (COMBRITBOR), 19 December 1962, the rebellion had been broken and there was little fear that it would spread across Sarawak and North Borneo.

> Of the original four thousand rebels, forty had been killed and some three thousand four hundred captured. The remainder had fled into the jungle and might be trying to reach the Indonesian frontier. Of the two principal leaders, Azahari had been away in the Philippines throughout the revolt, and Yassin Affendi was among the fugitives. [9]

Within three weeks of the start of the revolt, a sizable force had been assembled in Borneo. In Brunei and East Sarawak 1/2nd Gurkhas and the Queen's Own Highlanders had been joined by 40 and 42 Commando, together with 1st Royal Green Jackets, one company and HQ of 3 Commando Brigade, and a Royal Artillery battery serving in an infantry role. Supporting this force was the Brunei Army, the Sarawak Rangers, the police of the three territories, four thousand assorted tribesmen and, of course, the Royal Navy and the Royal Air Force.

Fig: 39 L/CPl P. Oberg, with Pte Woodall and a Recce Platoon patrol following, crossing a native bridge in the Borneo jungle. *P. Shield*

The revolt had been speedily dealt with, but there were those who feared that Borneo could become embroiled in a dispute with its immediate neighbour Indonesia, whose President Sukarno was vehemently opposed to the creation of Malaysia. Russia's increasing interest in South East Asia was demonstrated when its Defence Minister visited the Indonesian capital Jakarta, a move that caused concern throughout the whole region. In February 1962, the United States, fearing a communist take-over of South Vietnam, began committing military forces to assist that country in its dispute with neighbouring communist North Vietnam.[10] Meanwhile in Borneo, as the hunt for the remaining fugitive rebels continued, there were ominous signs of military activity on the Indonesian side of the border. Now that the initial impact of the revolt had been absorbed, Major General Walker took the opportunity to reshuffle his forces: the Queen's Own Highlanders and 1/2nd Gurkhas were to be relieved by 1st KOYLI and 1/7th Gurkhas.

Fig: 40 A patrol preparing for operations in the jungle. 2nd from L, Pte Trigg Nicholls, 4th from L, Cpl Milton Baden Powell Starky   *P. Shield*

The 1st KOYLI was transported to Brunei in the commando carrier *HMS Albion* and disembarked in Brunei Bay on the morning of 8 February 1963. From Brunei town the Battalion moved west to the oil town of Seria, where it took over responsibility for security of the Belait District from the Queen's Own Highlanders. In addition, 'A' Company's 2 and 3 Platoons moved to Meligan and Maliman in British North Borneo, 1 Platoon went to Long Akah, and the Mortar Platoon to Miri, both of the latter being in Sarawak. 'B' Company was initially employed to guard the power station, the airport, and to provide a reserve platoon, but it was not long before the whole company (less part of 5 Platoon) was taking part in 'Dirty Linen', an operation that was typical of many undertaken by the battalion during its tour in Borneo.

Moving first by boat, and when the river dwindled to a ditch, on foot, the object of operation 'Dirty Linen' was to collect illegal arms and gather intelligence in the Labi area, which lies some 40 kilometres south east of Kuala Belait. Few weapons were discovered, but information was obtained as to the whereabouts of two Tentera Nasional Kalimantan Utara (TNKU) rebels. Because the local Public Works Department (PWD), in particular its over-inquisitive manager, was suspected of being involved in rebel activity, it was necessary to mount a deception plan.

Fig: 41 Boats on the river are the main method of civilian transport in Borneo.   *Regt Archive*

Despite poor police security, the Company succeeded in the capture of one TNKU rebel (in a night-approach cordon, inserted without waking a single dog!) from the PWD quarters at Bukit Puan, the subsequent surrender of the other, the apprehension of the two PWD employees (known rebel sympathisers) and the eventual arrest of the local PWD manager and his foreman. The second TNKU rebel surrendered to the Regimental Band during a 'Hearts and Minds' visit to Bukit Puan! [11]

At the beginning of March, 'D' Company relieved 1, 2 and 3 Platoons taking over their patrolling and ambushing roles – especially 3 Platoon's patrolling along the river Baram towards the Indonesian border. In the middle of March, the Meligan and Maliman platoons were withdrawn and 'B' Company took over the Long Akah area, but of the six helicopters that should have been available, only two were serviceable. 'These air-lifted 5 Platoon to Lio Match (two days by boat up-river from Long Akah) and then broke down! It took 7 days to deploy the balance of the Company by boat.'[12]

Fig: 42 A KOYLI patrol making its way through the Borneo jungle.   *IWM*

'D' Company, commanded by Major J.M.S. Thain, was placed under the command of 2/7th Gurkhas and given the task of searching for the hard core of Brunei rebels led by Yassin Affendi. Despite strenuous efforts (16 Platoon spent 57 days in the jungle with only one break in camp), the only close contact with Affendi, who was thought to be living in the area northeast of Brunei town, was made by 2nd Lieutenant C.M.J. Deedes whose patrol located one of his recently occupied camps.

On Good Friday, 12 April, an urgent signal reached Major General Walker's HQ in Brunei. A party of thirty raiders had attacked a police station in the village of Tebedu, near the Indonesian border south of Kuching in Sarawak, and two policemen had been killed. 'A' Company 1st KOYLI, which had that very day been released as standby-by company in Brunei, was ordered to Kuching immediately. All Major S.D. Butterell's patrols were out in the jungle but, boarding a light aircraft that had been fitted with a loud hailer, the Major flew over the jungle trails recalling his men. To the astonishment of many sceptics, they all returned to their base in under four hours, and later that night the RAF flew the Company to Kuching. The identity of the attackers at Tebedu was unknown. They could have been part of a clandestine Chinese Communist Organisation (CCO) known to be strong in that area, the North Kalimantan National Army

(TNKU), or, more seriously, they could have been Indonesian regular soldiers: the raid was later proved to be have been planned and carried out by Indonesian regulars.

Whether it was the emergency at Tebedu, or the sudden transfer of 'A' Company to that area, which led to a degree of confusion at FARELF, but the resulting KOYLI movement orders proved to be quite bizarre. FARELF had previously decreed that in the third week of May a representative force from 1st KOYLI, to be known as 'H' Company, was to take part in the forthcoming South East Treaty Organisation (SEATO) exercise in Thailand. By 27 April, a partial movement of troops to produce this representative company had been made, but it was decided that the whole of 1st KOYLI be given three days notice to leave Borneo for Malaya on 1 May! As an added complication, a further order required that a composite company (Compo Company) from 1st KOYLI was to remain in Borneo.

> When the "force" assembled, it consisted of :- 45% A Coy (elements of 1,2,and 3 Platoons); 35% B Coy (Coy HQ, elements of 5 and 6 Platoons and the Anti-Tank Section); 12% C Coy (its Commander, Captain Wieler, acting as 2i/c, and a Mortar Section) and 8% HQ Coy (signallers and drivers etc.) Other than in the mortar section, no NCO had a sub-unit composed completely of his own men.[13]

On 1 May, as the main body of 1st KOYLI left Seria for Malaya in *HMS Albion*, the 'Compo Company', commanded by Major P.G. Fleming, joined 'D' Company 2/10th Gurkha Rifles in what was to be called 'KORGI FORCE'. The KOYLI platoons were deployed at Lubok Antu and Batu Lingtan from where they patrolled and ambushed trails leading from the Indonesian border.[14]

> 'B' Company HQ and its 6 Platoon under Sjt Richardson was deployed to Engkalili, where it took command of a police post and a platoon of 'Dad's Army' Dyaks, armed with an assortment of ancient shot-guns (these manned slit trenches that everyone took care to approach from the rear, no matter what time of day, the Dyaks being firmly ordered only to fire to their immediate front).[15]

Indonesian forces attempting to reconnoitre British positions across the border tried to complete their operations and return to Kalimantan (the name given by the Indonesians to that part of Borneo they inherited from the Dutch) before daylight.[16] To counter this, all British units in forward positions observed 'Stand To' from mid-night to 03:00 hrs. Unfortunately, this period usually coincided with the beginnings of a tropical downpour that filled slit trenches and resulted in the troops spending an uncomfortably wet and chilly three hours. Luckily, being under the command of 3

Commando Brigade, the careful insertion of 'Victualled IN' at the end of each signal request for re-supply produced basket-clad stone jars of Navy Rum nestling in the helicopter's supply nets. 'Whatever the medicinal merits, there's no doubt that "Up spirits" at three fifteen in the morning did wonders for the morale of Yorkshiremen and Dayaks alike. There was, of course, a subsequent reaction at HQ FARELF, but that's another story.'[17]

On 5 May, 'Compo' Company was withdrawn into reserve and attached to 40 Commando based outside Kutching. This was the first opportunity for the Company Commander to meet and organise its disparate elements. Of the many operations undertaken by 'Compo' Company, one of the more successful was 'Zebra Stripe', 8/9 May, which took place in the Bukit Tapang - Batu Kampong area, 17 miles south of Kuching. The Brigade Commander ascribed the success of this cordon and search operation to the KOYLI Company's speed of entry, which was achieved by the skilful use of the 'bale out' technique. This manoeuvre required the troops to leave their moving trucks, which continued along the road, then achieve complete surprise by doubling forward up the track towards the settlement as quietly as possible. In operation 'Queen Mary', 14-21 May, Lieutenant T.N. Bates, temporarily in command of 6 Platoon, insisted on searching an apparently locked-up house. His instinct proved to be correct and the search revealed an uncooperative Chinese woman who, after questioning, gave information leading to the arrest of the CCO's leader for the 19 Mile Bazaar area.

With the capture of Yasser Affendi on 18 May, the Brunei revolt finally came to an end, but the Emergency, and the threat of a more serious conflict with Indonesia was still very real. For 'Compo' Company, however, it was time to rejoin 1st KOYLI at Terendak Camp and, after almost a whole month of independent operations, on 23 May 1963, it embarked in LST (Landing Ship Tank) *Maxwell Brander* for the journey across the South China Sea.

The composite 'H' Company represented the Battalion at the SEATO exercise Dhanarajata in Thailand during June. In reality the exercises took the form of goodwill visits and ceremonial. At Ubon the Band performed while the 28th Commonwealth Brigade (including 'H' Company KOYLI) provided a guard of honour for the King of Thailand. One of the more spectacular events was the SEATO parade in Bangkok that involved 10,000 men from 72 units from many nations, the parade being watched by a crowd of 100,000 people.

> I was exercise adjutant for this deployment and recall that I had failed to tell those on the deployment to take their ammunition boots. These were needed for the parade but we got away with it by insisting that as Light Infantry marched quicker than anyone else we should march past last, after an interval carefully timed so that we would catch the rest of the parade up by the closing stages. We did this in true 'light troops' style wearing jungle boots. [18]

In July 1963 Lieutenant Colonel Rome was posted to Colchester at short notice as GSO1, 54th Division. He was relieved by Lieutenant Colonel G.R. Saltonstall OBE, but because the latter was not available until 1 November, the Second in Command, Major A.C. Elcomb acted as temporary CO in the interim. During October and November the 1st New Zealand Regiment left Terendak Camp, to be followed a short while after by 103rd Battery Royal Australian Artillery. It was generally assumed that 1st KOYLI would not be sent back to Borneo before the early summer of 1964, so it came as a surprise when FARELF announced that it would return to Borneo at the beginning of December. Two major Battalion exercises had been planned to take place in November and December, but this latest news curtailed most of this programme, the first phase only being completed by 23 November. The Colonel of the Regiment, Lieutenant General Sir Roger Bower, visited the Regiment at Terendak Camp and, despite the hasty preparations being made for the forthcoming move, Sir Roger managed to meet a considerable number of people during his short six-day visit.

The Federation of Malaysia was established on 16 September 1963. In elections held earlier in the year, which had been scrutinised by United Nations observers, Sarawak and North Borneo (which now changed its name to Sabah) voted to join the new Federation, but Brunei, despite strong urgings from Britain, wished to remain a British Protectorate. The most significant change for the British forces in the area was the handing over of supreme military authority from GHQ Singapore to the Malaysian National Defence Council in Kuala Lumpur.

The reaction of the Indonesian president, Sukarno, to the emergence of Malaysia was one of outrage coupled with violent threats of retribution. From this moment onwards, units of the Indonesian regular army organised and carried out an increasing programme of incursions into Eastern Malaysia. Although neither side made any formal declaration, there now existed a virtual state of war between the two Asian states. The first major incident was an attack by some 200 Indonesians, supported by about 300 unarmed porters, on the outpost at Long Jawi which was situated at the end of a river complex stretching from deep in the centre of Sarawak back to the port of Sibu on the western coast. The post, manned by six Gurkhas of the 1/2nd Gurkha Rifles, three policemen and twenty-one Border Scouts, was attacked on 27 September, the raiders killing two Gurkhas, two policemen and a Border Scout. With the two available wirelesses being destroyed, reaction to the attack was slow, and it was two days before reinforcements arrived. By the end of October, vigorous patrolling, and well-placed ambushes, had accounted for thirty-three of the raiders, together with an unknown number who must have perished when they were forced to flee into the jungle.

The 1st KOYLI MT section, plus the heavy baggage, left Terendak Camp for Borneo on 3 December, with the Tactical and Administrative Advance parties and 'A' Company leaving by air over the next eight days. The remainder of the Battalion left Terendak Camp on the morning of 7 December 1963, and approximately seven hours later were going on board *HMS Albion* for the two-day sea crossing to Brunei. Arriving off Labuan, 10 December, the troops were ferried ashore by LCTs (Landing Craft Tank) to be speedily transported south by RAF Beverleys to Anduki airfield near Seria. Three days later 'B' Company moved some 50 kilometres north along the coast to Tutong as Force Reserve, with one platoon on 15 minutes standby at Brunei airfield. 'D' Company went to Lutong to cover the coastal area including the towns of Miri, Niah, Bekenu and Bintulu. 'A' Company KOYLI relieved 1st Royal Green Jackets and deployed 2 and 3 Platoons, under the command of 3 Royal Malay Regiment, in the defence of Tawau, on the eastern coast of Sabah. The Assault Pioneers and Mortars were distributed throughout the Battalion while the Band and Bugles had important guard commitments in the Seria area.

The first President of Malaysia, Tunku Abdul Rahman, was over anxious to have Malaysian troops join in the defence of the newly formed state. The former Royal Malay Regiment had a few experienced NCOs who had served during the first Malayan Emergency, but the majority of the officers, particularly the junior ones, were young, enthusiastic, and very inexperienced. This inexperience was to have serious consequences for 3rd Royal Malay Regiment defending Tawau.

The town of Tawau, a prosperous trading centre, lies on the northern shore of Cowie Harbour, and opposite the island of Sebatik, half of which is Malaysian, the rest Indonesian. Five companies of Indonesian regular marines had been using the island to train volunteer terrorists, and the short sea crossing would enable them to reach any of their objectives on the mainland of Sabah. When the two KOYLI platoons joined 3rd Royal Malay Regiment and local gendarmarie in the defence of Tawau and the surrounding area, Brigadier J. Glennie, former Brigadier General Staff FARELF, and now Deputy Director of Operations, Brunei and Sabah, warned them to expect an attack. When speaking to 3rd Royal Malays and the gendarmerie, Glennie emphasized the importance of patrolling and creating a system of defence in depth. Both KOYLI platoons moved straight up to positions controlling centres of communication near the Indonesian border and began patrolling and improving their defensive positions. Just before 23:00 hrs on 29 December, a force of 35 Indonesian regulars and 128 volunteers, which had entered Sabah about eight days earlier, attacked a platoon and two sections of 3rd Royal Malays in their post at Kalabakan while they were engaged in domestic activities. Opening up with automatic fire and using grenades, the Indonesians killed eight Malays, including the company commander, and wounded nineteen: ten minutes later the 15 defenders of the nearby police garrison managed to fight off an assault on their station without incurring any casualties. Major General Walker arrived the following day and immediately sent a signal to the C-in-C, Admiral Sir Varyl Begg, for reinforcements. Already under Walker's command was 'B'

Company KOYLI at Tutong, which despatched 5 Platoon, the standby platoon, to Sapulut in central Sabah where it joined a force of 1st Leicesters and 1st Royal Green Jackets in the hunt for 80 terrorists. While the Leicesters and Green Jackets patrolled to the south, 5 Platoon constructed a series of mutually supporting defensive trenches covering all approaches to the village, after which it too carried out patrols to the south and east. On New Year's Day, 'B' Company moved to the Tawau area to deal with another incursion, a task that was to occupy it until the end of the month, while platoons from 'A' Company moved to join Company HQ at Bareo airfield. By the end of January 1964, one month after the incident at Kalabakan, all but six of the enemy involved in the raid had been killed, captured, or had surrendered.

Fig: 43 Helicopters and fixed wing aircraft on the airstrip at Bareo, 1964.   *IWM*

After Christmas 1963, 'D' Company moved from Lutong to Bintulu, a town on an estuary into which flow two river systems, the Batang Kemena and the Tatau. These rivers, and their numerous tributaries, are navigable for over 80 miles inland and provided ideal routes along which insurgents could travel. Patrols from 'D' Company moved up and down these waterways, staying out for up to two weeks at a time, in an effort to prevent enemy incursions.   From January 1964 onwards, British battalions became increasingly involved in patrolling and ambushing operations to prevent the cross-border activities of Indonesian regulars. This increased activity prompted the British government to take a closer look at the problem and, early in the New Year, the Secretary of State for Defence, Peter Thornycroft, and the Secretary for War, James Ramsden, visited Brunei. During his tour, the Secretary of State visited 'A' Company, 1st KOYLI, at

Fig:44 This elevated machine gun position formed part of the defence system
guarding the important airstrip at Bareo.   P. *Shield*

its base on the airfield at Bareo near the Indonesian border. The situation in
Brunei was in fact war in all but name. In response to an appeal from the
Secretary-General of the United Nations, Malaysia and Indonesia agreed to
a cease-fire, which came into effect from 25 January. During the whole of
the six weeks of the supposed cease-fire, the Indonesians continued with
their operations inside Eastern Malaysia and in early March instructions
were given to Major General Walker to resume full-scale operations.

In mid January, 'D' Company moved to the Meligan area of Sabah in
response to Indonesian incursions but, by the end of February, it briefly
returned to Lutong before joining the rest of the Battalion in the Bareo
sector.

Throughout February many of 1st KOYLI's platoons made hasty dashes to
various parts of Borneo and Sabah to deal with incursions, but by the end of
the month the Battalion's companies were beginning to settle into fixed
areas of responsibility. 'A' Company was established at Bareo airfield, an
important location in the plan of operations with several good routes into
Indonesia, these latter also made it a very vulnerable target. In late
February, 'B' Company moved to the south west of Bareo with 5 Platoon at
Lio Matoh, 6 Platoon to the south at Long Banga, and 7 Platoon and
Company HQ at Long Akah.

On the morning of 19 February, a helicopter took Private J. Cunningham
and his section to Long Rapung, north east of Bareo and close to the
Indonesian border, to join one of three patrols of 1 Platoon that were to try
to engage some insurgents thought to be hiding in the area. Setting off at
09:00 hrs Cunningham's patrol, led by Company Serjeant Major Reynolds,

moved towards the border, but finding no sign of the intruders it began its journey back to base. As it did so,

> Quite suddenly shots broke the jungle silence and I felt a burning sensation in my left wrist. I looked down at it and saw a hole. I stood dumbfounded, then turned towards the firing, raised my rifle to shoot and was hit again – this time in the shoulder. I fell to the ground, bleeding profusely, shocked that it was I who had been shot. The firing was going on until a voice called cease, it was quiet. I crawled away from the ambush area to join everyone else near the stream. There I found that Pte Alan Chandler had been shot too. When we had both been fixed up with bandages the long painful march back to our patrol base began. [19]

Ten minutes after reaching their base a helicopter from Bareo evacuated Cunningham and Chandler to Brunei airfield. Ambulances took them to Brunei hospital and by 15:00 hrs they were both undergoing operations. Four days later both men were transferred to Labuan and after a stay of 24 hrs were flown to the British Military Hospital, Singapore. 'Our wounds healed quickly and our sufferings were reduced to the minimum. For this we are deeply thankful.' [20]

Exactly two weeks later, 5 March, a firm contact was made with Indonesian insurgents at one of 'A' Company's three bases – Pa Lungan, not far from the recent encounter at Long Rapung. At 16:15 hrs on a very wet day, a party of approximately ten Indonesians approached an ambush position set by 1 Platoon, led by Serjeant W. Ashcroft. The local population had given warning of the enemy's presence and 1 Platoon was well prepared. The action was short and effective. When the enemy was in range the platoon opened fire killing five and wounding one. Of the others, all managed to escape, although it was thought that at least two had been wounded. In recognition of the part Serjeant Ashcroft played in this operation, his name was Mentioned in Despatches. One month later in the same Pa Lungan area, a patrol from 13 Platoon, led by Serjeant Kemp, ambushed two Indonesians killing one and capturing the other.

The ultimate success of the operations in Borneo was due in large part to two important characteristics of the British Army. First, and foremost, there was the high degree of training, especially in the techniques of jungle warfare, that resulted in highly effective patrolling. However, while maintaining a strict regime of professionalism, the British soldier's innate response to the needs of the indigenous population counted for much. The policy of winning the hearts and minds of the local population was of vital importance to the success of the whole enterprise.

The airfield at Bareo suffered from persistent low cloud and, as the number of troops grew from the initial 80 to approximately 320, the problems of air supply (mainly weight and weather) multiplied.

> Every single item of food, ammunition, medical equipment, clothing and all other requirements were supplied by air. Our Battalion alone was supplied with many hundreds of tons of barbed wire and pickets for the construction of defences.
> Forward troops seem to spend most of their time between airdrops thinking up almost impossible requests... Each Platoon was using as many medical stores each week as a battalion in normal circumstances. They were mainly used on treating the local civilian population and were all put to good use. [A long catalogue of requests ended with a response to the OC 3 Pl.] PLEASE NOTE: Your indent for "22 yards of MULTICOLURED CLOTH for Sarongs, at a cost not to exceed 1 Dollar 50 Cents per yard" has not been approved. [21]

The character, and background, of the troops involved can often produce unforeseen benefits.

> What had been achieved? There had been some tough patrolling through rain, rivers, and terrain that ripped and rotted clothing and jungle boots to shreds in days. Mostly it was a matter of 'hearts and minds' and showing the flag. The junior NCOs, commanding the patrols, proved outstanding in their leadership and navigation. The West Riding soldiers produced 'doctoring' and diplomatic skills no one, including themselves, knew they had. [One possible] long-lasting side effect of the deployment was that subsequent visitors to the longhouses along the BARAM were enchanted to be entertained by the children rendering 'One Man Went To Mow' and 'Ilkla Moor Baht At' in authentic West Riding accents. [22]

After four months, 1st KOYLI's second tour of duty in Borneo ended. Between 13 – 25 April the Battalion was transported back to Malaya using a variety of modes of transport that included aircraft, the frigate *HMS Loch Killisport*, the *Motor Vessel Auby* (a converted merchant ship) and an LST. It was later decided that all ranks who had served in Borneo during 1963 and 1964 were to be awarded the General Service Medal 1962 with the clasp 'Borneo'.

The 28th Commonwealth Infantry Brigade formed part of the military arm of SEATO and, since Malaysia's confrontation with Indonesia was not strictly the concern of SEATO, the absence of 1st KOYLI from the Brigade had implications for its ability to carry out its designated role. When the Battalion returned to Terendak Camp, Brigade was more than anxious to have it retrain in its SEATO role immediately.

The first exercise, May Bug, was thoroughly disliked by all concerned. Over a five-day period the Brigade deployed on Bukit Tapah, a 3,000 feet high mountain over which an imagined force of 100 communist terrorists was making its way south to blow up a railway line. The 1st KOYLI was chosen to occupy the summit, which it did despite the extremely difficult climbing conditions it encountered. The exercise was completed successfully, but the highlight for the Battalion was the delivery by helicopter to the DZ (the summit of Bukit Tapah) of iced Tiger beer, a morale boosting move ordered by the CO, but one which earned him a 'rocket' from Brigade HQ.

As 1st KOYLI settled down into its prescribed role in Malaya, fresh negotiations were taking place in Tokyo between the Malaysian and Indonesian governments. These talks broke down on 20 June and within 24 hours, the Indonesians launched an assault in which five Gurkha soldiers were killed and five wounded. News of this latest incident brought down the Battalion's movement notice from 12 hours to almost immediate notice to return to Borneo. Fortunately the expected increase in Indonesian activity never materialised and within days the Battalion was stood down to a less exacting degree of notice.

On 17 June, 'A' Company left Terendak to spend almost three weeks at the Jungle Warfare School at Kota Tinggi, carrying out Nuclear Clothing trials. The trials began with two physically exhausting phases, but at the conclusion of these the Company returned to base to the accompaniment of the KOYLI Band and Bugles. 'Despite the dirt, tiredness and garments we finished at the Light Infantry pace!!!'[23] The last exercise undertaken by 1st KOYLI in Malaya was codenamed 'Raven'. The report of the exercise in *The Bugle* contains two contrasting comments that may give some clue to its ultimate worth. After stating, ' The moves and counter moves that followed are full of hazardous muddle and would be dull to attempt to relate'. Nevertheless, the piece ends,

> Generally speaking it was agreed that Exercise Raven had been much more interesting than the usual jungle exercise we were used to. Here at least we were able to use our infantry tactics more fully and watch our supporting arms carry out their tasks especially the air and artillery, not to mention the fact that we were being watched ourselves. [24]

Return to the UK was drawing ever closer and, in August, a small advance party left Malaya. The Battalion was to be Air Trooped back to the UK, which meant that it returned in relatively small groups, unlike the days when one troopship would accommodate the entire battalion. Consequently, it took almost a month to complete the operation, although the period was extended when 'B' Company was ordered to stay behind for three weeks to support the Scots Guards, who would be under strength until reinforced by a company of the Irish Guards.

During those three weeks 'B' Company was kept extremely busy. From late September until it was relieved on 13 October, it was kept at 12 hours notice. Matters looked really serious on the night of 4/5 October when indications were that the Indonesians intended to land on the Malacca coast and 'B' Company was brought up to 30 minutes notice. Fortunately the weather intervened and the raiders were dispersed. After handing in their olive greens and their G 1098, the members of 'B' Company looked forward to a quiet flight home, but their journey was not to be completed without incident. As one of the aircraft passed over Italy it lost an engine, while another filled with smoke somewhere over Asia Minor.

The Depot and 4th Territorial Battalion

On 3 January 1962, the Depot at Pontefract assumed responsibility for the training of all adult recruits, and to assist in this task the Depot staff was partially replaced by staff from other Light Infantry Regiments. On 31 March, the KOYLI Regimental Depot closed and the following day the Light Infantry Regimental HQ assumed responsibility for all Regimental affairs. The KOYLI Regimental HQ was also established in the barracks at Pontefract and, on 1 April, Colonel Nic Pope became the Regimental Secretary.

Regimental planning was not focused exclusively on the 1st Battalion; the 4th Battalion was also busy with a very important event. In January 4th KOYLI learned that Her Majesty The Queen Mother had consented to present new colours to the Battalion sometime that summer, the Battalion's present colours being the original ones presented to it by King Edward VII at Windsor in 1909. Her Majesty presented the new colours on 3 August on the square at the Barracks, Pontefract. In her address to 4th KOYLI Her Majesty said

> On you, on the whole Territorial Army, devolves a tremendous responsibility. By your fitness for battle, by your willingness to sacrifice your leisure hours and by your ready answer to the call of duty in time of peace, you may dispel the threat of war.
>
> Yorkshire is the parent county of many celebrated fighting units but none is more famous than its Light Infantry Regiment and I am confident that you will uphold the traditions of your forebears and carry these new colours with pride and honour. [25]

Her Majesty later gave her permission for the old colours to be laid up in Wakefield Cathedral instead of the Regimental Chapel in York Minster, and this was done at a ceremony on 26 October 1963.

During 1962, Lieutenant General Sir Roger Bower chaired a War Office Committee tasked with studying the future of the Infantry. The problems facing the government were formidable and complex. Firstly, the cost of producing and maintaining an effective nuclear deterrent force was such that it cast doubt on the nation's ability to fund conventional forces in their current size and shape. This particular dilemma facing the government had troubled successive governments since the end of World War Two: how to deal with the nation's many overseas commitments, while at the same time making a significant reduction in conventional forces, especially the infantry? The government was seeking greater flexibility from its armed forces (a political euphemism for speedy expansion, and contraction) and, it was argued, if Corps such as the Royal Artillery, Royal Engineers and Royal Signals could be varied in size quickly, why not the Infantry? Here, once again, lay the seeds of the Corps of Infantry, a system that was common to the United States army and most of those on the continent, but one that would spell the demise of the Regimental system in the British Army. Secondly, there was the problem of the future of the Regimental Associations. With regiments now having only one Regular and one Territorial battalion, no Regimental Depot, and officers and men being cross posted within the Light Infantry Brigade, it would become increasing difficult to maintain the viability of the individual Regimental Associations. Financially, the Regimental Associations were at this time very dependent on generous help from the Army Benevolent Fund.

The Army Council set its face against a Corps of Infantry, preferring instead amalgamations, or the formation of existing Brigades into large Regiments. The Colonel of the Regiment admitted there were advantages and disadvantages to all these schemes and concluded.

> I have examined them all with very great care over a period of months, and I have come to the conclusion that the formation of a Light Infantry Regiment from the Light Infantry Brigade would be the best way that we could prepare for the conditions of the future.[26]

By the summer of 1962, the Council of Colonels of the Light Infantry Brigade had met and agreed to lend their support to the creation of a Light Infantry Regiment. The Colonels also agreed that any further amalgamations or disbandment were totally unacceptable, and it was felt that if old regimental titles had to be abandoned, then battalions could become numbered battalions of the Light Infantry Regiment.

> Brigades which are functional (eg. Light Infantry, Fusiliers, etc.) would find it easier to merge into a Large Regiment than would the County Brigades whose ties are not generally so intimate. Thanks to the foresight of General Sir Charles Deedes, the Light Infantry Club, which he did so much to found and foster thirty years ago, will provide an excellent starting point for a change of this kind, and for this we owe him our grateful thanks. [27]

The Army Council reported to the government in July, and the Secretary of State for War answered questions on the subject in the House of Commons on 14 November. The Secretary of State said that, while the Army Council did not at this stage wish to commit itself to any one solution, it did favour the formation of Large Regiments from existing Brigades.

On 19 March 1963, Lieutenant Colonel Lossock handed over command of 4th KOYLI to Lieutenant Colonel A.R. Wilson, who had joined the Battalion in 1947 from the 3rd Parachute Battalion.

The British Railway's steam locomotive 'King's Own Yorkshire Light Infantry', named on 20 May 1939 by Lady Deedes, had completed over 900,000 miles, and had been recently retired. In its place was a new Deltic Locomotive No 9002 and, at a ceremony on platform 14 of York station on the afternoon of 4 April, Lieutenant General Sir Roger Bower was asked to name it. After the ceremony the Colonel of the Regiment accepted from British Rail one of the nameplates of the old steam engine and, at a reception later that day, he also accepted a painting and a scale model of the engine as mementoes.

The following day, 5 April, the Light Infantry Depot held its final passing out parade at the Barracks, Pontefract. Indeed, the Barracks had come to the end of its useful life and after 85 years was to be disposed of. At the final passing out parade the Colonel of the Regiment paid tribute to the West Riding of Yorkshire, and Pontefract in particular, for the interest, loyalty and support that each had given to the Regiment during the 75 years that it had used the Barracks as its Depot. Lieutenant General Bower told the parade,

> From these Barracks and through those gates behind you, have gone thousands of soldiers of this Regiment, many of them to fight in those great wars which have beset us since the Barracks were opened, and many, I regret to say, who have never returned. I think it is fitting for us to remember them today.
> I would like to say that soldiers who come from the West Riding of Yorkshire are finer than any I have known, and I say that honestly and sincerely. [28]

In two particulars the year 1963 was to end on a disappointing note. Throughout the year, the Regiment had managed to recruit only 90 adult and boy soldiers, although this was only a reflection of Army recruitment as a whole. For some years Lieutenant General Sir Roger Bower, and his predecessor, Lieutenant General Sir Harold Redman, had tried to ensure that when the Light Infantry Depot moved to Shrewsbury, and the RHQ was set up at Pontefract, it would be possible to establish 4th KOYLI HQ alongside the RHQ at Pontefract. Unfortunately this very worthy scheme came to nought for reasons that, at the time, appeared to lack logic and were overlaid with difficulties.

Although 1964 saw an increase in numbers for the Regular Battalion and the TA, there were still problems to be faced. The Regiment was top of the recruiting table, but regular recruits were now joining the Light Infantry Brigade and after training were posted to whichever Regiment was most in need at the time. By April, 4th KOYLI had 125 new recruits, despite large increases being made to the recruiting areas of the other West Riding TA battalions. At the annual camp, which was held for the second year in succession at Greenfield Camp, Garelochhead, over 400 volunteers (82%) attended, a fine achievement for the largest TA unit in the West Riding.

Yet another solution to the age-old problem of quickly reinforcing regular battalions in times of emergencies had been introduced in April 1962. The 'Ever Ready' TA soldiers were expected to train to such a level that they could quickly reinforce the Regular Army in the period between the start of an emergency and the arrival in the field of the main TA units. Exercise 'Travelman' began on 26 September 1964, when four men of 4th KOYLI left to join 1st Duke of Wellington's Regiment (DWR) for two weeks in BAOR, Germany. The exercise, which included both battalion and brigade strength attacks (with troops carried into action aboard APCs), was deemed a success by all who took part.

---

[1] Buglers of the SCLI, ferried out aboard a fire tender, greeted the arrival of the *Nevasa* at Gibraltar.

[2] The original name, Fort George, was changed to Terendak Camp to avoid any perceived imperial overtones.

[3] Gascoigne, Pte F. *'A' Company*. Memoir. Regt. Archive.

[4] *The Bugle*, 1962, Vol. 54. 3 p 9 The 'Wally' referred to was, of course, Major Gen Walter Walker.

[5] *Ibid*, Vol. 54.3 p 7

[6] Preston, Brig. R.St. C. Memoir. Regt. Archive.

[7] *The Bugle*, 1962 Vol. 54.3 p 6

[8] Pocock, Tom. *Fighting General*, Collins, 1973 p 127

[9] Pocock, Tom. *Fighting General*, op cit   p 135

[10] Following the defeat of the French at Dien Bien Fu, French Indo-China was divided at the 17th parallel into communist controlled North Vietnam and French influenced South Vietnam. The elections of 1956 were intended to lead towards a unification of the two halves of the country, but these were postponed by South Vietnam. Eventually the North decided to achieve unification by force.

[11] Fleming, Lt Col P.G. *Commentary on Operation 'Dirty Linen'. 5 –20 March 1963* (Summary) Memoir. Regt. Archive.

[12] Fleming, Lt Col P.G. *Border Surveillance From The River Baram, 28 March-20 April* Memoir. Regt. Archive.

[13] Fleming, Lt Col P.G. *Commentary on Operations in Sarawak by "Compo" Company, 1 KOYLI 27 April-23 May, 1963.*

[14] Lubok Antu is approximately 60 kilometres east of Tawai, and Batu Lingtan is some 25 kilometres south of Tawai.

[15] Fleming, Lt Col P.G. *Commentary on Operations in Sarawak by "Compo" Company, 1 KOYLI 27 April-23 May, 1963.*

[16] The name is used by Malays and Indonesians to refer to the whole of the island of Borneo. Politically, it only applies to that part of the island that is Indonesian.

[17] Fleming, Lt Col P.G. *Commentary on Operations in Sarawak by "Compo" Company, 1 KOYLI 27 April-23 May, 1963.*

[18] Preston, Brig. R.St. C. Memoir. Regt. Archive.

[19] *The Bugle*, 1964, Vol. 56.2 p 23 Account written by Pte J. Cunningham

[20] *Ibid*, Vol. 56. 2 p 23

[21] *Ibid*, Vol. 56. 2 p 18

[22] Fleming, Lt Col P.G. *Border Surveillance From The River Baram, 28 March-20 April* op cit

[23] *The Bugle*, 1964, Vol. 56.3 p 20

[24] *Ibid*, Vol. 56. 3 p 22

[25] *The Bugle*, 1962, Vol. 54.3 Colonel-in-Chief's Address to 4th KOYLI, Supplement to *The Bugle*

[26] *The Bugle*, 1963, Vol. 55.1 p 1 Notes by the Colonel of the Regiment – Lt Gen Sir Roger Bower.

[27] *Ibid*, Vol. 55.2 p 1

[28] *Ibid*, Vol. 55.2 p 21

8

Tidworth and Aden

'With Air Trooping, a Battalion does not "move" from one station to another. It slowly disintegrates as each plane leaves, re-assembling some two months later in its new station.'[1] As a direct consequence, 1st KOYLI left Malaya in September 1964 and, following an extended leave period, did not re-assemble until 1 December. Originally ordered to move to Aldershot, a change of plan by the Ministry of Defence sent the Battalion to Lucknow Barracks, Tidworth. The prospect of living in Tidworth, with its close proximity to the bracing air of Salisbury Plain, was not to everyone's liking. The 1st KOYLI had last occupied Lucknow Barracks just 30 years earlier, and during the intervening years it appeared there had been little exterior change to Tidworth.[2]

The role of the modern infantry battalion was entering a period of significant change, with one particular requirement, rapid deployment, having important and immediate implications for the Battalion. The possibility of becoming the 'Spearhead Battalion' in the New Year meant that clearly defined levels of physical fitness, individual skills, and tactical methods had to be attained as soon as possible. Cross-country runs every Tuesday afternoon and route marches on Thursdays were in sharp contrast to the slow pace needed to conserve energy in the heat and humidity of the Far Eastern jungle.

A change in the roster allowed a generous Christmas leave to be taken but, on 4 January 1965, intensive training resumed. An air mobility exercise, 'Olympic Torch', saw the Battalion loading vehicles, packing kit, checking documentation then moving through the Movement Control Check Point at Devizes before boarding aircraft of RAF Transport Command for a short flight. This test of the Battalion's ability to undertake its Strategic Reserve Commitment was completed satisfactorily; recent experience of cooperating with the RAF in the Far East obviously producing dividends.

The death of Sir Winston Churchill brought with it an opportunity to provide a detachment to line the route of his funeral procession. On Saturday 30 January, the detachment, under the command of Major A.C. Elcomb, and led by the Bugles and Band of 1st KOYLI, marched into Fleet Street to take up its position on either side of the route to be taken by the cortege. The Colours were uncased in Fleet Street, the Queen's Colour being carried by Lieutenant C.M.S. Kaye and the Regimental Colour by 2nd Lieutenant H.N.G. McLeod. Despite the short period available for polishing and drill (rifle exercises for State Funerals not featuring prominently in the normal rifle drill syllabus), the occasion proved to be a unique experience for all who took part, and a particular honour for the Regiment.

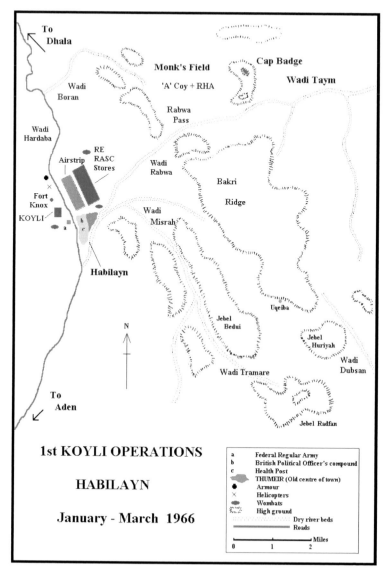

Map: 8. **Habilayn January – March 1966**
The area surrounding Habilayn and the airstrip.

On 4 February, 1st KOYLI became the Strategic Reserve Battalion, and, for the next six weeks, it had to be ready to fly to any trouble spot in the world at degrees of notice varying from 24 to 72 hours. To check its readiness, the Battalion held a mobilisation rehearsal on the very first day of this period. February also saw the introduction of the WOMBAT, a much lighter version of the Battalion 120 mm Anti Tank Gun; in addition, all ranks were required to re-train from the Light Machine Gun to the General Purpose Machine Gun (GPMG).

During exercise 'Rouse Stakes', which began on Salisbury Plain on 24 March, 'B' Company proved to be a very effective enemy, giving the rest of the Battalion, and 'B' Squadron, 5 Royal Tank Regiment, a stern test of their skills. At one point in the exercise a reconnaissance party consisting of Captain A.C.H. Bennett, Serjeant Denton, Corporal Stanton, and Privates Bouse and Sykes was given a brief, but unforgettable, experience. Arriving at what was believed to be the objective, the party suddenly came under live artillery fire. 'According to them, shells were bursting all round them (in reality they were only 200 yards away) and there was no need to teach them the "down, crawl, observe, fire"!!!' [3]

Whilst exercises could be exciting, the highlight of the period at Tidworth was the visit of Her Majesty, Queen Elizabeth the Queen Mother on 14 April. With the Battalion formed up in line on the square, Her Majesty inspected the front line and, much to the pleasure of all, said that she would like to inspect the second rank. On this occasion, one of the Yeomen Warders on duty on the parade ground was a veteran of the KOYLI, Company Serjeant Major J.P. Howson MM.[4] In her address to the Battalion Her Majesty commented on the apparent reversal in roles of the infantry and the cavalry.

> While the Infantry were accustomed to a more static life, the cavalry were often engaged in exciting forays against the enemy. Now I feel, the balance is much more even. Today, the cavalry operate to a great extent in their tanks and armoured cars in the mainlands of the world, and it is the Infantry who are able in a matter of hours to be in the far corners of the globe.[5]

Within days of these comments, the Battalion was indeed on the move, although not quite to the 'far corners of the globe'. Exercise 'Easter Lightning' began with 1st KOYLI being airlifted over a two-day period from airfields at Benson, Abingdon, and Colerne to Northern Ireland. The exercise required 5th Brigade to deal with an imaginary dissident uprising centred in the Antrim hills behind Belfast. The whole of 39th Brigade was employed in guarding vulnerable points and preventing riots, and the task for 5th Brigade was to search out the dissidents and neutralise them. This was to be achieved by active patrolling, direct attacks on large parties of the enemy (sometimes using air support), ambushes, cordon and searches, and roadblocks, all of which were standard infantry counter terrorist techniques. At the end of ten days, the dash and energy of the Battalion earned it the congratulations of the GOC Southern Command, Lieutenant General Sir Kenneth Darling KCB CBE DSO.

Elaborate celebrations for the 150th Anniversary of the Battle of Waterloo began in London on 12 June with a floodlit display on Horse Guards Parade by Colour parties and Bands drawn from those Regiments that had taken part in the battle. This was followed six days later by a memorial service on the battlefield at Hougoumont Farm (the Regiment was positioned close by on the day of the battle, 18 June 1815). The final event was a dinner at the Guildhall in London on 21 June attended by Major J.M.C. Hutton, Serjeant Burnet, Corporal Maddison and Private Grist.

After a period of nine months in the UK, 1st KOYLI was ordered abroad, destination, Aden. But within days of the departure of the advance party, and on the direct orders of the GOC, the Battalion was set one final test by 5th Brigade HQ. All ranks were to undertake a six-mile route march over part of Dartmoor, in full equipment and carrying personal weapons, the whole exercise to be completed in one hour. The Battalion accomplished this task successfully.

Fig: 45 Searchlight and trailer landed by helicopter on one of the highest buildings in Maalla, 1965.   *Regt Archive*

Orders for the unaccompanied nine-month tour to Aden had been confirmed in the spring of 1965, and 1st KOYLI flew out from Gatwick over the period 10 to 20 August. Uncertainty regarding the future of the Crown

Colony had been finally resolved when the British government announced that it intended to grant independence to the Aden Federation no later than 1968. The plan may have satisfied Whitehall, but it failed to meet with the approval of the population of the Federation, nor with their Yemeni neighbours. In the period leading up to the end of British rule, two rival factions – one sponsored by Egypt's President Nasser, the other a Marxist organisation – attempted to influence events by the usual terrorist means. The Battalion was about to face problems that would be similar to those it had faced in Malaya, Kenya, Cyprus, and Borneo; the only change would be the climate.

Tidworth in mid-August had been pleasantly warm, but on arrival in Aden the contrast was felt immediately one stepped off the plane. Even for those who could remember the previous short tour, the burning heat of Aden in high summer came as a shock. Nevertheless, the Battalion deployed quickly, smoothly, and purposefully. From its base at Radfan Camp, 1st KOYLI was responsible for the Port of Aden and was required to provide companies for Internal Security, Guard duties, and Reserve; 'C' Company's Reconnaissance Platoon being used for 'special duties'. The Internal Security Company, based in the naval shore establishment of *HMS Sheba* in Tawahi, was in overall control. Mobile and foot patrols were deployed and, when requested, the 'Road Block' Platoon could swiftly bring the bustling traffic to a complete standstill while searches were made for arms, ammunition, and likely suspects. So called 'Third Dimension' parties occupied strategic positions on balconies and rooftops in Maalla and Tawahi from where they could spot curfew breakers, and judge the direction of hostile fire by sound or muzzle flashes. The inhabitants were much amazed by the use of a helicopter to place a searchlight onto a dominant roof above the Maalla road from where observers could locate grenade throwers, or anyone intent on subversive activities.[6] A detailed roster ensured that everyone performed, endured, or enjoyed whatever duty was required of them.

The knowledge that British forces would leave the colony in 1968 to some extent compromised the usual practice of trying to win the hearts and minds of the local inhabitants. Even though 1st KOYLI had been dealing with similar problems for many years past, it was still difficult to accept certain situations.

> When there is an incident, the victims are usually innocent passers-by who have no stake in either the perpetuation of colonialism or the struggle for 'liberation'; a Somali woman and Arab children are typical examples. It is at these times that one is inclined to become angry and to wish that the grenadier or gunman were within easy reach. It is difficult to acquire the detachment of the professional policeman within a few weeks.[7]

The task of the security forces in Aden was made more problematical by the presence of a large number of service families, especially children. Guards were provided for daily journeys to and from schools, as well as protecting wives visiting vulnerable locations such as the NAAFI shops and cinemas. On one occasion, a mobile patrol in Tawahi discovered the dangerous back streets crowded with British tourists from a visiting cruise liner. Most of the tourists were women and, when told their safety could not be guaranteed if they remained there, one responded by asking, "What yer carrying guns fer?" Foot patrols were often involved in 'Snap, Seal and Frisk' operations that needed to be carried out at speed if concealed weapons were to be discovered on those caught in the sealed off area.

To facilitate the movement of the colony's security forces, and improve the trade route from Aden to Dhala, 73 Squadron RE was building a road. The chief hazard to the free flow of traffic on this road was the laying of mines, and the best counter measure was to have it covered with tarmac as soon as possible. Intent on deterring the engineers from completing this task, dissident tribesmen took to sniping at them, which prompted the engineers not only to shoot back, but also to request the provision of heavier defensive weapons. Mortars were used against the tribesmen, and in due course, 'A' Company's mortar section took over from the mortar section of 1st Royal Sussex Regiment. The RE camp at Al Milah, at the foot of the Radfan Hills, had well sandbagged mortar sangars at each corner from where the guns covered every approach road. The nightly curfew outside the camp allowed unrestricted fire to be brought down on any likely targets, and the occasional round from a borrowed Wombat added greatly to the overall effect. On one occasion, a night attack by a group of about 12 tribesmen was driven off by combined mortar and Wombat fire; the dissidents having one killed and at least one wounded.

A reconnaissance party, consisting of Majors M.R. Wade, D.M.F. Rouse and Captains M.J.A. Wilson and A.R. Aird, flew to Mukeiras, 7,000 feet up in the mountains and approximately two miles from the border with Yemen. (The camp at Mukeiras had first been sited and occupied by 'D' Company, 1st KOYLI in 1955.) Their purpose was to arrange for 'B' Company, 1st KOYLI, to take over from 'A' Company, 1st Royal Sussex Regiment. Unfortunately the planned move was cancelled, but this did not prevent the party visiting the local market. Here they moved, unarmed, among tribesmen who were themselves armed to the teeth, and the group was reminded of the British Army's history in the region when it found a number of army jackets for sale – one in almost pristine condition having formerly belonged to 2nd Somerset L.I. circa 1913. The local butcher's shop had meat on display that was almost obscured by swarms of flies, but possibly most curious of all was the sight of the permanent RAF mail corporal who spoke fluent Arabic and carried out his duties dressed in a shirt and Arab dhats.

On 10 September, 14 Platoon, commanded by Lieutenant C.M.J. Deedes, left Aden for the island of Perim, which lies at the southern end of the Red Sea, almost blocking the exit to the Indian Ocean. Four miles long and two miles wide, the island was home to some 300 inhabitants of mixed Arab and African origin. The role of the British troops was to guard the 20 or so Europeans, and their families, who operated the island's relay station; the station having been attacked by Yemenis some 18 months earlier. Platoons from Aden carried out two-week tours on the island and, as night duties were the main task, the daytime could be given over to swimming, fishing, and relaxation.

Also in September the actions of one officer of 'D' Company deserved, and was given, due recognition. The citation for the award of the Queen's Commendation read,

> On the morning of 29 September, 1965, 2Lt. H.N.G. McLeod took charge at the scene after an Army vehicle crashed and caught fire in Maalla Straight. At considerable personal risk he unloaded weapons, radios and magazines of ammunition from the blazing vehicle. Ammunition was exploding around him and he well knew that the vehicle load included a box of grenades. 2Lt McLeod did not leave the vehicle until further explosions and a flaring up of the fire made further recovery work impossible.[8]

On 3 October it was the turn of 7 Platoon and 'D' Company's mortar section to move to Al Milah to provide protection for the RE building the Aden-Dhala road.

> During the first five days we were given a right royal welcome. One small attack and one rather large one. In the second one most of the local village turned out to support the dissidents until a GPMG gave the Naib's (local headman) fort a fairly long burst. However, the next morning all the locals were laughing and smiling and obviously considered that the previous night had been very entertaining.[9]

Christmas saw a change to the format of the usual celebrations. The formation of an Officers, WOs and Serjeants Platoon for Christmas Day allowed 200 members of the Battalion to accept invitations from dozens of service families in Maalla and Tawahi to enjoy Christmas dinner with them. Unfortunately, for 'D' Company, which was on detachment with 45 Royal Marine Commando at Habilayn, Christmas celebrations had to be delayed.

Towards the end of December, the Reconnaissance Platoon took to the sea carrying out raids on unsuspecting Arab boats in the constant search for illegal arms, ammunition, or hidden terrorists. On 21 January 1966, 1st KOYLI handed over responsibility for internal security in Aden to 1st Welsh

Guards and, on 28 January, moved 'up country' on the next phase of its tour.

A fleet of buses set out northwards carrying Lieutenant Colonel Saltonstall and 1st KOYLI along the road to Habilayn. The new area of responsibility being the size of Somerset, it was thought necessary to reinforce the Battalion by placing No 2 Company, 1st Coldstream Guards, under its command. Against a background of sporadic attacks by dissident tribesmen – many of who were in the pay of President Nasser's Egyptian government, and rarely needed an excuse to shoot at anyone whether friend or foe – the Battalion set up its HQ at the airfield at Habilayn.[10] The Battalion's objectives were to keep the Aden-Dhala road open and free from mines or ambushes; prevent the disruption of road building in the area; guard the airfield; maintain the peace, and harass the dissidents by ambushes and helicopter-borne mobile operations.

Fig: 46 The 'Cap Badge' picket overlooked the Wadi Taym, 1966.   *P. Shield*

The airfield was an extremely busy one dealing with a constant flow of supplies of every kind, and numerous visitors of varying importance. In and around the airfield was the defence company and the Coldstream Guards company while to the north and east of the road was another rifle company in the Monks Field area. Pickets were placed on four of the highest hills overlooking the airfield while, further north platoon sized pickets on nearby mountaintops, 'Hotel Ten' and 'Cap Badge', guarded the route to the Wadi Taym. Rifle platoons provided 'aggressive defence' for the RE camp at Al

Milah, and were assisted in this by a troop of Saladin armoured cars of 4/7th Dragoon Guards and the mortar section of No 1 Company, Coldstream Guards. 'B' Company, under the command of Captain Tinson, was detached to Dhala and came under the command of 5th Battalion Federal Regular Army (FRA). Because of its previous experience with 45 Royal Marine Commando, 'D' Company had the more interesting role of Mobile Company and was given the task of patrolling the surrounding area on foot, and occasionally being airlifted by helicopter to investigate reported incidents.

Fig: 47 'B' Company on a training march. L:R. Pte Street, Cpl Mellors, Pte Curtiss, Sjt Moss, Ptes Alder, Healey, Mountain, Wroe and Brant, 1966   *Regt Archive*

The poor condition of the roads made the laying of mines a relatively easy task for the local dissidents, which, together with sniping from the surrounding hills, meant that all vehicles had to travel in convoy. Each movement was treated as a military operation and normally had an armoured car escort, piquets on the high ground; artillery and mortar cover together with air surveillance. As a result, daytime operations by the tribesmen were rare – superior firepower, helicopter cover, and the threat of attack from RAF Hunter strike aircraft being sufficient to deter all but the foolhardy. At night, however, most camps came under varying degrees of rifle, machine gun, rocket propelled grenades, and sometimes, medium mortar fire. Usually, the reply was left to the GPMGs and the mortar teams from their sandbagged sangars, but occasionally the company at Monk's Field was assisted by the 105 mm howitzers of the supporting battery

155

provided by the senior gunner battery in the Regular Army – Chestnut Troop, 1st Royal Horse Artillery. The command post of the defence company at Habilayn, known as Fort Knox, had an observation post at the top called the bridge. (This is not to be confused with a similar command post at Dhala administered by 45 Royal Marine Commando.)[11] The Royal Marines were thought to have begun the original construction, but many units had subsequently added to its design and when 1st KOYLI arrived, all defensive fire from Habilayn was controlled from the bridge.

> Each night at 18:50 hrs a rehearsal was held. Major Cowley pacing the bridge with a cigar between his lips peering out 'to sea' issuing orders, "15. DF X3, one round normal fire," "T3, DF 21 fire", "No 2 Sangar DF 10", " No 3 Sangar DF 16", "12E fire DF 4", "12F three rounds 2 in smoke to the north-east". Starting off with small arms fire and, rather like a conductor of an orchestra, bringing in the GPMGs and 2 in mortars, and building up to a great crescendo with the 81 mm mortars, the Wombat, the Saladins, the Saracens and perhaps the 105 mm howitzers from Monk's Field. The '1812 Overture' had nothing on this.[12]

The true identity of the original constructors of the bridge must be questioned in the light of the following description of some of the activities that took place on the bridge.

> The bridge must have been constructed by the Welsh Guards for Major Cowley had great difficulty in seeing over the parapet and had to sit on a high stool to achieve any success in controlling fire. Cpl Forsyth, manning the defence net, achieved all round vision by standing on six old A41 batteries. Capt Charlesworth was the only one who had no difficulty at all. The bridge has seen some rare sights when the camp has been attacked. The Commander Area West in a sarong, the Commanding Officer in a stunning pair of blue silk pyjamas peering into the night with bullets whirling overhead, and Major Cowley calling down defensive fire with one hand in his pocket (holding up the trousers which he had hastily put on).[13]

Friendly fire, that scourge which is seemingly impossible to eradicate from military action, can be visited upon the most diligent and well-trained units.

> During this time 'up country' we accidentally engaged one of our own patrols with mortar fire. Lieutenant C. Kaye was the patrol leader. We suffered a handful of minor casualties. I remember visiting them in the hospital at RAF Khormaksar where they were nearly all obliged to lie on their stomachs as they, having been

prone on the ground during the incident, had received most of the mortar fragments in their backsides.[14]

In late February, the Colonel of the Regiment, Lieutenant General Bower, visited the Battalion and toured around the various company locations 'up country'. Lieutenant General Bower was struck by the 'close similarity between this country and that of the Khyber Pass and also the Mohmand region of the North West Frontier, with which many old 2nd Battalion members will be familiar.'[15]

Fig: 48 'A' Company going up country from Radfan Camp, 1965.   *P. Shield*

In the first week of March, the Battalion returned to its internal security duties on the streets of Maalla and Tawahi. With growing encouragement from external sources, and regular supplies of arms, the various groups of terrorists continued their internecine assassinations and attacks on the security forces. A number of cordon and search operations were undertaken in a densely populated area of Maalla where it was suspected that both terrorist and arms dumps had been hidden. In each instance, once the cordons were in place the flushing and screening operations inevitably produced the usual quota of suspects who were duly processed by the police and members of the Special Branch.

While the majority of the Battalion returned to their internal security duties, a platoon of 1st KOYLI finally arrived at Mukeiras for a short period on detachment. No 6 Platoon, 'B' Company, spent three weeks in this remote outpost on the Yemeni border with the local garrison, 1st FRA, and a gunner detachment. During this time, little happened to disturb the peace of 6 Platoon, if one discounts the discharge of four magazines of LMG tracer over their camp by the FRA as they celebrated the festival of Id. Nevertheless, there was a constant threat from dissidents and, six miles away, over the border in the Yemeni town of Badar, there was a whole company of Egyptians with two large Russian guns each capable of putting shells into Mukeiras.

In June 1965, when the battalion was at Tidworth, it had taken part in the production of a training film dealing with 'Tactical Air Transport Operations'. Designed to show an infantry battalion of the Strategic Reserve responding to a sudden emergency and being airlifted to Aden, the Battalion was the obvious choice to be the featured battalion. 'A' Company was chosen to take the major part, and filming had taken place in the barracks at Devizes and at RAF Lyneham. In mid-March 1966, the film crew arrived at Habilayn and filming continued there, on the Dhala airstrip, Khormaksar airfield in Aden, and in Radfan Camp.

Fig: 49 L/Cpl Loveday and part of 'D' Company, waiting to be taken by helicopter from Habilayn airstrip, 1966.   *P. Shield*

The Battalion took part in a far more satisfying airlift operation when it returned to the UK at the end of its Aden tour. Between 11 and 18 May, 1st KOYLI handed over its duties in the Port of Aden to 1st Battalion Cameronians (Scottish Rifles), groups leaving at intervals for the UK. On arrival at Gatwick, each group was processed and then departed for a well-deserved leave for the next six weeks before reassembling at Tidworth.

One small group, however, decided they would forego the comfort of a VC10 flight from Aden to the UK for the excitement of a six-week overland trek in two army Land Rovers. For political and security reasons the MOD suggested that Captain R.G.H. Chetwynd Stapylton, 2nd Lieutenant A.H. Penny, and Privates Spencer, Driver, Woods and Smith, begin their journey from Bahrain rather than trying to leave Aden via the Yemen, or any of the other Arab states of the South Aden Peninsular. The party successfully completed its journey and thoroughly enjoyed visiting the ancient city of

Petra in southern Jordan, Jerusalem, Damascus, Istanbul, Athens and Rome, before embarking on a 900 mile, 26 hour trip to the port of Ostend.

The Depot and 4th Territorial Battalion

Towards the end of 1964, 4th KOYLI's 'Ever Ready' Platoon had over 50 members. With the news that the TA could now enlist 17 year olds, prospects for future recruitment looked promising. The Battalion's skills were on display at the Divisional Weapons Meeting in the autumn when it won the Divisional Team Championship for the third year running; this success was repeated the following year with the addition of the Young Soldiers Team Championships, the Open Individual, and Young Soldier's Individual Competitions adding to its haul of trophies.

In the spring of 1965, the MOD finally decided that the Barracks and playing fields at Pontefract would be disposed of. Attempts by the Colonel of the Regiment to discover the MOD's intentions regarding the future of the Territorial Army failed to elicit any firm decision. The government of the day, maintaining the practice of governments down the ages, was seeking to make substantial savings in its defence budget. Every peacetime government since the Haldane reforms of 1908 had faced the same insoluble problem; how to reduce the inevitable time lapse between a declaration of war, and the moment when the Territorial forces were sufficiently trained to take the field. The KOYLI's representatives of the latest stopgap solution, the 'Ever Readies', spent one week at the 1965 annual camp, followed by two weeks training with 1st DWR stationed in Osnabruck, Germany. While this level of training was useful, it did not completely solve the problem of achieving a speedy integration in times of emergency. Another worrying aspect of the problem was later highlighted when in

Fig: 39 4th KOYLI on exercise at Thetford camp, 1965. L:R. -?-, Major J.M.P. Naylor, Sjt Oates, Lt T.J. Crowther   *Regt Archive*

September a fitness exercise (a country hike of 17 miles over the moors of upper Wharfedale) was arranged. Of the fifty 4th KOYLI 'Ever Readies', only 28 volunteered, and of these only 17 arrived on the day. Not one of the participants completed the course.

The full extent of the government's thinking was outlined in a White Paper published in December 1965 by the Defence Secretary, Dennis Healey. In bald terms, it suggested that a Territorial Army trained to fight a conventional war in Europe was no longer needed in the current nuclear age. Furthermore, it claimed that, in the event of a nuclear attack the Territorial Army would be unable to provide assistance to the civil authorities commensurate with its current costs. Consequently, the government decided to replace the TA, and the Army Emergency Reserve (the Ever Readies), with an 'Army Volunteer Reserve', which would supplement the Regular Army Reserve and reinforce the Regular Army in time of need. Almost before the ink was dry on the White Paper, the government had a change of mind and proposed the formation of a lightly armed force for home defence. Given the two main planks of the White Paper's argument for disbanding the TA, the question arose, just what role could this lightly armed home defence force perform in the event of a nuclear attack? The passing of the Reserve Forces Act in 1966 was the first step towards the reorganisation, reduction, and near destruction of the Army's reserve forces. It may have been with some sense of relief that, on 18 March 1966, Lieutenant Colonel Wilson handed over command of 4th KOYLI to Lieutenant Colonel S. McL. Richardson whose unenviable task it would be to guide 4th KOYLI TA through the coming changes.

On 12 October 1966, the Council of Colonels of the Light Infantry met at the Royal Military Academy, Sandhurst, where once again the topic for discussion was the creation of a Large Light Infantry Regiment. It was unanimously agreed that nothing was to be gained from disrupting the present system of close association between the Light Infantry Regiments, but a review of the situation could be made in the light of future developments.

For the Reserve Forces, the die had been cast. Commencing 1 April 1967, the Territorial Army Volunteer Reserve Battalion (TAVR IIA), was to be known as the Light Infantry Volunteers, and would have its HQ and HQ Company at Shrewsbury. The rifle companies of the Light Infantry Volunteers would be located at: 'A' Company, Truro; 'B' Company, Wakefield; 'C' Company, Hereford, and 'D' Company, Durham. On the same date, 4th (Territorial) Battalion King's Own Yorkshire Light Infantry (TAVR III) would be formed under the command of Lieutenant Colonel S. McL. Richardson TD. The 4th (Territorial) Battalion KOYLI was to have one company at Pontefract, one at Dewsbury, and its HQ and HQ Company at the Wakefield drill hall, which it would share with 'B' Company (Yorkshire) Light Infantry Volunteers. 'B' Company (Yorkshire) The L I Volunteers was to be under the command of Major C.G. Delany TD. The organisation of the new reserve battalions and their companies, and the ease with which they were brought into existence, were developments that gave the Regular Army much food for thought.

---

[1] *The Bugle,* 1956, Vol. 56.3 p 14

[2] This opinion, recorded in *The Bugle,* may have been that of Cpl Mycock, a medical orderly who had joined 1st KOYLI on the last day of 1936, and did his basic training at Tidworth. After 28 years service (not all of which was with the KOYLI), and surviving the infamous retreat with 2nd KOYLI in Burma, Cpl Mycock left the Battalion for civilian life in January 1965.

[3] *The Bugle,* 1965, Vol. 57.2 p 19

[4] CSM Howson served with 2nd KOYLI in Burma and was a survivor of the retreat to India in 1942.

[5] *The Bugle,* 1965, Vol. 57.2 pp 15/16 Address by the Colonel-in Chief, KOYLI to the 1st KOYLI, Tidworth, 14 April 1965.

[6] Maalla (current spelling Ma'alla) was the native harbour, Tawahi (current spelling At-Tawahi) the business section, and Crater the old commercial quarter.

[7] *Ibid,* Vol. 57.3 pp 17/18

[8] *The Bugle,* 1966, Vol. 58.1 p 16

[9] *Ibid,* Vol. 58.1 p 23

[10] Nasser had been elected President of Egypt in June 1956.

[11] The camp at Dhala, which was under the command of 45 Royal Marine Commando, was shaped very much like a ship with the Bridge being located near the centre. 'B' Company maintained the tradition of using naval terms, thus, Light Infantrymen could be heard referring to the galley, or the heads, a foc'sle, and request men and defaulters instead of levee. However, the adoption of a suggestion that the sangars be called 'turrets' was rejected outright.

[12] *The Bugle,* 1966, Vol. 58.1 p 28

[13] *Ibid,* Vol. 58. 1 p 28

[14] Makepeace-Warne, Maj-Gen A. Memoir. Regt. Archive.

[15] *Ibid,* Vol. 58. 1 p 1

9

Tidworth – Berlin

The Last Post

When 1st KOYLI reassembled at Tidworth in June 1966, after its nine-month tour in Aden, it learned that the next move would be an accompanied tour to Berlin in the spring of 1967; a decision that was greeted with some enthusiasm. On 24 May, the CO, Lieutenant Colonel Saltonstall, was succeeded by Lieutenant Colonel A.C. Elcomb; only one of a number of changes that would take place that year. On 8 March, Colonel M.A.C.P. Kaye relinquished his Honorary Colonelcy of 4th KOYLI, and was succeeded by Colonel H.E. Barker, and on 18 March, the 4th Battalion's CO, Lieutenant Colonel Wilson handed over command to Lieutenant Colonel S. McL. Richardson TD.

On Minden Day, 1966, Major General C. J. Deedes succeeded Lieutenant General Sir Roger Bower as Colonel of the Regiment. Possibly no other regiment of the British Army could boast of having both father and son as their colonels, both Generals, and with a third generation of two sons serving in the Regiment.

In mid-October, the Battalion spent two weeks in night training at Stanford in Norfolk. Turning night into day added an extra twist to the usual map reading exercises, although navigation using the stars was considered by some to be the exclusive province of the padre since, 'He should know, it's his area.' In November, the Battalion visited Sennybridge, on the edge of the Brecon Beacons National Park, which had been chosen as the location for field firing training. The facilities at Sennybridge were excellent, 'D' Company even managed to carry out a company attack, and the rain, bogs and regular soakings failed to dampen the general enthusiasm for the exercise. What was not appreciated by anyone was the return journey to Tidworth. The rifle companies visited Sennybridge one at a time, and each made the 140-mile return journey on foot. (Actually the march was only 113 miles, the remaining distance being completed in three-ton lorries.) When 'A' Company returned, the second day's 43-mile march was completed in gale force winds that blew the rain horizontally.

> The actual passage across the Severn Bridge was dramatic in the extreme. The wind howled and roared through the slender steel structure making the suspension rods swing violently a foot out of true and setting the bare metal pedestrian pavement shuddering and vibrating. Two hundred feet below the Severn crashed in a flurry of broken white water and line after line of breakers extended seawards into the gathering afternoon gloom.¹

162

In early December, the Battalion was allotted five Wessex helicopters for company training. Given good communications, the ability of these aircraft to move small groups of infantrymen quickly and efficiently to the scene of operations was readily appreciated. Though some groups needed to hone their night techniques (pick up and landing points often resembling Piccadilly Circus), those who had used the Wessex in the Radfan found their skills and experience particularly valuable.

One week after returning from Christmas leave the Battalion undertook a ten-mile forced march, much to the regret of those who had over indulged during the festive period. Support platoons also had an opportunity to use the Sennybridge facilities and were lucky in that it did not snow during their two-week stay. In February, the Annual Inspection took a more modern and enlightened form than in previous years. Each company was allotted a different task – tactical platoon moves, battle efficiency tests, and preparation of men, vehicles, and freight for transportation by air. Each exercise came under the detailed scrutiny of the Brigade Commander who pronounced himself well satisfied with what he had seen.

During the March exercise 'Stardust', the Battalion acted as a dissident rebel guerrilla group, which the rest of 5th Brigade was ordered to eliminate. The absence of foliage on Salisbury Plain, and the provision of 34 transport helicopters for the Brigade, meant that concealment was a particularly tricky problem for the KOYLI guerrillas. 'B'Company specialised in lying low during the day, only ambushing and attacking at night. 'A' and 'D' Companies also harassed their opponents by night, but never offered themselves for direct attack, and were so successful that 5th Brigade's final dawn attack was launched against thin air. The Brigade was given a realistic and stern test of its counter insurgency techniques by a battalion that had learned much in its forays overseas; a fact that was much appreciated at Brigade and Divisional level. Before leaving for Germany, the Divisional commander, Major General A.J. Deane-Drummond, told Lieutenant Colonel Elcomb that 1st KOYLI was the best battalion in the Division; praise indeed since the Division included the Parachute Brigade.

The transfer to Berlin took place in April 1967. The Battalion occupied Montgomery Barracks, Kladow, considered by many to be the best barracks in West Berlin. Hemmed in between the Havel lake and the border between West Berlin and the Russian Zone of East Germany (about one quarter of the barrack's perimeter fence formed the boundary between the British sector of Berlin and Russian Zone), 1st KOYLI's HQ was some 13 miles from the centre of the city. One hundred miles to the east of the main BAOR forces, most British soldiers enjoyed their period of duty in West Berlin with its comfortable barracks, plenty of opportunities for sports, and all the attractions of a modern cosmopolitan city.

The main duties of the Battalion were little changed since the previous tour in 1953, and fell into two main categories – routine guard and observation, and regular ceremonial. The daily routine consisted of patrolling the boundary between the Allied and Soviet sectors, and demonstrating the Allies' right of unlimited access to East Berlin. As in the 1953-54 tour, the Battalion was equipped with Ferret scout cars which, together with the ubiquitous Land Rovers, were used to patrol the wire border, a journey of almost 22 miles that could take as long as three and a half hours on a busy day. A further example of the Allies' insistence on their right to freedom of movement was the British Military Train. Each morning an engine and seven coaches, each with one occupant, left West Berlin bound for Brunswick in West Germany. Guarded by one officer and four soldiers, the train returned each night, but its journey was regularly interrupted by the Russian's insistence on carrying out various checks. A regular charade took place at Marienborn station where, following the usual formalities, the Russian CO often conducted an unauthorised exchange of anything from postage stamps, or fishhooks to newspapers.

The Battalion was required to take its turn in providing a 27 strong platoon to guard the 73 year-old Rudolph Hess, the only prisoner remaining in Spandau Prison. Externally the building continued to present an aura of impressive strength, but once through the huge doors it was obviously in a state of terminal decay. Only one floor of the four- storey main building was in use, and most of the windows in the unused parts were missing. Large mounds of fallen masonry, plaster, and general rubble were to be seen everywhere, and the soldiers guarding Spandau's only prisoner could see little point to the whole exercise. ' "Let me give him a ladder sir," is one of many expressions that illustrated their feelings for this guard duty'. [2]

The ability to mount impeccable military parades was the duty of all units in the former German capital, which, during the post war years had developed a critical eye for such ceremonial. Having only recently arrived, 1st KOYLI was spared more than a token involvement in the 1967 Allied Forces Day Parade, but 'A' and 'D' Companies were called upon to provide two guards for a very long, slow, and dignified piece of ceremonial for the Queen's Official Birthday Parade in June.

In the mid 1960s, the British economy had entered yet another period of crisis. During talks in June 1967 between the Prime Minister, Harold Wilson, and the American President, Lyndon Johnson, the President agreed to assist the British economy, on condition that Britain maintained a presence east of Suez. Wilson accepted but, despite American help, the economic problems persisted and the government was forced to consider further reductions in public spending. In addition, in June of that year the Ministry of Defence announced its plans for a further reorganisation of the Army. The most important change involving the KOYLI was the coming together of the Light Infantry Brigade and the Royal Green Jackets to form the Light Division. Precise details of the changes were not made public, but the new pattern for the Territorial Army, which had come into operation on 1 April that year, gave a strong clue to what the future might hold for the Regular Army.

On 10 June, 'B' Company LI Volunteers joined the LI Volunteer Battalion for its first camp, which was held at Sennybridge. During the two weeks, the Volunteers carried out the usual field firing, night firing, night patrol and defence exercises, but were also introduced to a number of activities that were new to reserve forces. Anti-terrorist cordon and search drills were carried out, and a helicopter airlift into battle of almost the whole Battalion was an experience that few thought they would ever have.

During the last week in July, 4th KOYLI began its annual camp at Hornsea. Following the reorganisation, the first camp was to last only eight days, but it was appropriate that on this occasion it should coincide with Minden Day. At the traditional ceremonial parade, Lieutenant General Sir Geoffrey Musson, KCB, CBE, DSO, GOC Northern Command, took the salute. In the second week, a 24-hour exercise ended with an assault that was watched by the Parliamentary Under Secretary of State for Defence (Army), Mr James Boyden: the helicopter airlift of casualties from the cliff top and their transfer into waiting rescue craft being the highlight of the whole exercise.[3]

On 15 July, 1st KOYLI began a three-week period at Sennelager where it completed a full programme of field firing exercises. Minden Day provided the opportunity for the whole Battalion to travel from Sennelager to visit the Minden battlefield. At the annual ceremony, held by the local dignitaries at the Minden memorial a little way north of the town, the Regiment was represented by Lieutenant Colonel Elcomb who laid a wreath of bay, laurel and white roses, the full Bugle Platoon sounding Last Post and Reveille.

Fig: 51 Pte Lloyd and Pte Matthews (driver) on a stretch of the Berlin border.   *Regt Archive*

While the Battalion was at Sennelager, a number of soldiers from 'D' Company were able to have a short period of attachment to other Allied units stationed in Germany. Private Sanderson and Lance Corporal Walker (Bugles) found the pay scales of the 509th US Airborne Battalion were to be envied, but the American's constant desire to shake off army life, and 'being woken up each day at 04:30 hours!' proved to be a decided disadvantage to joining them. The spotlessly clean barracks of the 214th German Panzer Brigade was little compensation for Private Wilkinson and Private Matthews (Recce), and the ghastly food persuaded Wilkinson that, 'I don't think I could last two weeks on that food!' The Danish Life Guards appeared to Privates Richmond and Dodson to be using old World War Two kit. Despite being the King of Denmark's palace guard, they seemed to accept that compared with the ordinary British soldier, they were only amateurs. Although the centre of attraction with his stories of active service in Aden, Private Richmond said, 'it was good to get back to a spring bed and good regular conner'.[4]

Returning from Sennelager, the Assault Pioneers were given the task of guiding the Battalion through a two-week Watermanship training course. Progressing from basic safety rules to using paddles then engines, each company carried out an assault across the Havel and attacked the beach at Schildhorn, much to the surprise of the Berliners who were sun bathing there. The construction of rafts proved to be a far more challenging task.

Fig: 52 Berlin Tattoo, 1968   *P. Shield*

When one of the engines of 'A' Company's Class 5 raft failed, it spun round in a circle, collided with an improvised raft and soon began to sink. Fortunately, the Anti-Tank Platoon crew managed to jump clear before the raft and its load of Unimog (German four-wheel drive vehicle) and anti-tank gun disappeared beneath the waves. A REME recovery unit managed to locate the wreck and retrieved the equipment before it settled too far into the mud of the Havel.

The Berlin Tattoo, a bi-annual British event that involved more troops than either the Royal Tournament or the Edinburgh Tattoo, took place in late September in the huge Olympic Stadium. The Tattoo was usually organised by the DAAG of the Berlin Infantry Brigade, and fate had decreed that Major J.M.C. Hutton, KOYLI, would be assigned to that post in 1967. Major Hutton was fortunate in having the assistance of Captain J.M. Parker, a very able young cavalry officer, and Lieutenant Colonel 'Jiggs' Jaegar, Musical Director of the Irish Guards and senior director of music of the Brigade of Guards – and formerly of the KOYLI. The 600-strong massed bands, under the direction of Colonel Jaegar, accompanied three major displays, the finale being Captain Parker's fictitious Napoleonic battle, acted out to the accompaniment of the 1812 Overture. Sadly, as Major Hutton later recounted in *The Bugle*, 'Fate dogged us'. On the morning of the first performance, the wind blew down the wooden effigy of Moscow: fortunately, it was not too badly damaged and was successfully re-erected. Persistent rain that week turned the centre of the stadium into a quagmire and, at the opening of the final performance, a huge Union Jack (weighing nearly half-a-ton) held aloft by an American helicopter, broke free and descended onto a small section of the crowd injuring about nine people, one fatally.[5] Despite these behind the scenes difficulties, the Tattoo was warmly received by the huge crowd, which included a party from the Regimental Association that was paying a visit to the Battalion that week.

The Ministry of Defence finally published its plans for the formation of the Light Infantry within the framework of the new Light Division. The new regiment was to be formed on 10 July 1968, the day that Sir John Moore assumed command of the Light Brigade at Shorncliffe in 1803. The four Regular battalions of the Light Infantry Brigade would merge and form four new battalions to be called, 1st, 2nd 3rd and 4th Battalions, The Light Infantry. Initially the four battalions would be formed around the existing Regiments, 1st LI (SCLI), 2nd LI (KOYLI), 3rd LI (KSLI), 4th LI (DLI), but these distinctions would disappear, especially in 1970 when the Light Infantry Regiment was to be reduced to three battalions. No change was made to the titles of the Light Infantry Volunteers, or the 4th (Territorial) Battalion KOYLI. The Light Division's HQ was to be established at Winchester (the Depot of the Royal Green Jackets), and the Light Infantry RHQ was to be formed at Sir John Moore Barracks, Shrewsbury. The KOYLI Regimental HQ would be renamed the Light Infantry Office (Yorkshire) and was to remain at Wakefield Road, Pontefract, where it continues to this day.

Once these decisions had been reached, it was not difficult to arrange the other stages of the operation in descending order of importance and priority. Her Majesty The Queen appointed Her Majesty Queen Elizabeth The Queen Mother as Colonel-in-Chief, The Light Infantry, and Her Royal Highness Princess Alexandra as Deputy Colonel-in-Chief. The Colonel Commandant of the Light Division was to be Lieutenant General Sir Anthony Read KCB, CBE, DSO, and the Colonel, The Light Infantry, General Sir Geoffrey Musson KCB, CBE, DSO. The four battalions each provided a Deputy Colonel, Major General C.L. Firbank CB, CBE, DSO, DL (Somerset and Cornwall), Major General C.J. Deedes OBE, MC (Yorkshire), Brigadier A.J. Hardy CBE, (Shropshire), and Major General A.H.G. Ricketts CBE, DSO, DL (Durham). Each of the existing regiments was to have ten selected battle honours on both the Regimental and the Queen's Colour, the following being selected for the KOYLI –

Regimental Colour: Minden; Corunna; Fuentes D'Onor; Pyrenees; Nivell; Orthes; Pegu; Ali Masjid; Burma, 1885-87; Modder River.

Queen's Colour: Le Cateau; Ypres 1914, '15.'17,'18; Cambrai 1917, '18; Havrincourt; Norway, 1940; Fontenay Le Pesnil; Argoub Sellah; Sicily, 1943; Salerno; Burma 1942.

The Regimental Motto 'Cede Nullis' to be embroidered in the centre design of the Regimental Colour.

The Regimental HQ would remain at Pontefract, and the Regimental Association was to continue and be administered from the Light Infantry Office (Yorkshire). The Regimental journal *The Bugle* would cease publication in the summer of 1968 and be replaced by the Light Infantry Journal *The Silver Bugle*. The regimental silver of all the Light Infantry regiments was to be redistributed.

Training away from the confines of Berlin, where frequent ceremonials and repetitive patrols were very limiting, was always welcome, but the idea of spending four weeks in November 1967 under canvas at Reinsehlen Camp and the Soltau Training area on Luneburg Heath caused some misgivings among the members of 1st KOYLI. As luck would have it, the weather was fine, dry, and very cold. It had been such a long time since the Battalion had worked with tanks, many members of the Battalion had little or no previous experience to draw upon. A squadron of the Royal Scots Greys provided the armoured excitement, but the ease with which the ground was churned up soon reduced many of the Soltau tracks to liquid mud. The activities of the Reconnaissance Platoon were badly affected, their Ferret scout cars finding the mud far too difficult to get through. Whilst there had been much hard marching throughout the training period, there was more once it had been completed. The Battalion was to march the 100 miles from Reinsehlen Camp to Helmstedt Station, on the border with the Russian Zone, from where a train would take it back to Berlin. The Battalion was divided into two groups: HQ, with 'B' and 'C' Companies marched off on 23 November, 'A' and 'D' Companies setting out the next day. Many sore feet were endured, and many traditional marching songs were revived, but few men dropped out. Sadly, during the march, a passing car struck three young soldiers from 'B' Company; Privates R.W. Limb and N.C. Wilson were both killed and Private Armitage was seriously injured.

During the first two months of 1968, winter skiing at Garmisch, southern Bavaria, Silberhutte in the Harz mountains, and over the tiny nursery slopes created in Berlin, proved to be a novelty for a battalion that had spent much of its time over the past years in hot climates.

Fig: 53 Allied Forces Day Parade, 1968.   *Regt Archive*

It had long been the practice that battalions in Berlin had two spells of training outside the city. At the instigation of the GOC, General Sir John Nelson, a third opportunity was to be given, but the scheme would differ from the norm in that each rifle company would spend the two weeks away, independent of the Battalion. 'A' Company was the first to go in March/April 1968, and travelled to the Eiffel region, on Germany's border with Luxemburg and France. Internal security exercises, escape and evasion exercises, ambushes, and cooperation with other units, all formed part of the two weeks training undergone by each company in its turn.

The morale of the 'B' (Yorkshire) Company, Light Infantry Volunteers in Wakefield had been maintained during the winter months by the introduction of new equipment, and the prospects of closer ties to the new Light Infantry Regiment. The 4th KOYLI, who had assumed that the 1967 reorganisation had provided them with an assured future, discovered that this was not to be the case. Further government thinking had resulted in a decision to place the whole of the Territorial Army on a 'care and maintenance basis'. To ensure some form of comradeship, should the Battalion's existence be threatened in the future, an Officers' Club and a WO's and Serjeants' Club had been formed, and every soldier had been made a life member of the Regimental Association.

Vesting Day for the new regiment was 10 July 1968, but before this day arrived there was much to be done. The 1968 Allied Forces Day Parade, in which British, American, and French troops, plus their tanks and vehicles paraded through Berlin, took place on 18 May in torrential rain. At the Queen's Birthday Parade, Saturday 8 June, 1st KOYLI trooped its own Colour for the final time, with the CO mounted on a borrowed German police horse and the Colour Guard being drawn from representatives of all the companies. The Colour Party consisted of Lieutenant R.R. Saltonstall, Colour Serjeant Gale, and Serjeant Cohen, with Captain C.M.J. Deedes the parade adjutant and Regimental Serjeant Major Lee the parade RSM; Major S.P. Eller and Major J.A. Hare commanded the two guards, and Major General Bowes-Lyon took the salute.

Fig: 54 Vesting Day, 10 July, 1968.   *P. Shield*

As the RHQ in Pontefract prepared to make the necessary changes for the smooth transformation from KOYLI to Light Infantry, unwelcome visitors to the Regimental Museum, housed within the RHQ, stole items that were irreplaceable. Missing were Major C.A.L. Yate's, and Serjeant J.W. Ormsby's VC medals, together with two revolvers, Nazi daggers, and a number of other medals. Fortunately, by 14 June, the revolvers had been recovered, and three days later, both VC medals were returned by post: two men were later arrested and charged.

A pageant had been arranged for Vesting Day, which portrayed incidents from the history of all the regiments that were to be drawn together to form the Light Infantry. On the eve of the pageant fire destroyed part of the background set, nevertheless, on the day some 1,500 guests representing all sections of the British, American and French Garrison of Berlin, as well as prominent Berliners, assembled to witness the carefully prepared spectacle.

On receipt of the Army Board's decision to amalgamate the four Light Infantry Regiments, the Commanding Officer 1st KOYLI, Lieutenant Colonel Elcomb, spoke to the Battalion gathered in Montgomery Barracks, Berlin. After giving details of the forthcoming changes, Lieutenant Colonel Elcomb recalled the resentment and bitterness generated by the Cardwell reforms of 1881, which led to the officers of the 51st presenting the Regiment with a silver snuff box in the form of a coffin mounted on a gun carriage. He added that such a reaction must not be repeated when 1st KOYLI became the 2nd Battalion The Light Infantry. As far as he was concerned, 1st KOYLI was better than either the 51st or the 105th, and if 2nd LI were to be no better than 1st KOYLI, the fault would lie with those serving in that Regiment. On the last night, Lieutenant Colonel Elcomb's orders were carried out, and, no ceremony took place to mourn the passing of the Regiment. 'Not a drum was heard, not a funeral note.'[6]

> Every man had been issued with his new badge and, after dark, all notices and signs relating to the KOYLI were replaced with the 2nd LI signs.[7]

As darkness descended, more than two hundred years of Regimental history drew to a close. Whether fighting in Europe, or in the farthest corners of Empire, in peace and war the KOYLI could look back with pride on its service to Sovereign and Country. Two hundred years earlier, in July 1768, the 51st Regiment of Foot was in Dublin, Ireland, in the fifth year of a twelve-year period of peace. Anticipating a move under the Secretary at War's recently introduced system of relief for regiments, the platoons continued to practise the reduced number of evolutions required in loading and firing their muskets, an innovation that had recently been introduced in all infantry regiments. One hundred years earlier, the 51st were halfway through a six-month stay at Aldershot having returned from India the previous year. Fifty years earlier, in July 1918, the 2nd, 1/4th, 2/4th, 5th, 9th and 12th Battalions had weathered the storm of the German army's final assault on the Western Front and were preparing to launch their own offensives.

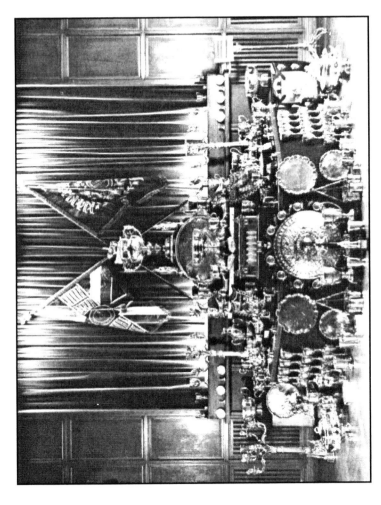

Fig: 55 Colours and Regimental Silver of 1st KOYLI

Regt Archive

These would see the defeat of the German army in the field, and bring about the signing of the Armistice on 11 November. Twenty-five years earlier, World War Two was at its height and, on 10 July 1943, 1st KOYLI and 53rd LAA (5th KOYLI) landed in Sicily, while 2/4th KOYLI and 57th LAA (5th KOYLI) re-equipped in North Africa before joining them in Italy. In England, 1/4th KOYLI and 94th LAA (8th KOYLI) trained for the invasion of France, and 2nd KOYLI and 149th RAC (7th KOYLI) trained in India for their planned return to the struggle against the Japanese.

The 23 years following the end of the Second World War had been for the majority of the British population years of peace. But for her armed forces, particularly the Army, 1968 was to be the only year to pass without a British soldier being killed on active duty.[8] As we have seen, the Regiment had sustained its share of men killed and wounded in the many actions in which it had been involved while serving overseas. The soldiers of The King's Own Yorkshire Light Infantry, whether Regular, National Service, or Territorial had, like their forebears from Minden to Malaya, done their duty. After 213 years, the final words must rest with Major C.W. Huxley who, writing in the last edition of *The Bugle* said,

Farewell The King's Own Yorkshire Light Infantry – Welcome The Light Infantry.

Cede Nullis

---

[1] *The Bugle*, 1967, Vol. 59.1 p 15

[2] *The Bugle*, 1968, Vol. 60.1 p 18

[3] One of the assault boats being used to rescue the casualties was itself in danger and had to be assisted by the RAF when its engine failed.

[4] *The Bugle*, 1967, Vol. 59.3 pp 22/23 The word 'conner' was Regimental slang for food.

[5] *The Bugle*, 1967, Vol. 59.3 p14

[6] The first line of the poem *The Burial of Sir John Moore*, by Charles Wolfe. 1791-1823

[7] Makepeace-Warne, Maj-Gen A. *Exceedingly Lucky, The History of the Light Infantry, 1968-1993*, Sidney Jary Ltd, Bristol 1993 p 18

[8] This sad statistic holds true to the present day - 2005

Colonels of the Regiment

51st Regiment of Foot

Rank	Name	Date of Appointment	
Lieutenant General	Robert Napier	19 December	1755
Lieutenant General	Thomas Brudenell	22 April	1757
General	Archibald Montgomerie, 11th Earl of Eglington	24 June	1767
Lieutenant General	Anthony George Martin	2 December	1795
General	William Morshead	9 May	1800
General	Thomas Hislop Bt, GCB	4 June	1822
Lieutenant General	Sir Benjamin D'Urban GCB, KCH	25 December	1829
General	Sir Thomas Willshire Bt, GCB	26 June	1849
General	Sir William Henry Elliott GCB, KH	1 June	1862
General	John Leslie Dennis CB	28 March	1874
General	Arnold Charles Errington	27 September	1879

2nd Madras European Light Infantry

General	Sir Hoptoun S. Scott KCB	5 October	1839
Colonel	Archibald Brown Dyce	1 April	1848
Major General	Richard Budd	4 July	1858

Following the Indian Mutiny 1856-1858, all regiments raised and funded by the Honourable East India Company were absorbed into the British Army.
The 2nd Madras European Light Infantry became 105th Madras Light Infantry on 1 April 1861.

105th Madras Light Infantry

Major General	Richard Budd	1 April	1861
Lieutenant General	Archibald Brown Dyce	30 September	1862
General	George Alexander Malcolm CB	10 March	1866
General	Arnold Charles Errington	3 June	1888

On the death of General G.A. Malcolm, 2 June 1888, General A.C. Errington became 'Colonel' of both battalions.

The King's Own Yorkshire Light Infantry
51st and 105th

General	Arnold Charles Errington	27 September	1879
General	Thomas Addison CB	1 April	1890
General	James Daubeney CB	18 November	1890
Lieutenant General	Sir Robert Hume GCB	14 September	1893
Lieutenant General	Frederick George Thomas Deshon CB	18 January	1903
General	Sir Arthur Singleton Wynne GCB	4 April	1913
General	Sir Charles Parker Deedes KCB, CMG, DSO	10 March	1927
Major General	William Robb CBE, DSO, MC	9 August	1947
Lieutenant General	Sir Harold Redman KCB, CBE	1 August	1950
Lieutenant General	Sir Roger Bower KCB, KBE	1 August	1960
Major General	Charles Julius Deedes CB, OBE, MC	1 August	1966

Honorary Colonels

Militia, Volunteer and Territorial Battalions

1st West York Militia

Henry Pleydell Dawnay, Viscount Downe	24 July	1758
Sir George Savile	4 November	1763
Charles, 11th Duke of Norfolk	3 May	1787
William, 2nd Earl FitzWilliam	10 March	1798
Lieutenant Colonel J. Dixon	15 April	1809
Richard Fountayne Wilson	26 May	1824
John 2nd Baron Wharncliffe	22 June	1846
Lieutenant Colonel Hon E.G. Monkton	17 May	1853
Major A. Aitken	13 April	1872

In the Army reorganisation of 1881, 1st West York Militia became 3rd King's Own Light Infantry (South Yorkshire Regiment), which in 1887 became 3rd King's Own Yorkshire Light Infantry.

1st Volunteer Battalion

With the permission of the Lord Lieutenant, this Battalion was formed in Wakefield, 17 November 1859, as the 9th West Riding of Yorkshire Rifle Volunteers. In 1880, the Battalion's number was changed from 9th to 5th, and in 1881 it became the 1st Volunteer Battalion King's Own Light Infantry (South Yorkshire Regiment). In 1887, it was renamed the 1st Volunteer Battalion King's Own Yorkshire Light Infantry. In 1908, the Militia and Volunteer forces formed the basis of the Territorial Force, later to be known as the Territorial Army. The Battalion had no Honorary Colonels.

King's Own Yorkshire Light Infantry

3rd Battalion

Colonel	A. Aitken	1 June	1881
Colonel	M.G. Johnstone	12 July	1907

4th Territorial Battalion

Colonel Rt. Hon.	C.G. Miles Gaskell	1 April	1908
Colonel	E. Hind VD	1 April	1909
Colonel	H.J. Haslegrave TD	1 April	1913
		1914 – 1918	
Colonel	H.J. Haslegrave CMG, TD	12 August	1922
Colonel	The Viscount Allendale KG, CB, CBE, MC	3 November	1928
		1939 – 1945	
Colonel	T. Chadwick MC, TD, DL, JP	9 March	1948
Colonel	M.A.C.P. Kaye TD, DL	8 March	1955
Colonel	H.E. Barker TD	8 March	1966

5th Territorial Battalion

Colonel	A. Sturrock	1 April	1908
Colonel	J.R. Shaw	1 April	1909
		1914 – 1918	
Colonel	C.C. Moxon CMG, DSO	1 January	1919
Brigadier General	Brooke C.R.I. CMG, DSO, MP	25 June	1924
Colonel	W. St. A. Warde-Aldam DSO	14 September	1935

1939 – 1945

In 1938, 5th KOYLI was converted to Royal Artillery and became 53rd Light Anti-Aircraft Regiment, which, with its second line regiment, 57th Light Anti-Aircraft Regiment RA, served throughout the Second World War.

Commanding Officers
1st : 2nd Battalions

4th Territorial Battalion

1945 – 1968

1st Battalion	Date of Appointment	
Lieutenant Colonel N.S. Pope DSO	26 August	1944
Lieutenant Colonel D.G.B. Ridout OBE	1 February	1946
1st Battalion disbanded	1 February	1948

2nd Battalion		
Lieutenant Colonel B.W. Wood	19 April	1944
Lieutenant Colonel W.S.F. Hickie OBE	11 December	1945
Lieutenant Colonel A.B. Brown OBE	1 January	1948
1st and 2nd KOYLI amalgamated to form 1st KOYLI	18 November	1948

1st Battalion		
Lieutenant Colonel A.B. Brown OBE	18 November	1948
Lieutenant Colonel J.C. Preston DSO	17 November	1950
Lieutenant Colonel N.S. Pope DSO, MBE	17 November	1952
Lieutenant Colonel C.J. Deedes OBE, MC	1 June	1955
Lieutenant Colonel S.H. Kent OBE	1 August	1957
Lieutenant Colonel S.N. Floyer-Acland	7 December	1959
Lieutenant Colonel H.C.I. Rome	1 November	1961
Lieutenant Colonel G.R. Saltonstall OBE	1 November	1963
Lieutenant Colonel A.C. Elcomb	24 May	1966

4th Battalion Territorial Army		
Lieutenant Colonel M.A.C.P. Kaye TD, DL	1 May	1947
Lieutenant Colonel J.R. Haslegrave OBE, TD	14 January	1951
Lieutenant Colonel H.H. Barker TD	13 January	1954
Lieutenant Colonel M.P. Robinson	14 January	1957
Lieutenant Colonel W.H. Lossock	14 January	1960
Lieutenant Colonel A.R. Wilson	19 March	1963
Lieutenant Colonel S. McL. Richardson TD	18 March	1966
Lieutenant Colonel J.D. Carter TD	31 March	1968

The King's Own Yorkshire Light Infantry Soldiers Killed In Action Or Died While Serving

1st January 1946 – 10th July 1968

Number	Rank	Name		Location	Date	
4523205	Private	Smith G.	1st Batt.	Germany - Neuengamme	19 March	1946
14798407	Private	Beevers H.	2nd Batt.	India - Malthone	2 April	1946
14818306	Private	Heathcote D.	2nd Batt	India - Malthone	2 April	1946
14410289	Serjeant	Crosse B.	46th Div HQ att	Austria - Graz	6 July	1946
14892817	Private	Fletcher T.	1/4th 'Z' Coy	Austria - Vienna	25 July	1946
14997334	Private	Yates J.M.	2nd Batt.	India - Deolali (BMH)	5 December	1946
19060770	Private	Williamson J.	1st Batt.	Germany - Vögelsang	26 May	1947
14879386	Lance Corporal	Swansbury		Germany - Minden	17 September	1947
19033400	Private	Morton J.S.	2nd Batt.		11 November	1947
19038765	Private	Mayoh D.	2nd Batt.	Malaya	11 November	1947
4686645	Private	Elgie T.W.		UK	12 March	1948
4689198	Colour Serjeant	Price D.A.		Malaya	27 April	1948
19078500	Private	Foley J.		Malaya	27 April	1948
19040918	Private	Marritt J.R.		Malaya	31 May	1948
21072300	Private	Rimmington H.		UK	15 June	1948
19577791	Private	Guy R.	KSLI att	Malaya	31 July	1948
22548740	Private	Elliott J.		Malaya	6 August	1948
113776	Captain	Lock D.G.	Som LI att	Malaya	2 October	1948
21127814	Lance Corporal	Hutchinson K.		Malaya	2 October	1948

Number	Rank	Name	Notes	Location	Date	Year
19040217	Private	Dobson A.		Malaya	2 October	1948
19152767	Private	Woodhouse H.		Malaya	2 October	1948
4686645	Private	Elgie T.W.		UK	12 March	1949
4535833	Serjeant	Gilpin J.		Malaya	25 July	1949
22007418	Private	Gee		Malaya	4 August	1949
19031974	Private	Ward K.W.		Malaya	9 November	1949
19036879	Private	Carter A.		Malaya	3 December	1949
19043915	Private	Kelly H.		Malaya	3 December	1949
19039099	Private	Mills J.		Malaya	3 December	1949
14247304	Private	Godfrey J.J.H.	ACC att	Malaya	3 December	1949
19047466	Private	McAdam A.		Malaya	27 January	1950
21124024	Lance Corporal	McGee		Malaya	1 April	1950
19045452	Private	James R.A.		Malaya	18 April	1950
19089487	Private	Boden W.J.		Malaya	10 June	1950
14190046	Private	Gough J.E.		Malaya	10 June	1950
22124535	Private	Harrison C.M.		Malaya	10 June	1950
19044014	Private	Jones D.		Malaya	10 June	1950
22192195	Private	Hall R.L.		Malaya	10 June	1950
22134701	Private	Hudson J.K.		Malaya	10 June	1950
22273408	Private	Brown V.		Malaya	16 June	1950
409088	2nd Lieutenant	Pymont D.S.	Som LI att	Malaya	9 July	1950
22184662	Private	Hicks D.C.		Malaya	24 October	1950
2138873	Serjeant	Baddeley W.C.		Malaya	21 November	1950
22348095	Private	Gregory J.D.		Malaya	1 December	1950
19013444	Lance Corporal	Whitehead J.D.		Malaya	26 January	1951
22373010	Private	Fee A.J.		Malaya	20 February	1951

Appendix 3

Number	Rank	Name	Notes	Location	Date	Year
14444957	Corporal	Marsden D.		Austria	24 March	1951
4689561	Serjeant	Briggs G.C.		UK	11 May	1951
19034147	Corporal	Heathcote J.B.		UK	14 May	1951
22154382	Private	Walker C.		Malaya	20 May	1951
24925	Lieutenant	Hobson W.H.		Egypt - Canal Zone	30 January	1952
22651758	Private	Kendall N.		Germany	7 August	1952
22513172	Private	Everett-Proctor P.D.		Germany	7 August	1952
14474093	Lance Corporal	Hudson R.	DCLI att	Germany	17 September	1952
4699910	Serjeant	Beaumont R.	Som LI att	Malaya	23/27 January	1953
22530574	Private	Henry P.		UK	30 July	1953
22340455	Private (TA)	Ripley D.		UK	29 July	1954
22973278	Private	Thompson W.W.W.		UK	24 August	1954
22530875	Corporal (TA)	Jackson I.B.		UK	17 November	1954
22883336	Private	Blackburn D.		Kenya	6 May	1955
4699919	Serjeant	Morris N.S.		Aden	30 December	1955
23055301	Private	Callaghan P.M.		Aden	30 December	1955
22557118	Bandsman	Musgreave R.		UK	16 January	1956
22971924	Lance Corporal	Russell C.		Cyprus	29 January	1956
19034149	Serjeant	Wade L. DCM		Cyprus	27 March	1956
23274694	Private	Ashe J.		Cyprus	28 May	1956
23274732	Private	Townend D.		Cyprus/Home	3 September	1957
23442902	Private	Britton A.	att to DLI	Cyprus	28 October	1958
23047581	Private (TA)	Greaves G.		UK	20 February	1959
14458527	Colour/Serjeant	Robson R.F.		UK	24 February	1959
23370287	Private (TA)	Haley A.G.		UK	14 July	1959
22855106	Corporal (TA)	Horncastle N.		UK	16 November	1959

181

Appendix 3

23732540	Private	Smith A.P.	UK	23 November	1959
23478666	Lance Corporal	Long J.P.	UK	19 December	1959
465896	2nd Lieutenant	Beaumont J.S.	Germany - Norway	12 May	1961
23835964	Private	Reynolds A.	Germany - Norway	12 May	1961
23735964	Private	Smith J.	Germany - Norway	12 May	1961
23695996	Private (TA)	Holmes B.	UK	1 February	1962
23869715	Private (TA)	Heeps R.G.	UK	31 March	1962
23227315	Corporal	Sambrook G.	Malaya	14 July	1962
22971777	Private (TA)	Webster C.	UK	10 September	1962
23782368	Private	Linaker D.E.	Malaya	26 September	1962
23882716	Private	Kirk W.	Malaya	13 November	1962
23652645	Private (TA)	Haigh W.	UK	9 December	1962
23882983	Private (TA)	Robertshaw F.	Brunei	16 February	1963
23867972	Bugler	Lockwood C.P.	UK	5 September	1963
23668255	Private	Casey B.	UK - Tidworth	12 December	1964
23846204	Private	Elliott G.	UK - Tidworth	25 December	1964
23652692	Private	Edwards B.	UK - Tidworth	2 January	1965
23854670	Corporal	Cross R.P.	UK - Tidworth	5 August	1965
23699079	Private	Robinson P.	UK - Tidworth	14 August	1965
23734516	Corporal	Ford L.J.	UK	19 December	1965
24033392	Private	Cowin G.A.	UK	4 January	1966
24114994	Private	Limb R.W.	Germany - Berlin	24 November	1967
24114993	Private	Wilson N.C.	Germany - Berlin	24 November	1967

The King's Own Yorkshire Light Infantry

Affiliated Regiments and Battalions

553rd (KOYLI) Light Anti-Aircraft Regiment
557th Mixed (KOYLI) Heavy Anti-Aircraft Regiment
Royal Artillery
Territorial Army

On 1 May 1947, the former 53rd and 57th Light Anti-Aircraft (LAA) Regiments, which had been placed in suspended animation at the end of World War Two, were reactivated. The new regiments were numbered 553rd (KOYLI) LAA Regiment, RA (TA), to be commanded by Lieutenant Colonel W.J. Nutter, and 557th Mixed (KOYLI) Heavy Anti-Aircraft (HAA) Regiment RA (TA), commanded by Lieutenant Colonel W.F. Bracewell. (The term 'mixed' indicated that the unit would contain members of the Auxiliary Territorial Service (ATS), later known as the Women's Royal Army Corps.) Both of these units were to have their headquarters at Scarborough Barracks, Doncaster and were to be part of 65th AA Brigade under the command of Brigadier A. Smith OBE, TD. It was the government's intention that time expired National Servicemen would serve as reservists in TA units such as these.

As the nation began to come to terms with the aftermath of six years of war, its armed forces were not allowed the luxury of a period of relaxation. The nation was faced with many uncertainties and needed to guard against new threats that were perceived to come from its former allies in eastern Europe. The Territorial AA Regiments were to return to training for the task that had been assigned to them during the Second World War: the defence of fighting units against aerial attack. In the early years of the Cold War, improvements in aircraft design, especially their speed of attack, had to be countered by a number of innovations that resulted in an increasing reliance on the Radar control and guidance of the guns.

The annual firing camp in 1953 took place at Towyn, North Wales, the 557th (KOYLI) HAA attending in May and the 553rd (KOYLI) LAA in June. The 553rd LAA had the honour of being one of the first LAA units to use the new Bristol Bofor No 12 guns at Towyn, which may have accounted for a certain amount of erratic firing. Later in the year a weekend camp at RAF Church Fenton allowed 553rd LAA to combine with other LAA units in airfield defence. Shortly before Remembrance Sunday 1953, the Regimental Band was fortunate enough to have almost all its instruments replaced with new ones. 'The only instrument not changed was Gnr. Mathers' euphonium. The distinction here is that Gunner Mathers (who is 62 years old and considered the Father of the Regiment now) played this same instrument when he joined the band as a boy in 1908, and his instrument was merely reconditioned.'[1]

The changing pattern of defence requirements resulted in 557th HAA being converted to a LAA Regiment on 31 March 1954. When the members of 557th HAA learned of the forthcoming change they expressed a certain degree of concern. Some comfort was obtained from the news that, because of their historic association with the KOYLI, they, together with the 553rd LAA, would be allowed to wear a green whistle cord: sadly, because of their long exposure to the ways of the artillery, they mistakenly, but understandably, referred to it as a lanyard. In addition, on their No 1 Dress, they were allowed to wear KOYLI buttons, both dispensations recalling and reinforcing the origins and long association of the units with 5th KOYLI.

In early May, a visit to RAF Lindholme demonstrated the difficulties of engaging low flying jet aircraft with the standard and Bristolised 40 mm Bofors; aircraft recognition also proved to be difficult when speeds of 400 mph or more were involved. Later that year, at the 1954 'RAF at Home', held on Battle of Britain Saturday at RAF Lindholme, 553rd LAA demonstrated its skill at engaging low-flying attacking aircraft; the guns, of course, using blank ammunition.

As the Western Powers and the Soviet Union improved their ability to strike at each other with nuclear weapons, it became clear that such threats could not be effectively countered by any conventional system of AA fire. Despite constant changes and refinements to the basic systems of defence against aerial attack, the cost effectiveness of conventional AA units brought about fundamental changes. In late 1954, the government announced the disbandment of Anti-Aircraft Command, which had existed since 1938 when many infantry battalions were converted to LAA regiments in an attempt to counter the threat of a sustained aerial attack from the German Luftwaffe.

The 553rd and 557th LAA Regiments now faced an uncertain future. 'Much of our present time is taken up with new bombs – Atom and Hydrogen. All ranks are being instructed in their effectiveness and ways of minimising the damage they cause. It has revealed some very sobering thoughts in case of another war.'[2] Within six months, the fate of the two AA regiments had been decided. Faced with the need to economise, the two regiments were to be amalgamated into a single battery within 323rd LAA Regiment. The KOYLI connection would be maintained, the War Office giving approval for the new LAA Regiment to retain not only the title KOYLI, but also the Colours of 5th KOYLI, and its Regimental silver: the battery was to remain at the Scarborough Barracks, Doncaster. The reduction in establishment meant that all surplus non-volunteer National Servicemen were to be posted to the Army Emergency Reserve, and for the volunteers a place would be found in the Mobile Defence Columns. The new LAA Battery was to be known as 'R' (KOYLI) LAA Battery RA (TA), and was to be commanded by Major F. Wood TD, RA, (TA).

Appendix 4

Inevitably, the need to adapt to changing circumstances meant that long held traditions and associations would eventually end. On 29 June 1957, the Commanding Officer, Adjutant, and a Colour Party from the Regimental Depot of the KOYLI at Strensall, arrived in Doncaster for the formal return by 'R' (KOYLI) Battery 323 LAA Regiment RA (TA) of the 5th Battalion KOYLI Colours to the Regiment. The Gunners marched on to the parade ground at Sandford Road Barracks with the Colours of the 5th Battalion KOYLI then, the Colour Party from the Depot – Lieutenant S.P. Eller, Queen's Colour, Lieutenant J.A. Charlesworth, Regimental Colour, Company Serjeant Major Cocliff, Serjeant Studd and Serjeant Moore, marched on to the parade ground and halted in front of the Colours. Captain A.W. Taylor, an old member of the 5th Battalion, who had had the honour of receiving the Queen's Colour on behalf of the Battalion from King Edward VII in 1909, then took the Colours from the Gunners and handed them back to the Regimental Colour party.[3] After the playing of the Nation Anthem, the Colours were marched away to the accompaniment of the KOYLI Regimental March played by the band of the 323rd LAA Regiment.

---

[1] *The Bugle,* 1954, Vol. 46.1 p 42

[2] *The Bugle,* 1955, Vol. 47.1 p 35

[3] *The Bugle,* 1957, Vol. 49.3 p 89 The 5th KOYLI Colours were received from Edward VII at a ceremony at Windsor Castle in 1909, not 1907 as recorded in *The Bugle.*

The King's Own Yorkshire Light Infantry

Allied Regiments and Battalions

Canadian Army
1st Battalion The Saskatoon Light Infantry (MG)

The 105th Regiment (Fusiliers), a reserve force battalion of the Canadian Army, was formed from a number of Militia units in a general expansion of the Militia in April 1912. In the following spring, a further expansion saw the former Saskatoon companies of the 105th becoming the 105th Regiment (Saskatoon Fusiliers). It was at this time that the 105th established its alliance with the King's Own Yorkshire Light Infantry; the connection stemming from the original regimental number of 2nd KOYLI, which was formed from the 105th Madras European Light Infantry.

On the outbreak of the First World War, the 105th Regiment (Saskatoon Fusiliers) became part of the 11th Overseas Battalion and, together with the 16th Light Horse from Battleford, and several other former Militia cavalry units, it was used to reinforce the 5th Battalion, Western Cavalry. As part of 2nd Brigade, 1st Canadian Division, the 5th Battalion fought as infantry due to the lack of horses. With the high percentage of men coming from Saskatchewan, the 5th Battalion later became known as the Red Saskatchewan.

Arriving in France on 14 February 1915, the Battalion received its baptism of fire in the German gas attack at Ypres, 25 April 1915. Despite having no gas masks the 5th Battalion held the line on the Gravenstafel Ridge, thus allowing the remainder of the 2nd Brigade to fall back to defensive positions. Later that year, during the attack at Festubert, the Battalion succeeded in capturing a German strong point but at the cost of every officer and senior NCO being either killed or wounded.

The Battalion served with distinction throughout the 1916 Battles of the Somme, and in April 1917, during the spectacular assault and capture of Vimy Ridge, it was part of the successful attack on the enemy position known as the Pimple. Later in the same year, the Battalion took part in the Third Battle of Ypres, which ended in November with the Canadian Corps' capture of the Passchendaele Ridge.

It was during the Battle of Amiens, which began on 8 August 1918, that Sergeant Raphael L. Zengal MM of the 5th Battalion won the Victoria Cross (9 August). The 5th Battalion was part of the victorious Final One Hundred Days, which saw the defeat of the German Army in the field. Under the command of Lieutenant General Sir Arthur Currie, the Canadian Corps, part of the British First Army, captured Valencienne at a cost to the Germans of 800 dead and 1,800 prisoners; the Canadians lost only 80 killed and 300 wounded.

In 1923, the 105th became 1st North Saskatchewan Regiment and formed an alliance with the Duke of Wellington's West Riding Regiment (DWR). The following year came yet another change of name, this time to the shorter Saskatoon Light Infantry (SLI) and, in 1925, resumed its alliance with the KOYLI.

During World War Two, the SLI was part of 1st Canadian Division, which arrived in England on 17 December 1939, and initially moved into Tournai Barracks, Aldershot. His Majesty King George VI inspected the Battalion at Aldershot on 24 January 1940, and in February, General Sir Charles Deedes, Colonel of the KOYLI, visited the SLI and presented the Battalion with a camp flag of the KOYLI. On 8 April, the SLI was inspected by its Colonel-in-Chief, Her Majesty Queen Elizabeth, who gave her permission for the Saskatoon Light Infantry to wear KOYLI buttons and whistle cords (referred to by the Canadians as lanyards) as part of their dress regulations. A further tangible link with the KOYLI was demonstrated on 24 October 1941, when Her Majesty Queen Elizabeth visited the SLI at Caterham and presented the Battalion with new Colours.

The evacuation of the British Expeditionary Force from Dunkirk in May 1940 halted plans for 1st Canadian Division to cross to France, and in August, the Division was the only completely mobile, equipped, and trained formation in Britain. Between May 1940 and June 1943, 1st Canadian Division remained in England training. The SLI's early training included amphibious warfare techniques, and between 24 August and 2 September 1940 the Battalion was involved in Operation Gauntlet. During this secret operation, some 1500 men were successfully landed on the islands of Spitzbergen and Bear Island where they destroyed not only the coalmines, but also the weather and radio stations. Having prevented these facilities falling into German hands, the 2000 resident Russian miners were evacuated to Archangel, while 800 Norwegians were taken back to Britain.

The 1st KOYLI formed part of the Allied force that invaded Sicily on 10 July 1943, and, on 13th July, it was joined by the SLI, which was now known as 1st Canadian Division Support Battalion (Saskatoon LI). The three support groups of the SLI were deployed at Company strength using the Vickers Machine Gun, the 4.2 inch mortar providing direct and indirect fire support to the infantry. The groups immediately went into action, and it was to be 26 August before the last group was withdrawn. The Battalion also took part in the invasion of the Italian mainland, landing at Reggio on 3 September 1943. As part of 13th Corps, 8th Army, the SLI fought in the campaign that slowly cleared the Germans from the eastern side of Italy. It took part in the drive towards Campobosso and eventually reached Ortona, where it was taken out of the line on 4 January 1944; after which 1st Canadian Division underwent a complete reorganisation.

A return to the name 1st Saskatoon LI (MG) was made during the period of reorganisation, and on 25 August 1944, the Battalion returned to the line and crossed the Metauro. Fierce German resistance met the Allied attacks on Rimini and Cattolica (the latter being observed by Winston Churchill) before 1st Canadian Division was relieved as it reached the Ronca. The 1st SLI (MG) moved back into the line on 28 November and by Christmas had arrived on the banks of the Senio, where it stayed for the remainder of the winter. In late February 1945, the Division was relieved by 8th Indian Division and made its way south to Leghorn, from where it left to join 1st Canadian Army in western Europe.

Arriving at Hoogstraaten, Belgium, on 4 March 1945, the Division moved north then eastwards along the Ijssel to eliminate German resistance in northwest Holland. With the surrender of the German Army in Holland on 5 May 1945, 1st SLI (MG) travelled to Rotterdam and eventually sailed for the UK on 10 May 1945. On 20 September, the Battalion embarked at Southampton for Halifax where it was disbanded on 3rd October 1945.

In August 1947, Colonel G. Chamier, OBE, joined the British Army Staff in Washington, USA, and took the opportunity to visit the reformed 1st SLI in Saskatoon. In his speech of welcome, Lieutenant Colonel P. Reynolds, the Commanding Officer of 1st SLI, said how proud the Battalion was to wear the green lanyards. In his reply, Colonel Chamier pointed out that when, as a young subaltern in 1926, he had made a similar mistaken reference to the whistle cord in the Officer's Mess of 2nd KOYLI in India, he had been debagged by his brother officers. Obviously, this was one tradition that was not maintained on this occasion.

In the winter of 1952, a platoon of 1st SLI – by which time it had become a machine gun battalion – was asked to test a variation of the Canadian Army's winter equipment. The platoon was to camp out for the night – even if the temperature was 40 below! The conditions were certainly in sharp contrast to those experienced by 4th KOYLI during its annual camp.

> Also interesting is the fact that pyjamas are made to wear in the daytime ... the soldier in the northland goes to bed exactly as he was born, sleeping in two bedrolls, which are light and very warm. Reason for this strange procedure is that the soldier is warned against putting on anything in the daytime which he has worn at night ... it might contain some moisture and that's fatal in 40 or even 20 below weather.[1]

During the course of a visit made by Lieutenant Colonel S.H. Kent to 1st SLI (MG) in July 1954, the Canadian Reserve Army made certain changes, which resulted in the Battalion becoming part of a Militia Group rather than a unit of a Reserve Brigade. In common with the periodic changes to the British Army, the Canadian Army was also obliged to accept reorganisation and, in 1958, 1st SLI (MG) had yet another change of name, becoming 2nd Battalion, The North Saskatchewan Regiment (Saskatoon Light Infantry). The OC the KOYLI Depot, Major J.S. Wood, sent to the new 2nd Battalion a number of whistle cords, for which the CO, Lieutenant Colonel J.L.

Summers, duly thanked him. Lieutenant Colonel Summers also said that the Battalion had reverted to being an infantry battalion and had lost its good old Vickers machine guns, but the more startling news was that it had an authorized band of Pipes and Drums. The Colonel went on to reveal that the Seaforth Highlanders had granted permission for 2nd NSR (SLI)'s Pipe and Drum band to wear the Mackenzie Tartan, but, 'I sincerely trust this will in no manner weaken our ties with the KOYLI, for we value our affiliation most highly.'[2]

When the Honorary Colonel of 4th KOYLI, Colonel M.A.C.P. Kaye, visited 2nd N. Saskatchewan Regiment (SLI) in January 1959, he received a very warm welcome from Lieutenant Colonel J. L. Summers, who was also the chief pharmacist at the local hospital. Colonel Kaye was escorted round the Battalion's Depot, known as the Stadium, Saskatoon, and noted many items of Regimental memorabilia illustrating the close ties between the two Regiments. Attending the dinner given in Colonel Kaye's honour were many of the Battalion's officers who had driven in arctic conditions up to 150 miles from the outlying companies. The huge distances involved meant that the Militia was organised on a geographical basis, rather than the usual Divisions and Brigades, and a military group might consist of a number of small sub-units with perhaps only one major unit. While there were obvious differences, the Battalion was of a similar size to 4th KOYLI, and experienced the same problems. Both approached their difficulties in the traditional spirit of the Volunteer, and both displayed the Territorial ethos of training, social events and camaraderie.

When the KOYLI became part of the Light Infantry Regiment in 1968, the Light Infantry maintained the association with the 1st Saskatoon LI.[3]

Australian Infantry
51st Infantry Battalion (The North Queensland Regiment)

A number of volunteer mounted infantry units from Western Australia served in South Africa during the Boer War. The 51st Battalion, Australian Imperial Force (AIF) was raised at Tel-el-Kebir, Egypt on 1 March 1916 from half the 11th Battalion and reinforcements of the 11th and 28th Battalions, all personnel being Western Australian volunteers. Since the 51st Battalion's volunteers came from the same region as the Western Australian Mounted Infantry, the Battalion was deemed its successor, and as such was allowed to bear the Mounted Infantry's Battle Honour – South Africa 1899-1902.

The 51st Infantry Battalion served with distinction on the Western Front from August 1916 until the end of the war. The Battalion lost 389 men in a two-day counter-attack at Villers Bretonneux, 24/25 April 1918, during which action it won one Victoria Cross and 41 other decorations. For the remainder of the war the badly depleted 51st Battalion was amalgamated with the 52nd Battalion, which had also sustained heavy casualties.

In the inter-war years, the Battalion was reformed at Subiaco, Western Australia in 1921; converted into a Militia unit at Launceston, Tasmania, 1922; relocated to Gladsville, Sydney, New South Wales in 1924, where it became a member of the 8th Brigade, 1st Division. A further amalgamation took place in 1930 when the 51st was joined with the 30th Battalion (New South Wales Scottish) at Ryde, before finally amalgamating with the 18th Battalion in 1935 to become the 18th/51st Battalion.

On 1 October 1936, at Cairns, Queensland, the 51st Battalion Far North Queensland Regiment (FNQR) was formed, and retained the motto 'Ducit Amor Patriae', which had been given to the 51st Battalion in 1927. An Army Order of 1937 records that the 51st Battalion was affiliated with the King's Own Yorkshire Light Infantry. Although no records exist, the most likely reason for this affiliation was that the KOYLI was formerly the 51st Regiment of Foot which, sometime in the 1840s, had detachments stationed in Tasmania and Western Australia, two previous homes of the 51st FNQR.

When war was declared in 1939, the 51st Battalion lost many of its militiamen to the 2nd AIF as volunteers. The Battalion continued to train for its Militia role but, when Japan entered the war in December 1941, it was placed on full time duty and tasked with the defence of the area from Port Douglas to Gordonvale. Further reductions in numbers resulted in an amalgamation with 31st Battalion The Kennedy Regiment (Townsville) on 12 April 1943; the new Battalion was renamed 31st/51st Battalion. The Battalion embarked for overseas duty on 20 June 1943 and saw action in Dutch New Guinea until 24 July 1944 when it returned to Australia. In December 1944, it embarked for Bougainville in the Solomon Islands and, on 8 June 1945, 'A' Company, together with part of 'C' Company, was involved north of Bougainville at Porton Plantation in what proved to be the Battalion's heaviest engagement of World War Two. Of the 190 men who took part in the action, 23 were killed or missing and 106 were wounded: the survivors were evacuated on 11 June 1945. The GOC 2nd Australian Corps, AIF, Lieutenant General S.G. Savage, said of them, 'The bravery of the men in the Porton operation has not been surpassed by Australian troops in either World War One or World War Two'. On the surrender of the Japanese in September 1945, the Battalion was dispersed, with elements in Nauru, Rabaul and Ocean Island. The $31^{st}/51^{st}$ finally returned to Australia in June 1946 where it was disbanded at Townsville and Cairns.

Some doubt exists as to the exact date of the re-raising of the 51st Battalion, Far North Queensland Regiment (FNQR), but it was presented with its Colours, which incorporated the Battle Honours of all its predecessors, in 1950.

On 17 May 1955, Mr John Dalton, an ex-officer of the Australian Army, and Honorary Member of the 51st Battalion FNQR's Serjeants' Mess, visited the KOYLI's Regimental Depot at Strensall. During his visit Mr Dalton presented a suitably inscribed pewter tankard to the KOYLI Serjeants' Mess, a gift from the Serjeants' Mess of the 51st FNQR. Notes sent to the Regimental Depot by the CO of the 51st FNQR, Lieutenant Colonel H.S. Williams, painted an interesting picture of the area in which his battalion, which was organised along similar lines to the British Territorial Army, operated. Obvious contrasts between the 4th KOYLI and 51st FNQR were: in Australia the annual camp that year would take place 380 miles south of the Battalion HQ at Cairns; the Brigade HQ was 240 miles away, and the next senior HQ, Northern Command, was in Brisbane, 1,400 miles away![4] When Lieutenant Colonel S.H. Kent visited the 51st Battalion FNQR in August 1956, he was shown the site of the forthcoming annual camp where the accent would be on jungle training, a programme that would have been very difficult to simulate for a 4th KOYLI annual camp.[5]

On 18 August 1957, and before a crowd of about 7,000 people, 500 men were on parade when the Queen's and the Regimental Colours were presented to the 51st Battalion by Field Marshal Sir William Slim, GCB, GCMC, GCVO, GBE, DSO, MC, Governor General of Australia.[6] Just before Christmas 1957, a number of whistle cords were sent by the KOYLI to the 51st FNQR to be worn by the Officers, Warrant Officers, and Serjeants of the 51st Battalion.

More reorganisation took place on 3 June 1960 when the 51st was again integrated with the 31st Battalion, the Kennedy Regiment, the 42nd Battalion and the Capricornia Regiment, forming 2nd Battalion, The Royal Queensland Regiment, with Battalion HQ at Townsville. When another bout of reorganisation took place, and the 2nd Battalion Royal Queensland Regiment was expanded, the 51st was reformed at Cairns on 24 May 1965 as 51st Battalion The Royal Queensland Regiment. Minden Greetings were exchanged by the 51st Battalion and the KOYLI on 1 August 1965, the CO of the 51st, Lieutenant Colonel S.E. Davis, expressing great pleasure at the increase in numbers of his battalion whose four rifle companies were now almost up to full strength.

The 51st Battalion continued training until a general reduction in the size of the Australian Army took place on 31 July 1976 when it became the 51st Independent Rifle Company, The Royal Queensland Regiment. A change of title and duties occurred on 1 October 1985 when the 51st Independent Rifle Company became the Royal Force Surveillance unit in North Queensland and was renamed the 51st Battalion The Far North Queensland Regiment (51 FNQR). The 51st Battalion has not only survived, but has expanded and now, 2004, has four companies. In 1985 it adopted the colour patch of the original 51st Battalion AIF and the badge and motto of the original 51st Battalion Far North Queensland Regiment, the new badge being surmounted by the Queen's crown instead of the King's crown of the original.[7]

---

[1] *The Bugle,* 1952, Vol. 44.5 p 17

[2] *The Bugle,* 1958, Vol. 50.3 p 81 The KOYLI Regimental March – 'With Jockey to the Fair' had been adopted by the 2nd NSR (SLI). The usual Light Infantry tempo for this march, 140 paces to the minute, must have presented the Battalion's pipers with a challenge.

[3] Information compiled from – Origins and Lineage – Saskatoon Light Infantry, Regiments of the British Empire, contributed by Major M. Young, Deputy CO, Saskatoon Light Infantry.

[4] *The Bugle,* 1955, Vol. 47.4 pp 13/14

[5] *The Bugle,* 1956, Vol. 48.4 pp 128-130

[6] *The Bugle,* 1957, Vol. 49.4 p 129

[7] Information compiled from History of 51 Far North Queensland Regiment. http:/www.army.gov.au/51FNQR.html

Appendix 6

The Minden Post
1948-1951

Editors
Captain H.C.I. Rome
Captain G.H. Hulme
Captain J.M. Hutton
Lieutenant G.M. Betts
Serjeant Winter : Serjeant Hazel : Serjeant Greenfield

In May 1948, when 2nd KOYLI took over Glugor (later re-named Minden) Barracks in Penang, Malaya, from 2nd West Yorks, there was general approval for the latter's weekly regimental gazette, which had been professionally printed locally. It was decided that 2nd KOYLI would start publication of its own official regimental newspaper to be titled *The Minden Post*. The duties of the 2nd i/c HQ Company were considered suitably broad to include editorship of the paper, given that an Education Serjeant who had been taken over with all the other paraphernalia from the outgoing battalion would assist him.

The first edition of the new weekly paper came out on 12 June and, four days later, the Emergency in Malaya was declared. While based in Taiping over the past months, the Battalion had been engaged in routine internal security activities, and had some operational detachments in place. But, with the official Emergency, rifle companies dispersed to various locations on mainland Malaya, and so *The Minden Post* immediately provided a useful link for the men in their out-stations. As the battalion (re-titled 1st KOYLI from October 1948) was to be involved in widespread operations against the Communist Terrorists for the next three years, it soon became clear that the weekly paper's role was of some significance.

The four page paper, of our national tabloid page-size, was printed on the presses of the *Straits Echo*, Penang's national daily, and was an impressive production, headed by the Regimental crest, and with photographs. The front page would cover major events of the week, both Regimental and international, and occasionally a learned article with a military theme. For example, when the marvellous *Letters of Private Wheeler of the 51st* were discovered and edited for publication in 1951 by Captain B.H. Liddell Hart (9th KOYLI in the First World War), *The Minden Post* was able to publish a series of the letters a year earlier, about Wheeler's experiences during his service (1809-1828) in the Peninsular War and at Waterloo; a tremendous coup to publish one of the Regiment's very own. Page Two would lead with an editorial, sweated over (in good journalistic tradition!) by 2i/c HQ Company, along with news snippets from Britain and a column of jokes,

193

invariably somewhat 'corny'. Page Three was reserved for 'the heart of the matter', the notes from all companies, whether based on the mainland or, perhaps temporarily, on the island, and from the specialist groups such as the Regimental Band and the Signals Platoon. Page Four was devoted to sport, Battalion, British, and international. Pages One, Two and Four were the responsibility of the editor and his assistant, backed up by the typing of HQ Company Clerk, whilst companies and specialist groups were urged to ensure that their weekly contributions reached the editor well in time for printing and publication on Page Three. Active service conditions, with constant jungle patrolling, were often an inhibiting factor to the regular receipt of Company Notes and this proved to be the most frustrating factor of the whole exercise. But, it must be admitted, that there were some outstanding pieces of prose submitted from time to time during the three years of the *Post's* production.

The production process would begin on Monday morning with the selection of articles and news items, which could be typed up in advance of the Friday night printing. As the week progressed, editorial staff would become apprehensive about material as deadlines came and went, with the result that Friday was always a very hectic day. The paper was actually run off on the *Straits Echo* presses after that paper's Saturday edition had been 'put to bed', usually around midnight, but often much later. Before this, *The Minden Post* material would have to be set up by lino-type machines onto hot lead pieces (a fascinating process to the layman) and then arranged according to the layout of each page. All this activity was carried out by the *Straits Echo* staff – Chinese, Malays, Indians, and Eurasians. They were a splendid bunch of skilled craftsmen working at speed in the noisy, hot, humid atmosphere, with ink and oil fumes from rather ancient presses. The operation would require the presence of one or both of the *Post's* editorial team throughout the evening of Friday and the early hours of Saturday, in order to proof-read and correct the page-sheets before the presses could be fed with the final approved pages of lino-type and several hundred copies run off for Battalion readers. Fortunately, the *Straits Echo* was situated in the heart of Georgetown, among the many bars and cabarets, so that sustenance and relaxation were on hand for pressurised editorial staff to indulge in occasional breaks during the long night's work! Once the bundles of newspapers were ready, often as dawn was breaking, the staff would climb into the jeep and return to barracks, where the papers would be delivered to Penang messes and offices in time for breakfast, and loaded onto company vehicles about to journey to their out-stations on the mainland.

It was a useful weekly operation with enough tension to keep the editor and his assistant on their toes, especially on those Friday mornings when only one set of company notes had arrived – or perhaps none! There was a commercial aspect too, whereby, to offset the printing costs (partially only, no doubt), the *Post* published display advertisements from local Penang shops, cinemas, bars, etc on every page. The editorial staff became adept at finding and retaining advertisers, a pleasant occasional routine of gentle persuasion over the odd noon-day Tiger Beer!

The very last edition of *The Minden Post* was published on 28 July 1951, just before the Battalion sailed home, the last of about 160 editions. It was a worthy contribution to the Battalion's myriad activities during the Malayan Emergency and generally appreciated. Every Saturday morning, a sleepy serjeant despatched copies of the paper by airmail to the Colonel of the Regiment, and to the Regimental Association, among others. Today, some copies are held in the Regimental Museum at Doncaster, and it is pleasing to record that the Department of Documents of the Imperial War Museum in London has a complete set of *The Minden Post*, all available for public viewing.

In May 2001, at the KOYLI Malayan Veterans' Re-union at Doncaster, in the 50th Anniversary year of 1st KOYLI's departure from Malaya, over one hundred Photostat copies of the last edition of *The Minden Post* (28 July 1951) were circulated among those attending. It brought back a few memories to ageing ex-Regular and ex-National Servicemen.

John Barnes
Former Education Serjeant (Assistant Editor)
1st KOYLI
Penang, Malaya. 1948-1950

The Minden Post, Saturday, July 15, 1950.

195

Postscript.

When 2nd KOYLI was stationed in Deolali, India, prior to sailing for Malaya in late 1947, it produced a single page information sheet entitled 'Bugle Call' under which title was printed the Regimental motto, Cede Nullis. Lieutenant Colonel W.S.F. Hickie used this publication to issue his 'Letter from the Commanding Officer', after some members of the Battalion had threatened to write to their Members of Parliament complaining of the slow pace of demobilization. Lieutenant Colonel Hickie's letter was published in a special edition of the newssheet entitled 'Special Bugle Call', which was dated – Monday 18 November 1946. This edition was shown as Vol. 5 No 15, which suggests there had been at least 74 editions printed before this date.

Appendix 7

The King's Own Yorkshire Light Infantry

Army Cadet Force
KOYLI

The first post-war edition of *The Bugle,* published in January 1946, reported that five Army Cadet Force Battalions had been raised and were affiliated to the Regiment; also affiliated were units of the Army Cadet Force (KOYLI) at Batley and Wheelwright Grammar Schools, and Silcoates School. The ACF in war time did not have WOs and sergeants, all units were commanded and trained by officers, nearly all of whom were school teachers, ex-WOs or ex-senior NCOs, local government officers, and the like. They had seen ACF service as their contribution to the war effort alongside their civilian occupations, but when hostilities ceased, their commitment to the Force came to an abrupt end. Their departure left a huge gap that was not easily filled, but this was not the only shock in store for the ACF. Many returning ex-servicemen objected strongly to their sons or brothers becoming involved with the ACF, and this reaction had a significant effect on numbers. By 1947, the lack of numbers, and suitable instructors, reduced the ACF units to 2nd Battalion ACF (KOYLI), (companies at Earlsheaton, Ravensthorpe, Thornhill and Dewsbury) with its HQ at the drill hall, Dewsbury , and 4th Battalion ACF (KOYLI), (companies at Batley, Ossett, and units at the three schools) with its HQ at Batley.

The Minden Day celebrations of 1947, which were attended by the Colonel-in-Chief of the Regiment, Her Majesty Queen Elizabeth, included a service in York Minster to honour the Regiment's dead from World War Two. Taking part in the parade that followed the service were cadets from 2nd and 4th Battalions ACF (KOYLI) and Silcoates School ACF (KOYLI).

Each year, cadet activities followed a similar pattern to those of the TA battalion, but with obvious exceptions. Weekly attendance at the local drill hall, or cadet hut, for training, weekend courses, sporting activities and competitions were carried out within the overall structure of the local TA/ACF. During most years there were occasional weekends spent away from home when cadets could take part in training courses, sporting competitions or outdoor pursuits. In those years when there was a summer camp, the cadets were offered an extended period away from home and, in the decade immediately following the war, this was an opportunity not to be missed. The recruiting area of 4th KOYLI TA produced so many ACF units that in December 1947 it was extremely difficult to find sufficient instructors to deal with the needs of the ACF. Despite the limited funds available, great efforts were made to provide each unit with the necessary signs, badges, and flashes as worn by the Regiment.

On 1 December 1952, 2nd Cadet Battalion and 4th Cadet Battalion KOYLI amalgamated to become 4th Cadet Battalion KOYLI under the command of Major W.F.M. Clive, with HQ at Dewsbury. One obvious attraction for the cadets was having the opportunity to fire real guns, albeit under strict supervision. In a competition open to ACF units from the whole of the British Isles, a team representing 4 Company (Wakefield), 4th Cadet Battalion KOYLI, won the 1954 *News of the World* Trophy for small bore shooting with a score of 946 out of 1,000. In the same year, the senior team representing 4th Battalion ACF came second in the annual West Riding Championships while the junior team won its section.

During the Whitsuntide weekend of 1956, 4th Cadet Battalion spent a weekend at the Regimental Depot at Strensall, York, where the cadets had an opportunity to zero rifles and fire Bren and LMG. Platoon schemes on the common were organised, but the highlight of the visit must have been the opportunity to fire the new FN self-loading rifle, which was being issued to all units of the Regular Army. The 4th Cadet Battalion's summer camp in 1957 was also held at the Regimental Depot, Strensall. Nights spent in bivouacs, night operations carried out against a defended position, and many initiative tests, all contributed to giving the cadets a realistic understanding of life in the army. The camp also coincided with Minden Day and, in keeping with Regimental tradition, the cadets wore white roses when they paraded for inspection by Major H.C.I. Rome before marching to the Garrison Church for a service conducted by the Battalion Padre, the Rev. K. Law MA, the Vicar of Ossett.

On 1 May 1958, 4th Cadet Battalion, with companies at Dewsbury, Batley, Thornhill, Wakefield, Normanton and Ossett, amalgamated with 5th Cadet Battalion which had companies at Pontefract, Fitzwilliam and South Kirkby. The new unit, under the command of Lieutenant Colonel W.F. M. Clive, was to have its HQ at Dewsbury. An article written in the February 1959 edition of *The Bugle* gave an insight into the activities of the Infantry Junior Leaders Battalion (IJLB) at Plymouth (later transferred to Oswestry), and acted as a guide for those cadets who were considering making a career in the Army. Intended for boys between the ages of 15 and 16, the aim of the IJLB was to help Junior Soldiers develop the firm foundations on which their progress towards the rank of NCO and WO could be based. Successful completion of the course usually resulted in accelerated promotion when the young soldier reached his own battalion.

The ACF was not immune to the changes that affected the Light Infantry regiments in the late 1950s. The creation of the IJLB was one of a number of such organisations, other units included the All Arms Junior Leaders Regiment, the Junior Tradesmen's Regiment, and the Light Infantry Brigade, Junior Soldiers Wing, which had its HQ at Shrewsbury and trained future buglers and bandsmen. Given the activities of the ACF and the possibilities offered by these other units, cadets were given a clear picture of the various training programmes available, which could lead to their joining the Army, and preferably the KOYLI.

When Her Majesty The Queen Mother visited 1st KOYLI at Pontefract, 28 October 1961, three officers, one adult WO, and 21 cadets attended the parade and lined part of the route when Her Majesty departed.

A further reorganisation of the ACF detachments of the KOYLI produced 'E' Company (from the former 4th Cadet Battalion) and 'F' Company (from the former 5th Cadet Battalion), with each detachment being wholly administered by its Company Commander. This arrangement was subject to further change in April 1963 when all detachments were made administratively fully independent and were renamed with 'F' Company, under the command of Major A. Leslie, coming under the Area Command of Major E.A. Woodhouse TD. The liaison between the cadets and 4th Battalion KOYLI TA became much closer, especially for those detachments that met at the local TA Company's Drill Hall.

In an attempt to improve Army recruiting figures, in 1964 each regiment was to provide a team of five whose task was to show the Army to its best advantage among Youth Organisations. The KOYLI team, known as 14 Army Youth Team (AYT), was under the command of Lieutenant J.B. Charlesworth. The team assisted with the programme of events for the nine ACF detachments in the Pontefract and Wakefield area, and the Yeomanry detachments in the Doncaster area. Plans for weekend exercises for both ACF and Youth Clubs were undertaken, together with training for the Duke of Edinburgh's Award scheme.

In January 1964, the adult RSM of 'F' Company ACF, RSM W. (Jerry) Delany, had the distinction of completing 42 years service, 24 years with the Regular Army, and 18 years with the ACF. At Imphal Barracks, York, on 29 November 1964, Lieutenant General Sir Edward Howard-Vyse, KBE, CB, MC, the newly appointed chairman of the Army Cadet Force, presented RSM Delany with the BEM, in recognition of his outstanding service to the ACF. In the summer of 1964 *The Bugle* recorded the fact that 35 cadets from the South Kirkby detachment had joined the regular Army since 1957 (a remarkable record for such a small community), and that a national campaign had been launched in the newspapers to attract officers and adult instructors for the ACF.

In 1965/66, upon the retirement of Colonel Clive and Major Woodhouse, 'E' and 'F' Companies were amalgamated to form the Light Infantry Area Yorkshire ACF under the command of Captain (later Lieutenant Colonel) G.P. Cresswell. Major Leslie was posted to South Yorkshire to command the Dearne Valley area ACF, which was re-badged as York and Lancasters.

On 4 February 1967, thirty Cadets from Wakefield, Pontefract, and Fitzwilliam were invited to the Passing Out Parade at the Light Infantry Brigade Depot at Shrewsbury, where the new Colonel of the Regiment, Major-General C.J. Deedes inspected the parade and then took the march past. Minden Day 1967 was celebrated at the annual camp, which that year took place at Burniston Barracks, Scarborough. Major J.S. Cowley, OC Cadet Training Team, and Captain R.J.R. Taylerson, OC 14 Army Youth Team, together with officers of the KOYLI ACF began the day with a champagne breakfast. At 10:00 hrs 140 cadets, their officers, WOs, and serjeants marched on to the parade ground to be inspected by the Deputy Commandant Colonel W.A.R. Hutton, TD.

In 1968, 14 AYT moved from Pontefract to Doncaster and significantly increased its contacts with youth clubs and schools throughout the area. For the ACF, the New Year brought the exciting news that the MOD might sanction a visit to 1st KOYLI in Berlin sometime in April. The MOD did approve, and 22 Cadets under the command of Captain G.P. Cresswell and Lieutenant A. Kemp travelled to Berlin, where they not only saw the historic sights, but travelled in Ferret and Saracen armoured cars, rode in tanks over the Royal Tank Regiment's training area, and spent time in assault boats on the Havel. The whole visit proved to be a wonderful experience for the boys, and one not readily available to their contemporaries at home.

Over the years the summer camps, shooting competitions, the Duke of Edinburgh's Award scheme, and a wide variety of sporting competitions and adventure training courses filled the yearly programmes for the cadets. Understandably, recruiting fluctuated, as did the number of officers and adults available to train the young boys. Many cadets joined the Regiment either directly, or by transferring to the Junior Leaders Battalion at Shrewsbury; but whichever route was chosen, the activities of the ACF KOYLI helped to maintain the important links between the Regiment and its recruiting area that had been in place for over two hundred years.

The Queen Mother's Banner

In 1947, the Colonel-in-Chief of the Regiment, Her Majesty Queen Elizabeth, presented the Regiment with a Banner, which was to be competed for annually. Various reasons prevented any meaningful competition being mounted at the time: 2nd KOYLI's move to Malaya and the ensuing Malayan Emergency, the amalgamation of 1st and 2nd Battalions, and it was not until 1960 that the form of the competition was finally determined.

The competition was to be held over a full year and include both military and sporting events. In 1960, the first of the competition, the events included:

Cross-Country	Basketball
Athletics	Hockey
Rugby	Cricket
Soccer	Shooting (Full Bore)
Shooting (Small Bore)	

Drill and Turnout	Administration and Discipline
First Aid	Nuclear Quiz

Battle Efficiency – This took the form of:
Forced march of approximately 10 miles

Field firing competition	Elementary map reading
March discipline	Physical fitness
Fire control orders	Fighting patrol

Lt Gen Sir Roger Bower, presented The Queen Mother's Banner
to Capt B.M. Lees, Commanding Support Company, the Champion Company
– Germany, December 1960.

Appendix 9
Corporal Joe Costello

Born: 1918
Joined 2/4th KOYLI - 1939
Fought in North Africa, Italy 1939-1945
Malaya, Korea, Kenya, Aden, Cyprus 1945-1962
Discharged (Corporal) 1962
Killed in a road accident 1970

The greatest individualist, or 'odd bod'.
Extract from *Jungle Campaign*, John Scurr.

Joe Costello, then 32 years old, [1950] was a huge, brawny fellow with magnificent bushy ginger moustache, an inexhaustible spirit, and constant good humour. After running away from home at the age of 14 to join the merchant navy, Joe had become a tramp prior to the 1939-45 war. He told me that he had tramped round Jamaica as well as many parts of England and that he never wore socks, not even in the army. In those pre-war days, Joe had been a Communist Party activist, but now ugly scars marked the spot on his hand where he'd had a hammer and sickle tattoo inexpertly removed. One time when one of the lads in the company mentioned his home town, Joe asked him which street he lived in, 'King Street,' the lad replied. 'King Street?' Joe exclaimed. 'I've knocked on every door in that street!'

[In the final months of 1950, when 'C' Company was at Kulim, Malaya, and training] Joe Costello, the former tramp, had left 'C' Company – indeed, with three others [he] had left the KOYLI – having volunteered for a new airborne unit that was just being formed: the Malayan Scouts. [SAS] After Malaya, Joe had soldiered in Korea, Kenya, Aden and Cyprus and at the Joint Service Staff College. Though he had also served in other regiments, Joe had begun and ended his army career in the KOYLI.

A year after his discharge in 1962, with the rank of corporal (previously busted from Serjeant), Joe returned to being a tramp, though one who bathed daily! He soon became a well-known personality, tramping the roads of Yorkshire. All burly and proud, with long ginger hair, moustache and beard, he always wore a donkey jacket festooned with his medals and regimental badges and pushed a pram, also adorned with badges, containing his belongings. On his travels, he peddled bootlaces, razor blades, needles and cotton and sometimes worked as a night watchman. Always jovial and well mannered, he was popular with the local people and especially with children wherever he went.

Then, on 30 August 1970, at the age of 52, Joe was fatally injured in a road accident in South Milford, near Doncaster. Two hundred people attended his funeral at South Milford cemetery. Among former comrades present was 'Taggy' Bell, who had been a Serjeant in 'C' company in Malaya. Members of the SAS acted as pallbearers, and two buglers from the

202

2nd Battalion Light Infantry sounded the 'Last Post' at the graveside. A fitting send-off for a great old soldier.

Memoirs of Captain N.C. Rowe KSLI att. 1st KOYLI 1956-1957
CBS Camp in Cyprus

There were so many complaints about the state of the tents that a high-level team was sent out from London to investigate. One Sunday this team toured the camp to look at the tents, ending up in the Officers' Mess. We then discovered a General was missing. Always embarrassing to lose a General, particularly in an internal security environment. But then I had an idea. My Company Storeman had once been the General's batman, so I hied off to my Company Store and, sure enough, there was the General sitting on an upturned box having a mug of tea with my storeman.

This Company Storeman was a great character. When due to leave the Army after 21 years service he was offered resettlement training. When asked what he was going to do in civilian life he said, "A tramp". Great excitement as the Army Education branch tried to work out the appropriate resettlement training to become a tramp. I understand he went on to be a much-loved tramp in Yorkshire with a good showing from all walks of life at his funeral.

The People 26 March 1967

A short article about Joe appeared in the above newspaper. The reporter confirmed that Joe was still tramping around the North Country, and that among the many articles he carried around was his own pewter tankard with the following inscription. 'Presented to Cpl J. Costello KOYLI by the Officers of the Joint Services Staff College 1962'.

Appendix 10

The King's Own Yorkshire Light Infantry

Bugle Calls

1st Battalion

2nd Battalion

4th Battalion (TA)   **As for 1st Battalion**

The Light Infantry Brigade

Brigade Depot Call

The Light Division Assembly

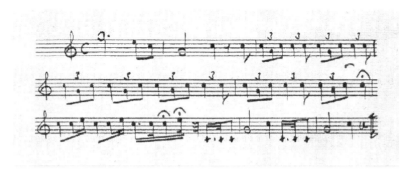

During the Peninsular War, this Light Division call was sounded to assemble Regiments on their Regimental Parade Grounds. In late 1954, it was suggested that this call be adopted for use as a prelude to the sounding of the 'Advance' upon which the battalion marches on parade to the Band and Bugle March 'Light Infantry'.

YIELD TO NONE

The History Of The King's Own Yorkshire Light Infantry

Volume VII
1945 – 1968

Bibliography

Journals, Regimental Histories, Official Sources

The Bugle Journal of The King's Own Yorkshire Light Infantry   Vols 38 – 60. 1946 - 1968

Ellenberger, Brig G.F.
The History of The King's Own Yorkshire Light Infantry 1939-1948
            Gale & Polden   Aldershot   1961

Makepeace-Warne, Maj Gen A.
Exceedingly Lucky,The History of the Light Infantry 1968-1993
            Sidney Jary Ltd   Bristol   1993

Pigott, Maj Gen. A.J.K.
Manpower Problems,   War Office   London   1948

Commonwealth War Graves Commission

General Works

Barnett, Correlli

Britain and Her Army	Cassell & Co	London	1970
The Lost Victory	Macmillan	London	1995

Beckett, I. & Chandler, D.
The Oxford Illustrated History of the British Army
            Oxford Univ Press   Oxford   1994

Carver, FM Lord
Britain's Army in the 20th Century   Macmillan   London   1998

Dupuy, R.E. & T.
The Encyclopaedia of Military History   Macdonald & Jane   London   1970

Fortescue, Sir J.
'*A Gallant Company', in The British Army, 1783-1802,* 19 vols.   London   1910

French, David
The British Way in Warfare 1688-2000   Unwin Hyman   London   1990

James, Lawrence
The Rise and Fall of the British Empire   Little Brown & Co   London   1994

Kirton, Peter
Normanton, Grit Grime and Courage   Author   York   2001

Pocock, Tom
Fighting General   Collins   London   1973

Scurr, John

Malayan Tales of the Yorkshire L.I.	Pentland Press	Durham	1997
Jungle Campaign	The Book Guild	Sussex	1998

Springhall, John
Decolonization since 1945 .   Palgrave   Hants   2001

Strawson, John
Gentlemen in Khaki   Secker & Warburg   London   1989

Electronically gathered information

Australian Army Website   *Far North Queensland 51ˢᵗ Battalion*
                           http:/www.army.gov.au/51FNQR.htm

Young, Major, M.   *History of Saskatchewan Light Infantry*
http:/www.regiments.org.regiments/na-canada/volmil/skinf/955Nsask.htm

Index of People

208

Dugmore, Lt Col, J.W.R., 48
Dunster, Sjt, 43

Eden, Anthony, Foreign Sec., 54, 61
Edinburgh, Prince Phillip, Duke, 47
Edward VII, King, 142
Edwards, Major, W. VC, 117
Elcomb, Major, A.C., 120, 135, 147, 162, 163, 165, 171
Elizabeth II, Queen, 47, 58, 63, 168
Elizabeth, HM The QM, 10, 14, 48, 53, 88, 111, 117, 142, 149, 168, 187
Eller, Major, S.P., 170, 185
Elliott, Pte, 95
Erasmus (priest), 103
Erskine, Gen Sir George, 68
Evans, P. (Malayan Police Force), 38
Everett-Proctor, Pte, P.D., 54

Farouk, King, 32
Firbank, Major Gen, C.L., 168
Fleming, Lt, P.G., 11, 133
Flint, Cpl, 113
Flint, Cpl, 'B' Coy, 30
Floyer-Acland, Lt Col, S.N., 112, 114, 116, 117
Foott, Sjt, C., 113
Forrester, Sjt, 47
Forsyth, Cpl, 156
Fothergill, Pte, A., 123 (fn16)
Fry, Pte (Ginger), 36

Gale, Colour/Sjt, R., 170
Gale, Gen, Sir Richard, 55
Gascoigne, Pte, F., 124
General China, Mau Mau leader, 68
Gent, Sir Edward, 21, 23
Georgadjis, 101
George VI, King, 53, 187
Glennie, Brig, J., 136
Gloucester, HRH, Duchess, 111
Gloucester, HRH, Duke, 110
Godfrey, Pte, J.J.H., 36
Good, Brig, I.H., 15
Goodall, 2Lt, A.D.S., 76, 81, 86, 94
Goodall, Cpl, 24
Gordon, Brig, 13
Gough, Pte, J.E., 39
Goulburn, Brig, C., 105
Gowans, Major, R.L.N., 48
Gray, W.N., Comm. of Police, 45
Greenfield, Sjt, 193
Gregory, Pte, J.D., 41
Grist, CSM, L., 118
Grist, Pte, R., 150
Grivas, Col. George, 91, 100, 101, 102
Guest RSM, 11

209

210

211

212

213

Thain, Major, J.M.S., 132
Thomas, 2Lt, D.R., 114
Thomas, L/Cpl, W., 10
Thomas, Terry (entertainer), 78
Thorne, 2Lt, J.P., 34
Thornycroft, Peter, MP, 137
Thurlow, Brig Lord, 72
Tinson, Capt, A.R., 59, 87, 109, 155
Tito (Josip Broz), Yugoslav Marshal and President, 4
Townend, Pte, D., 104
Turpin, Capt, J.R., 70

Unett, 2Lt, R., 27
Urquhart, Major Gen, R.E., 41, 45, 53

Vallance, Major, J.R.A., 30

Wade, Major, M.R., 126, 152
Wade, Sjt, L., 104
Walby, 2Lt, P.G.M., 34
Walker, C.V., Lord Mayor of Leeds, 6
Walker, L/Cpl (Bugler), 166
Walker, Lt Col, W., 24, 128, 130, 132, 136
Walker, Pte, C., 45
Walters, Cpl, T., 24
Walton, John, JP, Mayor of Pontefract, 120
Ward, Gen Sir Dudley, 111
Ward, Pte, K., 35
Waruhiuwa Kungu, (Kikuyu Chief), 66
Weiler, Brig, L.F.E., 120
Weiler, Capt, D.L.E., 126, 133
West, Lt Gen, Sir Michael, 117
Whistler, Major Gen, 15
Whitehead, Pte, J.D., 42, 43
Whitworth, Major, G.B., 14
Wigg, 2Lt, 32
Wilkingson, Pte, 166
Wilson, Harold, Prime Minister, 164
Wilson, Lt, A.R., 47, 144, 160, 162
Wilson, Lt, M.J.A., 112, 152
Wilson, Pte, N.C., 169
Wilson, Sjt, 37
Wingate, Major Gen, O., 6
Wingfield, Lt, J.J.R., 115
Winter, Sjt, 193
Wood, Lt Col, B.W., 6
Wood, Major, F. RA. (TA), 184
Wood, Major, J.S., 110, 118, 188
Woodfine, Pte, 116
Woodhouse, Major, E.A., 199
Woodhouse, Pte, H, 30
Woodland, Sgt, (2nd Coldstream Gds), 40
Woods, Pte, 158
Wright, Cpl, T., 15

214

Xenophontos, Nicos, 96

Yate, Major, C.A.L. VC, 171
Young, Major, M., 192 (fn3)

Zengal, Sgt, R.L. VC. SLI., 186

Index of Places

Abingdon, 149
Addis Ababa, Ethiopia, 80
Aden, 77, 78, 80, 81, 87, 124, 150-153
Ahmednagar, 10
Ahwar, 82, 84
Al Milah, 152, 153, 155
Aldershot, 63, 187
Ampang, 39
Amsterdam, 4
Anduki, airfield, 136
Athens, 159
Ayer Hitam, 41

Badar, 158
Baling, 34
Bangkok, 38, 134
Baram, river, 131
Bareo, 137-140
Barnard Castle, 48, 52
Barnsley, 118
Batang Kemena, river, 137
Batley, 12, 108
Batu Gajah, 39
Batu Kampong, 134
Batu Lingtan, 133
Bekenu, 136
Belfast, 149
Benson, 149
Bergamo, 8-9
Bergen-Belsen, 53
Berlin, 57-59, 61, 162, 163, 167-171
Berwick-on-Tweed, 4, 12
Bethmangala, 6
Betong, 38
Bidor, 30
Bintulu, 136, 137
Blackpool, 84
Bodney, 62
Bologna, 9
Bombay, 11
Borkenburg, 53
Bougainville, 190
Brilon, 54, 111
Brunei, 128, 132
Brunswick, 162
Buchen, 4
Bukit Puan, 131
Bukit Tapah, 141
Bukit Tapang, 134
Butterworth, airfield, 46

Cairns, 190, 191
Calais, 8

216

218

219

220